U.S. Agriculture & Third World Development

A Policy Study by the Curry Foundation

U.S. Agriculture
& Third World
Development
The Critical Linkage

edited by
Randall B. Purcell & Elizabeth Morrison

Lynne Rienner Publishers • Boulder & London

Published in the United States of America in 1987 by
Lynne Rienner Publishers, Inc.
948 North Street, Boulder, Colorado 80302

Library of Congress Cataloging-in-Publication Data

U.S. Agriculture and Third World Development.

  Bibliography: p.
  Includes index.
  1. Agriculture—Economic aspects—United States.
2. Produce trade—United States. 3. Agriculture—
Developing countries. 4. Agriculture and state—
United States. 5. United States—Commerce—
Developing countries. 6. Developing countries—
Commerce—United States. I. Purcell, Randall B.
II. Morrison, Elizabeth, 1959–
HD1765.U15 1987   338.1′09172′4   86-29860
ISBN 1-55587-011-2 (lib. bdg.)

Printed and bound in the United States of America

The paper used in this publication meets the
requirements of the American National Standard
for Permanence of Paper for Printed Library
Materials Z39.48-1984.

Contents

Part 3   Issues for U.S. Policy

Part 4   Policy Prescriptions

Figures and Tables

Foreword

With this volume, the Curry Foundation presents the third in a series of public policy studies that have examined the predominant issues in U.S. agriculture as they have unfolded since 1981. Those issues, in the order that we have seen them evolve, are domestic farm policy, agricultural trade, and now agriculture and the developing world.

This particular evolution reflects two powerful themes that in turn reflect what is perhaps most critical not only to the health of U.S. agriculture, but to the well-being of the economy of the United States as a whole: U.S. interdependence with the rest of the world, and the increasing importance of the developing nations in the global economy.

The United States is entering ever more difficult times in which these themes are salient; yet, the trend toward insularity in international affairs, and protectionism in international trade in particular, should warn us that these themes are increasingly under attack. We hope this volume helps illuminate the consequences of global interdependence and the importance of the developing nations for us all.

The editors and I would like to express our gratitude to my fellow members of the Curry Foundation Board of Trustees, whose guidance has helped steer the foundation toward such productive pursuits. We also want to thank the Farm Foundation, the Ford Foundation, Pauline Knox, the National Center for Food and Agricultural Policy at Resources for the Future, and Pioneer Hi-Bred International for their contributions. In particular, we express deep appreciation to the Rockefeller Foundation for their considerable assistance, which made this enterprise a success. We also add special thanks to the U.S. Agency for International Development, which made it possible for a number of our developing country friends to participate in the project conference.

As always, our final and very special gratitude goes to those members of the project Advisory Committee whose direction was indispensable to the project's success. And, of course, this project would in no way have been possible without the contribution in experience and knowledge of those writers and reviewers whose work this volume represents.

Charles E. Curry
Chairman
Curry Foundation

Introduction

Randall B. Purcell

For the second or third time in fifty years, food problems and questions about food—how much of it there is and who has it—have become part of the global Zeitgeist. The last time food was as visible an issue was in the 1960s when famine struck the Indian subcontinent and, later, ravaged Africa's Sahel. Then, the Malthusians at the Club of Rome warned that it was only a matter of time before the world's population outstripped its ability to feed itself. Now, for the first time in history, people are asking whether there will be a perennial surplus of food.

According to the U.N. Food and Agriculture Organization, world agricultural output increased 27 percent between 1974 and 1984 and reached an all-time high. In the last decade, developed country agricultural production increased 15 percent, and farm output in the developing world rose an astounding 38 percent. Most importantly, per capita food production has been rising steadily.

Such performance can be attributed to the use of vastly improved technology and greater incentives for farmers to produce. The Green Revolution took hold in Asia to make India nearly self-sufficient and, occasionally now, an exporter of wheat. China, under an incentives policy established by its new leadership, has increased its food production by 40 percent in five years. Bangladesh, once the world's basket case, is now self-sufficient in grains. While such gains are reflected in a 10 percent rise in food production during the last decade in Asia, the intensive use of existing land and the clearing of millions of new acres in Brazil and Argentina have contributed to a 16 percent rise in Latin America's food output during the same period.

Meanwhile, in the developed world, price policies enacted after the war by a half-starved European Economic Community, along with more recent improvements in crop yields, have made it an important exporter of food. Canada and Australia, always big food producers, also have had major output increases. And U.S. farmers have brought idle land back into production, have spent heavily on output-increasing investments, and have responded to government price and reserve policies to produce more food than ever.

Although increased food production has provided more people with more and better food, it has led to market surpluses that have greatly intensified competition among agricultural exporters. It also has contributed to a

1

decline in agricultural price levels that has severely debilitated farmers and farm economies everywhere.

Among developed countries the problem is worse in the United States, where surpluses are greatest and where agriculture has been affected disproportionately by the increase in world production. The United States traditionally has held much of the world's grain in carryover stocks, thereby providing the adjustment mechanism for balancing global supply and demand. Uniquely, too, U.S. agriculture has been stung by the strength of the dollar, which has put U.S. farmers at a competitive disadvantage relative to other exporters. These factors have combined with high U.S. price supports, selective import controls, subsidized exports on the part of U.S. competitors, the worldwide recession, and related debt constraints of developing countries to dramatically tilt the balance of U.S. agricultural trade. Total U.S. farm exports dropped to nearly $26 billion in 1986, down 12 percent from 1985 and 37 percent from a peak of $44 billion in 1981. For the first time, during three consecutive months of 1986, the United States—the largest food producer in the world—bought more food abroad than it sold.

The decline in foreign markets has contributed to a serious income problem in U.S. agriculture. In 1986, net farm income declined to its lowest level since the Great Depression. The loss of exports also has reinforced a severe financial crisis in agribusiness and rural banking, as expanded debt commitments of the 1970s, based on an export-driven expectation of continued prosperity, now are met with significant excess capacity, serious cash flow problems, and reduced equity as land values bottom out.

Most observers believe that the U.S. farm industry will have to be scaled down from its size of a decade ago. But few would argue that the country can maintain a vigorous, healthy agricultural industry without maintaining and, indeed, expanding foreign markets. Given that population growth in the United States has stabilized and domestic per capita food consumption is expected to rise only slightly during the next decade, only a small percentage of increases in incomes will be spent on food. It is estimated that future domestic demand will absorb only about two-fifths of the normal U.S. wheat crop, only one-half of the annual U.S. soybean production, and only two-thirds of the annual U.S. corn production. If exports are not expanded, costly government set aside and production control programs almost certainly will be needed, and there likely will follow a significant reorganization of agriculture with mass outmigration and painful dislocation from the sector. We already have witnessed some of the necessary shakeout as the cost of the government's farm program rose to $30 billion in 1986 even as thousands of family farms were foreclosed.

What is the solution for U.S. agricultural exports in an environment where many people are wondering whether world food production increases will continue indefinitely—indeed, wondering whether the bad news is that the Malthusian doomsayers were wrong? The future, as this book attempts to demonstrate, does not have to be a bleak one.

A number of factors should caution against predicting that food production will irreversibly continue to increase. Natural climatic variability has always made production erratic. Moreover, government policies and individual investment decisions cause production to fluctuate as unpredictably as the political and social environment in which such decisions are made. To be sure, most of the excess food on today's markets is the product of recent U.S. and European income and price supports. Most observers agree that such supports cannot be sustained, economically or politically, into the 1990s.

Other, more depressing factors should advise against viewing today's agricultural problem as fundamentally a problem of surplus. Although food supplies appear to be plentiful in the aggregate, food problems in some areas of the world are as severe as ever. Sixty percent of the population of less-developed countries still have caloric intakes below the standards established by the Food and Agriculture Organization. More dramatically, the food crisis in Africa persists, as population growth—close to 3 percent annually—continues to outpace the production of food, and drought continues to exact its toll in human lives.

The paradox between the millions of Africans, Asians, and Latin Americans who continue to suffer shortages and U.S. farmers who are accumulating huge mountains of food reveals the central tenet of this volume—that is, although the United States produces more food than it wants, it does not produce as much food as the hungry world needs. The United States simply produces far more than the hungry world can afford to buy.

That poor, hungry people in developing countries need but cannot afford more food should challenge those concerned about U.S. agricultural exports to find ways in which that need can be translated into effective market demand. This book takes up that challenge by exploring whether the Third World can become a market for U.S. agriculture and by articulating recommendations for U.S. policy that might help make it so. The writings here reflect the substantive part of a larger Curry Foundation project that aims to focus expert and political attention on these questions.

Our thesis throughout the project is one that has achieved wide approbation among agricultural, trade, and development economists but is only slowly gaining acceptance among U.S. farm and commodity groups and U.S. policymakers. We contend that the Third World in fact can become a substantial market for U.S. agriculture by—contrary to what common sense would at first indicate—the development of local agriculture in developing countries themselves. Because the majority of people in the Third World are employed in the agricultural sector, the development of this sector achieves a more even distribution of income than does the development of smaller, more advanced, hierarchical economic sectors. And in the early and middle stages of economic development a higher percentage of each additional increment of income is devoted to increasing and diversifying the consumption of food. But the strong demand for food created by income growth tends to outstrip the growth potential of local agriculture. The paradoxical result is that successful farm development in developing countries can often lead to larger farm import demands.

Recent experience bears this out. Developing country agricultural imports surged in the more favorable growth environment of the 1970s while at the same time developing countries were producing and exporting more. In fact, our study shows that during the "food crisis" decade of the 1970s, the historically positive balance of Third World agricultural trade actually strengthened.

It is important to stress, as we do in these pages, that the positive relationship between U.S. and developing country agriculture does not hold together in every case. Brazil, in the case of soybeans, and India and China, in the case of wheat, are a few of the more important examples of a negative relationship. However, the benefits to U.S. agriculture are usually long-term ones, as there is a time lag between marginal income growth and the demand for imports. Obviously then, even though Brazil, India, and China are net exporters of certain farm products, it is doubtful they can continue to export at the levels they have—and it is likely that they will increase their imports—as domestic income and the effective market demand for food among so many millions of people increase.

The realization of a positive relationship between U.S. and developing country agriculture is greatly dependent—in fact hinges on—developing country policy toward agriculture. Many countries in the Third World have rejected agriculturally based economic development in favor of import substitution–based industrial growth. This has been successful only for a relative handful of countries. Nevertheless, developing countries are only slowly realizing that agricultural sector development facilitates the kind of labor-intensive, capital stretching employment growth that is so crucial in creating and sustaining the demand needed to transform poor, rural societies into modern, industrial economies.

Although developing country economic strategies are dependent largely on the prejudices of developing country leaders, U.S. policy can make a difference. A carrot-and-stick approach to economic assistance and debt relief, for instance, can help force a policy dialogue that emphasizes the adoption of policies that favor agriculture. Once the transformation to an agricultural strategy is made, other more direct U.S. policies have a tremendous impact on the strategy's success. U.S. farm and farm trade policies, for example, often determine how much developing countries can afford to buy and sell on world markets. U.S. monetary and fiscal policies also act as a curse or a blessing. The appreciation of the dollar in the early and middle part of the 1980s, for instance, made some critical developing country imports almost unaffordable. And high real interest rates continue to compound the Third World debt problem, thus forcing many countries to restrict imports and limit the export-generating investments that might otherwise help pay off foreign debt. Consider this—the eighteen developing countries that make up the largest markets for U.S. farm products hold more than 60 percent of all problem debt. It is estimated that an easing of the debt problem could increase U.S. agricultural exports by as much as 20 percent.

The chapters in this book were collected in a manner that would engender a coherent set of recommendations for U.S. policy. Part 1 examines the global environment for trade. It analyzes the trends in food production and consumption, identifies the world's major agricultural importers and exporters, and attempts to determine what, how much, and under what circumstances the United States can expect to export to and import from the developing world. It is followed by an interesting, critical commentary.

Part 2 consists of regional analyses. In an effort to draw lessons about the links between economic development, agricultural development, and agricultural trade, each chapter in Part 2 examines successful and unsuccessful development policies of countries in one of four regions: Africa, Latin America, Asia, and the Pacific. These background writings were used to inform the authors of Part 3, who examine the principal issues in the U.S.–Third World agricultural relationship: macroeconomic and trade policy and food assistance. Commentaries follow chapters on both issues.

All seven chapters were reviewed by the author of the book's concluding chapter, whose charge was to prescribe policy options that would promote a harmonious relationship between U.S. and Third World agriculture. The author produced the chapter as a working draft. All writings were then discussed and criticized during a two-day working conference composed of almost one hundred experts in agriculture, trade, and development from the United States and selected developing countries. The gathering hammered out recommendations for a reworking of the final chapter, which serves as the project's final report.

The report, and indeed most of the writings in this book, demonstrates that the United States can expect to restore full health to its agricultural sector only as developing countries improve their own agriculture. But the problems afflicting farmers in the United States and poor people in the developing world are too serious to allow us to wait for a partnership between U.S. and Third World agriculture to develop. The groups most responsible for influencing U.S. farm and agricultural trade legislation on the one hand and U.S. policy toward developing countries on the other must start now to work together so that such a partnership can get off the ground. Unfortunately, the differences between the two groups mirror the distance that needs to be closed in the U.S.–Third World relationship itself. The powerful, conservative farm and commodity establishment in the United States must begin to promote more than short-term profits for its industry. Similarly, the liberal development establishment must begin to assert more than the humanitarian value of its cause. We hope that the mutual ground we have established here prompts both groups to stand behind, or at least think seriously about, the policies we have articulated.

part one

The Environment for Trade

chapter one

Global Trends in Agricultural Production and Trade

T. Kelley White
C. Edward Overton
Gene A. Mathia

The years since 1960 have been a period of evolutionary and, at times, revolutionary change in world agricultural production and trade, both of which have fluctuated widely. In order to understand agriculture during this period and to usefully and effectively project its performance in the future, it is necessary to understand the temporal and regional variations and factors associated with the changes that have occurred.

This chapter focuses on long-term trends in U.S. and world agricultural production and trade, paying special attention to the role of developing or less-developed countries (LDCs). The first section reviews aggregate agricultural production patterns, examines global production changes since 1960, and elaborates the differences in production among developed countries, developing countries, and the centrally planned economies (CPEs). The second section focuses more narrowly on the U.S. position in world agricultural trade. The third section looks at international markets from a commodity perspective. Here an attempt is made to identify the significant changes in the production, export, and import of commodities among the three major groups of countries. The fourth section explores the changes in the structure and performance of world markets, and the final section discusses future agricultural production and trade patterns.

World Production Patterns

The world agricultural system has not performed too badly since 1960. Aggregate world agricultural production has grown at an average compound rate of between 2.0 and 2.5 percent annually since 1960, a rate sufficient to lead to an improvement in per capita production. As illustrated in Figure 1.1, per capita production was relatively stable during the early 1970s, thereby leading many economists to conclude that the ability of world ag-

Figure 1.1   Agricultural Production Index—World

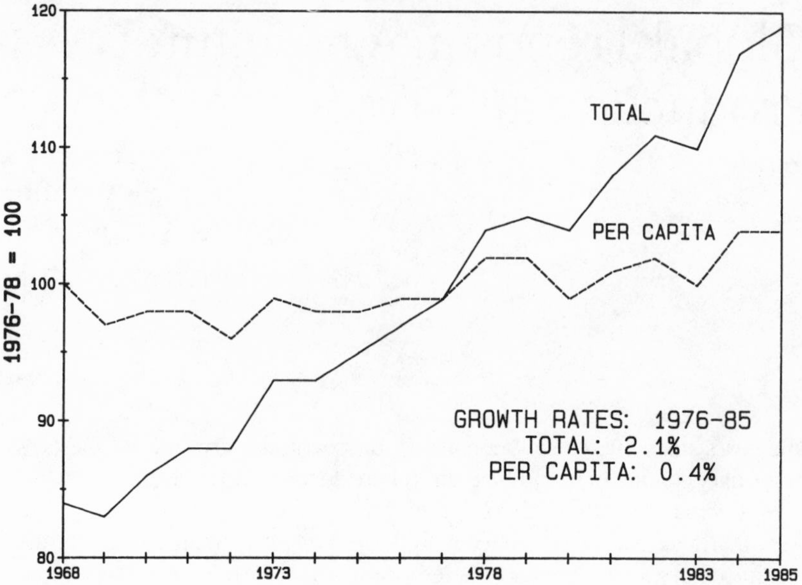

ricultural production to continue expanding at a rate sufficient to offset population growth was reaching its limit. Per capita production, however, increased steadily during the first half of the 1980s, falling only in 1983. This one-year dip is attributable primarily to the U.S. payment-in-kind program and abnormally poor weather, which resulted in a large decline in U.S. production.

In the years since 1960, all three groups of countries experienced aggregate agricultural production growth. Production actually grew more rapidly in developing countries and in the CPEs (Figures 1.2 and 1.3) than in developed countries (Figures 1.4 and 1.5). However, even though the developing countries experienced a 2.8 percent rate of growth in aggregate agricultural production, they enjoyed only a 0.3 percent growth rate in per capita production after 1976, due to rapid population growth. An exception is India, which not only experienced growth in aggregate and per capita production, but also became a net exporter of selected foods. The CPEs had a relatively favorable rate of agricultural production growth (2.4 percent), and a low rate of population growth, which resulted in a higher per capita production growth rate of 1.2 percent. China, for example, recently has shown great improvement in aggregate production and significant progress in limiting population growth. The developed market economies (excluding the United States), with their reasonably high rates of growth in agricultural production and low rates of population growth, also enjoyed rapid increases

Figure 1.2   Agricultural Production Index—LDCs

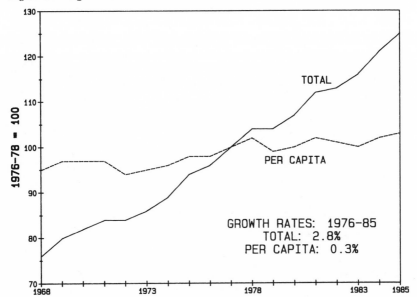

Figure 1.3   Agricultural Production Index—CPEs

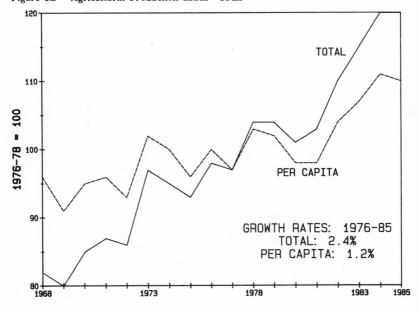

Figure 1.4   Agricultural Production Index—Developed Countries Excluding the United States

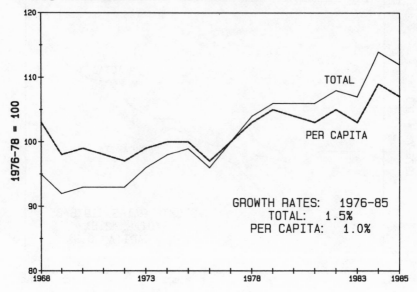

Figure 1.5   Agricultural Production Index—United States

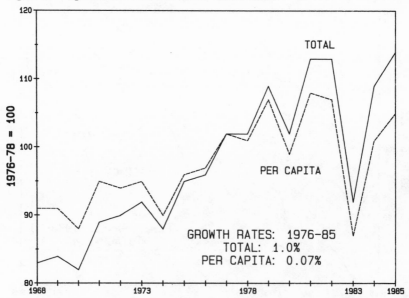

in per capita production. This resulted in growing excess supplies available for export or accumulation.

Agricultural production in the United States grew slowly during the 1960s. Supply control programs maintained relatively high prices and restricted production by withdrawing millions of acres of cropland, thereby keeping supply in balance with slow growth in demand. In the mid-1970s, world demand for agricultural imports grew more rapidly and resulted in higher prices that brought idle land back into production. Between 1974 and 1981, U.S. agricultural production increased 36 percent. Although the recession of the early 1980s then caused a slump in demand, U.S. production levels remained high as investments made during the 1970s came on stream and the government provided high target and loan rates and began to acquire stocks. These and other external forces have distorted market price signals to the U.S. farmer and have misled foreign producers. Favorable world prices, supported and stabilized partly by U.S. price policies, have provided a tremendous incentive to other countries to increase production and, in many cases, expand exports.

World Agricultural Trade

World trade in agricultural products grew more rapidly than production during the 1970s, which implied an increasing interdependency in agriculture. At the beginning of the 1960s, world agricultural trade represented only 10 percent of world production. Between 1960 and 1980 trade increased to approximately 17 percent of production. The aggregate value of agricultural trade doubled between 1970 and 1975 and almost doubled again by 1980 (see Figure 1.6), while real world agricultural prices were lower in 1980 than in the 1960s (Table 1.1). The 1980s, however, saw a rapid decline in the rate of growth in world agricultural trade. Both volume and value declined between 1981 and 1984 (see Table 1.2). This substantial turnaround has been accompanied by significant changes in trade patterns.

Developing Countries

Between 1960 and 1984, developing countries played an increasingly important role in agricultural trade. While imports from other developing countries declined from 32 percent in 1965–1967 to 28 percent in 1979–1981, imports from developed countries increased from 59 percent to 62 percent. Between 1970 and 1972, developing countries imported only 17 percent of global agricultural commodities; by 1984, their imports had increased to 25 percent. On the other hand, agricultural exports from the developing countries fell from 35 percent in 1967 to 30 percent between 1982 and 1984.

Figure 1.6   Value of Agricultural Trade—LDCs

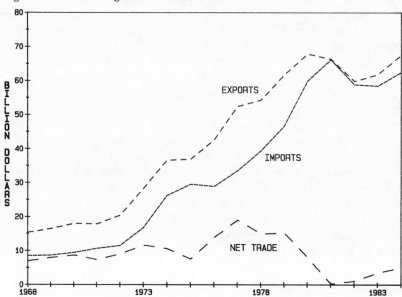

Table 1.1   Index of Commodity Prices in Constant Dollars, 1968–1985
(1976–1978 = 100)[a]

Year	Total Agriculture	Food	Nonfood	Petroleum
1968	82	76	108	24
1969	85	80	110	22
1970	85	82	96	20
1971	80	77	92	26
1972	86	85	88	27
1973	112	110	120	33
1974	153	163	110	112
1975	105	110	86	99
1976	103	102	107	104
1977	108	110	98	104
1978	88	86	93	90
1979	87	84	98	115
1980	105	107	107	173
1981	83	82	89	194
1982	68	63	80	194
1983	73	68	91	172
1984	73	69	87	171
1985	62	59	78	166

Source: World Bank published data.

[a]Weighted by developing countries' export values for 1977–1979 and computed from
data deflated by manufacturing unit value index.

Centrally Planned Economies

The CPEs have been net importers of agricultural products since 1968 (Figure 1.7). Since 1981, however, their imports have declined and their exports have been stable, yielding an improved net trade balance. The Soviet Union and the Eastern European countries decided in the 1970s to increase the availability of animal products in order to improve the quality of their citizens' diets. This required an expanding and stable supply of feed grains. The Soviet Union and China entered long-term trade agreements with major exporting countries, primarily the United States, Canada and Argentina. China opened up relationships with the West and utilized trade, including agricultural imports, to further its development.

CPE policy decisions were a very significant factor in the explosive growth of world agricultural trade during the 1970s and the fall in world agricultural trade during the 1980s. The decisions the CPEs make beyond 1985 are critical to the food surplus countries, especially the United States.

Developed Countries Other than the United States

The developed countries (excluding the United States) have experienced rapid economic growth, slow population growth, and, because they already had high income levels, relatively slow growth in domestic demand for food since 1965. Both their exports and imports have increased rapidly since 1968 (Figure 1.8), with a negative net trade balance during the entire 1968–1984 period. Exports began to grow more rapidly than imports in 1980, resulting in a slight upturn in the net trade balance. Increased growth in production in a few developed countries enabled them to help satisfy the rapid growth of import demand in the CPEs. Japan was an exception in both its production and trade patterns. Its demand for wheat and red meat outstripped its production capacity because of rapidly growing per capita incomes, changing diets, which previously were based largely on rice and fish, and a declining agricultural land base.

A high rate of growth in agricultural production relative to consumption in developed countries was in part a response to market signals that reflected growing world demand and in part a reaction to internal agricultural policies that provided relatively favorable domestic prices. Although these domestic prices were often greater than world prices, growing foreign markets could be tapped by subsidizing exports. Foreign markets provided outlets for surplus products, allowed farmers' productive capacities to be utilized, and maintained farm incomes and government subsidies at politically acceptable levels.

The United States

The United States, probably more than any other country, was in a strong position to respond quickly and efficiently to the strong growth in world

Table 1.2   Composition of World Agricultural Trade Value for Selected Years and Regions[a] (in percentage)

Exporter and Year	Exporter's Share of Import Market[b] Importer					Distribution of Exporter's Shipments[c] Importer				
	U.S.	Developed less U.S.	LDC	CPE	World	U.S.	Developed less U.S.	LDC	CPE	World
U.S.										
1965–67	0	16	32	3	16	0	63	35	2	100
1970–72	0	15	29	5	14	0	62	33	4	100
1975–77	0	17	29	11	17	0	58	34	9	100
1979–81	0	17	28	17	19	0	51	36	13	100
1982–84	0	17	27	12	17	0	51	40	10	100
Developed less U.S.										
1965–67	38	46	27	25	39	10	70	12	8	100
1970–72	40	52	35	23	44	9	71	13	6	100
1975–77	34	51	34	20	42	6	71	16	6	100
1979–81	37	54	39	28	45	7	65	20	9	100
1982–84	43	55	37	27	45	8	62	21	9	100
LDC										
1965–67	60	32	32	30	35	19	55	16	10	100
1970–72	59	28	29	32	32	19	54	15	11	100
1975–77	62	28	31	40	33	16	49	19	16	100
1979–81	60	25	28	31	29	17	46	22	15	100
1982–84	55	24	32	35	30	16	41	27	17	100

CPE										
1965–67	1	6	8	42	10	1	36	14	49	100
1970–72	1	6	7	40	9	1	37	13	49	100
1975–77	2	5	7	29	8	2	34	17	47	100
1979–81	2	4	5	23	7	3	32	17	48	100
1982–84	2	4	4	26	7	3	29	15	53	100
World										
1965–67	100	100	100	100	100	11	60	17	12	100
1970–72	100	100	100	100	100	10	61	17	11	100
1975–77	100	100	100	100	100	8	59	20	13	100
1979–81	100	100	100	100	100	8	54	23	14	100
1982–84	100	100	100	100	100	9	52	25	14	100

Source: UN trade data.

[a]The trade table was constructed using the reporting countries import values. Many CPE and LDC countries do not report either import or export values; consequently, trading partner values from the UN and total trade values reported by the Food and Agriculture Organization were used to adjust the LDC, CPE, and world trade.

[b]The LDCs imported 31 percent of their agricultural products from the United States.

[c]Thirty-five percent of the U.S. agricultural exports went to LDCs.

Figure 1.7   Value of Agricultural Trade—CPEs

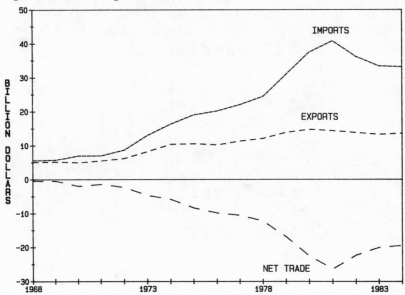

Figure 1.8   Value of Agricultural Trade—Developed Countries Excluding the United States

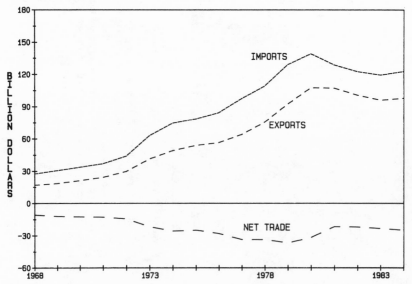

agricultural demand during the 1970s. At the beginning of the 1970s, the U.S. agricultural sector's resources were underutilized due to agricultural policies that had emphasized supply management. High inflation, low real interest rates, and favorable tax and credit policies encouraged additional investments to expand productive capacity. Total farm debts were relatively low, and capital gains were growing rapidly as a result of soaring land values.

U.S. farmers did respond to these incentives, as evidenced by the fact that U.S. agricultural exports increased from approximately $10 billion to more than $40 billion between the early 1970s and the early 1980s (Figure 1.9). The value of imports increased gradually during this period, but they have turned up sharply since 1983. The net trade balance increased greatly between 1977 and 1981, but since then has fallen sharply due to both declining export values and rising import values.

The growth in exports produced not only an era of prosperity with expectations for future export growth and rising land values, but also a growing U.S. dependency on foreign markets for the disposal of the burgeoning U.S. farm output. However, in the 1980s, U.S. farmers quickly became aware of the negative consequences of such dependence as demand growth slowed and U.S. agricultural exports declined. U.S. domestic economic and agricultural policies have since insulated farmers from world price signals. In addition, a rapidly rising U.S. dollar relative to other currencies has contributed to declining U.S. exports and market share. Other countries such as

Figure 1.9   Value of Agricultural Trade—United States

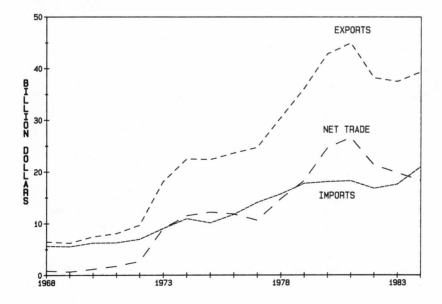

Canada, Australia, Argentina, Brazil, and the European Economic Community (EEC), provided with a price umbrella by U.S. agricultural policy and a price advantage by the strong U.S. dollar, were able to expand market share and total export volume.

World Commodity Markets

A closer look at commodity markets will throw some light on the historical importance of the United States in world markets and on the role the United States may play in the future. Trends in production, utilization, and trade are discussed in the following section, with special attention given to the U.S. role in each market and, where significant, to the role of the developing countries.

Food Grains

Wheat and rice are the major internationally traded food grains; wheat is by far the most important (Table 1.3). World wheat production has increased from 238 million metric tons in 1960/61 to a projected 504 million metric tons in 1986/87, an increase of 112 percent. Utilization has just about kept pace with production while total trade has increased by more than 115 percent. However, during this period U.S. exports increased less than 100 per-

Table 1.3   World Wheat Production, Utilization, Trade, and Carryover Stocks, 1986/87 and Selected Recent Years (million metric tons)

July–June Trade Years	Production	Utilization	U.S. Exports	Non-U.S. Exports	Total Trade	Ending Stocks[a]	Stocks as Percentage of Utilization
Projected (6/86)							
1986/87	504.4	503.4	30.5	61.0	91.5	125.3	24.9
Preliminary							
1985/86	502.1	494.3	25.0	60.9	85.9	124.3	25.1
1984/85	515.6	500.2	38.1	68.0	106.1	116.4	23.3
1983/84	490.9	486.4	38.9	63.1	102.0	100.9	20.7
1982/83	479.1	467.9	39.9	58.8	98.7	96.3	20.6
1981/82	448.4	441.5	48.8	52.5	101.3	85.0	19.3
1980/81	443.0	445.8	41.9	52.2	94.1	78.2	17.5
1979/80	424.5	444.3	37.4	48.6	86.0	81.0	18.2
1978/79	446.8	430.2	32.3	39.7	72.0	100.9	23.4
1976/77	421.4	385.9	25.8	37.5	63.3	99.8	25.9
1971/72	351.0	344.3	16.6	35.4	52.0	81.0	23.5
1966/67	306.7	279.8	20.3	35.7	56.0	82.1	29.4
1960/61	238.4	238.4	19.6	22.4	41.9	81.8	34.8

Source: U.S. Department of Agriculture, Foreign Agriculture Service, *Foreign Agricultural Circular, Grains* (Washington, D.C.: USDA, 1986).

[a]Excludes total stocks in most communist nations due to lack of published data. Stocks are an aggregate of individual marketing years and do not reflect stocks at a single point in time.

cent while the exports of U.S. competitors increased about 200 percent. (In 1981/82, the peak U.S. export year, wheat exports were 150 percent larger than in 1960/61, while the wheat exports of other wheat-producing countries were 135 percent higher.)

The United States, Canada, Australia, Argentina, and, in the last few years, the EEC have been the world's major wheat exporters. Although U.S. export volumes have declined since 1981, the U.S. share of the world market has dropped only slightly and stabilized at approximately 40 percent. The production increases of major U.S. competitors and a few importers, along with increases in the value of the dollar, have affected adversely both U.S. volume and share of wheat. Also, high target and loan prices in the United States have priced U.S. wheat above world markets and provided incentives for other countries to increase production and exports.

World production of milled rice has more than doubled since 1960/61. Utilization has grown less rapidly, however, thereby resulting in a gradual buildup of stocks, held primarily by the United States (Table 1.4). Trade in rice is a relatively small share of world production (about 4 percent in 1984/85). The United States is not a large rice producer, but it exports a large percentage of its production and normally accounts for 15 to 20 percent of world trade. Several developing countries have become self-sufficient in

Table 1.4   World Milled Rice Production, Utilization, Trade, and Carryover Stocks, 1986/87 and Selected Recent Years (million metric tons)

July–June Trade Years	Production	Utilization	U.S. Exports	Non-U.S. Exports	Total Trade[a]	Ending Stocks[b]	Stocks as Percentage of Utilization
Projected (6/86)							
1986/87	320.2	318.0	—	—	11.9	26.2	8.2
Preliminary							
1985/86	315.7	313.6	2.2	9.6	11.8	24.0	7.6
1984/85	318.6	314.0	1.9	9.6	11.5	21.9	7.0
1983/84	308.0	308.1	2.1	10.4	12.6	17.2	5.6
1982/83	285.7	289.6	2.3	9.6	11.9	17.3	6.0
1981/82	280.6	281.5	2.5	9.3	11.8	21.3	7.6
1980/81	271.0	272.3	3.0	10.1	13.1	22.1	8.1
1979/80	258.1	262.6	3.0	9.7	12.7	23.4	8.9
1978/79	263.7	258.6	2.3	9.7	12.0	27.9	10.8
1976/77	236.8	238.4	2.1	8.5	10.6	17.8	7.4
1971/72	216.4	218.8	1.8	6.9	8.7	15.4	7.0
1966/67	179.3	180.7	1.7	6.1	7.8	10.6	5.9
1961/62	147.3	147.7	0.9	5.4	6.3	7.0	4.7

Source: U.S. Department of Agriculture, Foreign Agriculture Service, *Foreign Agricultural Circular, Grains* (Washington, D.C.: USDA, 1986).

[a]Exports are computed on a calendar year basis.
[b]Excludes total stocks in most communist nations due to lack of published data. Stocks are an aggregate of individual marketing years and do not reflect stocks at a single point in time.

rice. In addition to Thailand, now an important exporter, the large producing countries of China, North Korea, India, and Laos are now self-sufficient and even marginal exporters, but even small percentage increases in their production, if exported, could cause havoc in the international rice market.

Coarse Grain

World coarse grain production has increased about 80 percent since 1960 (Table 1.5). U.S. exports have increased more than 200 percent while competitor exports increased by around 400 percent. This large increase in trade with a rather modest increase in world production suggests that most of the increased utilization of grain occurred in importing countries.

Major coarse grain exporters have been the United States, Canada, South Africa, and Argentina. The United States continues to be the dominant exporter but has experienced large declines in exports since 1980. Its share, although fluctuating between 40 and 70 percent, has hovered near 60 percent. Argentina has usually been the second largest exporter and has maintained its share since 1980/81 when total exports tailed off. As with food grains, the most notable changes in trade patterns for feed grains were the increasing importance of the developing countries and the CPEs and the declining importance of several developed countries (aside from the United States) as importers.

Table 1.5   World Coarse Grain Production, Utilization, Trade, and Carryover Stocks, 1986/87 and Selected Recent Years (million metric tons)

Oct./Sept. Trade Years	Production	Utilization	U.S. Exports	Non-U.S. Exports	Total Trade	Ending Stocks[a]	Stocks as Percentage of Utilization
Projected (6/86)							
1986/87	814.8	798.2	49.0	41.2	90.2	187.8	23.5
Preliminary							
1985/86	842.5	772.8	39.1	45.0	84.1	171.1	22.1
1984/85	808.5	779.5	55.5	46.4	101.9	101.5	13.0
1983/84	685.5	761.6	55.8	36.1	91.9	72.5	9.5
1982/83	779.1	751.4	54.0	35.9	89.9	148.5	19.8
1981/82	769.9	739.8	58.4	38.0	96.6	112.9	15.3
1980/81	732.0	742.1	69.5	38.5	108.0	82.8	11.2
1979/80	740.6	740.0	71.4	27.8	99.2	92.7	12.5
1978/79	751.7	746.0	60.2	32.5	92.7	92.2	12.4
1976/77	703.5	684.2	50.6	33.3	83.9	78.2	11.4
1971/72	629.9	616.2	24.2	25.1	49.3	87.0	14.1
1966/67	521.2	520.2	20.0	20.0	40.0	76.1	14.6
1960/61	447.9	437.2	15.7	8.3	24.0	109.7	25.1

Source: U.S. Department of Agriculture, Foreign Agriculture Service, *Foreign Agricultural Circular, Grains* (Washington, D.C.: USDA, 1986).

[a]Excludes total stocks in most communist nations due to lack of published data. Stocks are an aggregate of individual marketing years and do not reflect stocks at a single point in time.

Oilseeds and Oilseed Products

World production of oilseeds has increased by nearly 150 percent since 1972, and production of oilseed products has increased more than 80 percent with most of the increase occurring in U.S.-competitor countries (Table 1.6). Brazil and other countries (especially the EEC as a processor of imported beans) have accounted for a large share of the increase in protein meal output. It is important to note that a large share of increased U.S. soybean production has been exported as raw beans, while Brazil, and to a lesser extent Argentina, have emphasized the exportation of soybean meal. World oil production is distributed more evenly among crops than is protein meal. The world total has been growing, but most sources of oils have maintained their relative importance.

The United States still holds a large share of the world soybean trade, with more than 70 percent of the total since 1975. The recent decline in world soybean trade can be traced to the world recession that brought about several changes in the EEC import pattern. These include the increased feeding of surplus wheat to livestock, reduced dairy production, and the increased imports of high-protein, corn gluten feed. The developing countries have not increased their imports of soybean products since the 1981–1983 recession because of the large foreign debts these countries sustain, the higher real price of soybeans due to the appreciating dollar, and the slower growth rate in livestock production in developing countries.

Cotton

World cotton production has increased since the late 1960s from about 12 million metric tons to almost 15 million metric tons in the 1981–1983 period; in 1984, a sharp increase to almost 19 million metric tons occurred (Table 1.7). Since 1968, most of the major producers, with the exception of China, the Soviet Union, Pakistan and India, have maintained the same general level of production. The United States and the Soviet Union are the largest cotton exporters, although China's exports have grown dramatically since 1982. Pakistan, Australia, Egypt, and the Sudan are important exporters, but the bulk of exports is divided among a larger number of other countries. Eastern Europe, the EEC, other Western European countries, Japan, the Republic of Korea, and Taiwan are major cotton importers with 70–80 percent of the total. Taiwan, the Republic of Korea, West Germany, Portugal, the Soviet Union, and Indonesia are the only countries that have shown a significant increase in cotton imports.

Cassava and Pulses

The production of cassava and pulses is not very important for the United States but is an important source of food for many of the developing countries. World cassava production has increased in Asia and Africa but declined

**Table 1.6   World Oilseed Production, Crush, Trade, and Carryover
Stocks and Production of Oilseed Products for Selected Years
(million metric tons)**

Year	Production	Crush	U.S. Exports	Non-U.S. Exports	Total Trade	Ending Stocks
Oilseeds[a]						
Projected						
1986/87	196	158	22	14	36	27
Preliminary						
1985/86	194	154	22	12	34	26
1984/85	190	150	18	15	33	21
1983/84	165	137	22	11	33	16
1982/83	178	143	26	9	35	21
1981/82	169	138	27	9	36	19
1980/81	156	133	22	9	31	21
1979/80	170	135	26	10	36	19
1972/73	80	—	14	7	21	7

Oilseed Meals Production[b]	U.S.	Non-U.S.	World
Projected			
1986/87	25.0	81.7	106.7
Preliminary			
1985/86	25.2	78.5	103.7
1984/85	24.8	76.8	101.6
1983/84	22.6	70.4	93.0
1982/83	26.7	71.3	98.0
1981/82	25.2	68.8	94.0
1980/81	24.7	66.1	90.8
1979/80	27.5	65.4	92.9
1972/73	18.1	39.8	57.9

Major Vegetable and Marine Oils Production[c]	U.S.	Non-U.S.	World
Projected			
1986/87	6.3	44.1	50.4
Preliminary			
1985/86	6.4	42.6	49.0
1984/85	6.3	40.0	46.3
1983/84	5.8	36.7	42.5
1982/83	6.6	36.7	43.3
1981/82	6.2	35.3	41.5
1980/81	6.2	33.7	39.9
1979/80	6.7	32.9	39.6
1972/73	4.3	23.4	27.7

Source: U.S. Department of Agriculture, Foreign Agricultural Service, *Foreign
Agriculture Circular, Oilseeds and Products* (Washington, D.C.: USDA, 1986).

[a]Includes soybean, cottonseed, peanut, sunflower seed, rapeseed, flaxseed,
copra, and palm kernel.
[b]Includes soybean, cottonseed, peanut, sunflower seed, rapeseed, linseed,
copra, palm kernel, and fish.
[c]Includes soybean, palm, sunflower, rapeseed, cottonseed, peanut, coconut,
fish, palm kernel, and linseed.

Table 1.7   Cotton Production in the World and in Selected Major Producing Countries (thousand metric tons)

Year	World	U.S.	USSR	China	Pakistan	Egypt	India	Brazil	Turkey	Others
1968/69	12,430	2,379	1,953	2,351	529	437	1,039	718	435	2,589
1969/70	12,430	2,175	1,955	2,079	538	541	1,093	673	400	2,975
1970/71	12,040	2,219	2,345	2,286	544	509	1,017	490	400	2,231
1975/76	11,797	1,808	2,528	2,373	494	382	1,184	395	480	2,153
1976/77	12,341	2,304	2,615	2,086	418	396	1,066	550	476	2,430
1977/78	13,965	3,133	2,715	2,047	553	399	1,283	478	575	2,783
1978/79	13,032	2,364	2,593	2,166	464	438	1,402	580	475	2,550
1979/80	14,313	3,185	2,794	2,199	744	484	1,417	579	476	2,435
1980/81	14,153	2,422	2,939	2,700	719	529	1,376	622	500	2,347
1981/82	15,498	3,407	2,891	2,961	761	499	1,482	645	488	2,365
1982/83	14,818	2,605	2,598	3,592	823	461	1,525	650	489	2,075
1983/84	14,737	1,692	2,627	4,638	476	421	1,325	556	522	2,479
1984/85	18,913	2,827	2,343	6,249	1,008	401	1,725	970	580	2,811
Preliminary 1985/86	17,011	2,925	2,636	4,159	1,241	435	1,829	660	518	2,608
Projected 1986/87	16,464	2,395	2,656	4,289	1,154	435	1,742	672	478	2,643

Source: U.S. Department of Agriculture, Foreign Agricultural Service, *Foreign Agricultural Circular, World Cotton Situation* (Washington, D.C.: USDA, July 1986), FC 7-86.

in Latin America. Since 1975, overall cassava production increased from about 100 million metric tons to 129 million metric tons. Much of this increase has been utilized as animal feed. World production of pulses has been approximately 42 million metric tons since 1971, and world shares have essentially remained constant. In a few countries, notably Thailand, cassava has become a major export commodity (mainly to the EEC, where cassava is used as feed).

Red Meats and Poultry
World production of red meats and poultry since 1974 has changed less than has cereals (Table 1.8). Very few countries have developed a dependency on meat imports, preferring instead to import feeds and coarse grains to enlarge their domestic industries. Only poultry and pork production have increased worldwide. Between 1974 and 1984, pork production increased from about 41 to 52 million metric tons, with China accounting for most of the increase. The EEC has dominated world pork trade; Eastern Europe and Canada share the rest of the market. The United States has never been a major pork exporter.

Poultry production increased from 16 to 23 million metric tons annually during the 1974–1984 period. Production shares have remained fairly stable although output has increased. World poultry trade has been dominated by the EEC, but other important exporters are the United States, Brazil, and Eastern Europe. Brazil has shown the largest gains in export volume and market share since the mid-1970s. Total poultry exports almost doubled between the mid-1970s and 1985.

Beef and veal production remained at the 40-million-metric-ton level during the 1974–1984 period, with U.S. output falling slightly. World trade shares of beef and veal have been relatively stable since 1970. The major beef and veal exporters are the EEC, Brazil, Australia, and New Zealand. The EEC share has been increasing during the 1980s while Argentine and Australian shares have declined.

U.S. Commodity Markets

Exports
The United States has been and continues to be a major exporter of wheat, coarse grains, soybeans, rice, cotton, fruits, vegetables, and nuts (Table 1.9). Total export sales reached only $31 billion in 1984/85, which was a sharp drop from the 1980/81 peak of $43 billion but was still larger than the 1976/77 level. The decline was due primarily to reduced sales of coarse grains, oilseed, and wheat.

The drop in the sale of these commodities was analyzed by the U.S. Department of Agriculture's Economic Research Service to determine the effects of changing world conditions on trade. The indebtedness of many importing countries and foreign exchange movements (dollar appreciating relative to other currencies) were important factors for all three commodities but less so for wheat. The increase in foreign wheat production and changing U.S. loan rates may have been more important in explaining the reduction in U.S. wheat sales. However, population and income growth were good for U.S. exports of all three commodities. The effect of the EEC's export policy on declining U.S. sales was relatively small because that policy underwent little change during this period. Declining freight rates affected coarse grains trade more than they did wheat trade because a larger volume of coarse grains is shipped on foreign flagships with lower freight rates.

Major commercial markets for U.S. wheat are the Soviet Union, Japan, and Western Hemisphere countries; Africa is an increasingly important market for concessional sales. U.S. coarse grain exports have a similar pattern—Japan, the Western Hemisphere countries, and the Soviet Union purchase relatively large volumes. U.S. course grain exports peaked in 1979/80, fell sharply in 1982/83, but rose again in 1984/85 as the Soviets increased their imports.

Soybean exports are distributed among several countries including those in the Western Hemisphere and Japan, but the EEC is the most important customer. Volume peaked in 1981/82 at about 25 million metric tons but fell to less than 20 million metric tons in 1984/85. The EEC reduced its imports sharply in 1984/85.

The developing countries, as a group, have been the fastest growing market for U.S. grain since 1970. The importance of their markets actually has increased during the post-1980 period of declining U.S market share. The recent growth is, in part, due to large concessional sales to these countries. It is also partly due to the smaller increase, and in some cases decline, in the value of the dollar in real terms relative to developing country currencies.

U.S. exports of red meats and poultry are relatively small; Japan is the single most important importer of U.S. beef, veal, and pork. The trend in exports is up for beef and veal, but U.S. pork exports have been falling since 1980. Pork exports to Canada, already small, have declined recently, thereby causing a decline in total pork exports. Poultry exports peaked in 1980 and have been falling since, because of the decline in exports to Egypt.

Imports
U.S. imports can be divided into complementary products (those not directly competitive with domestic production) and supplementary products (those competitive with domestic commodities). Both types of imports have increased since the mid-1970s, but supplementary imports have increased

Table 1.8   Pork, Beef and Veal, and Poultry Production in Major World Producing Areas, 1974–1978 Average and 1980–1986 (million metric tons)

Area	1974–78 Average	1980	1981	1982	1983	1984	Preliminary 1985	Projected 1986
Pork								
United States	5.9	7.5	7.2	6.5	6.9	6.7	6.7	6.6
Other North America	1.5	1.8	1.7	1.8	2.0	1.8	1.8	1.8
South America	1.0	1.2	1.2	1.2	1.2	0.8	0.8	0.9
EC-10	8.2	9.1	9.5	9.4	9.7	9.7	9.9	10.1
Other Western Europe	1.9	2.4	2.3	2.5	2.5	2.5	2.5	2.5
Eastern Europe	6.3	6.9	6.6	6.4	6.6	6.5	6.5	6.6
Soviet Union	5.2	5.2	5.2	5.3	5.8	5.9	5.8	5.8
Asia (Excl. PRC)	2.0	2.7	2.6	2.6	2.8	3.0	3.1	3.1
Oceania	0.2	0.2	0.2	0.2	0.2	0.3	0.3	0.3
China (PRC)	8.7 a	N.A.	11.9	12.7	13.2	14.4	16.5	17.0
World Total b	40.9	37.0	48.4	48.6	50.9	51.6	53.9	54.7
Beef and Veal								
United States	11.5	10.0	10.4	10.4	10.7	10.9	11.0	10.5
Other North America	2.2	2.2	2.3	2.4	2.3	2.3	2.4	2.4
South America	6.1	6.3	6.6	6.2	6.1	6.3	6.3	6.3
EC-10	6.6	7.0	6.9	6.6	6.9	7.4	7.3	7.0
Other Western Europe	1.1	1.3	1.2	1.2	1.1	1.1	1.1	1.1
Eastern Europe	2.5	2.5	2.3	2.5	2.4	2.5	2.4	2.4
Soviet Union	6.7	6.6	6.6	6.6	7.0	7.2	7.4	7.4
South Africa	0.5	0.6	0.5	0.6	0.7	0.7	0.6	0.6
Asia (Excl. PRC)	0.8	1.0	1.0	1.0	1.0	1.1	1.1	1.1
Oceania	2.4	2.0	1.9	2.2	1.9	1.7	1.8	1.9
Total	40.4	39.5	39.7	39.9	40.3	41.0	41.4	40.7

Total Poultry

United States	5.3	6.5	6.9	7.0	7.1	7.4	7.8	8.2
Other North America	0.8	0.9	1.1	1.1	1.1	1.2	1.3	1.2
South America	1.0	1.5	2.0	2.1	2.1	2.0	2.1	2.2
EC-10	3.4	3.8	4.1	4.4	4.3	4.3	4.3	4.4
Other Western Europe	0.9	1.0	1.2	1.2	1.1	1.1	1.1	1.1
Eastern Europe	1.6	1.9	2.0	1.8	1.8	1.9	2.0	2.0
Soviet Union	1.5	2.0	2.3	2.4	2.6	2.7	2.8	2.9
Africa	0.2	0.4	0.5	0.5	0.6	0.6	0.7	0.7
Japan	0.9	1.1	1.1	1.2	1.3	1.3	1.4	1.4
Other Asia and Oceania	0.4	0.5	0.8	0.7	0.8	0.8	0.9	0.9
Total	16.0	19.6	22.0	22.4	22.8	23.3	24.4	25.0

Source: U.S. Department of Agriculture, Foreign Agricultural Service, *Foreign Agriculture Circular, Livestock and Poultry Situation* (Washington, D.C.: USDA, March 1986), FL&P 1-86.

[a]Average production for 1976–1980.
[b]Totals may not add due to rounding.

Table 1.9   Composition of U.S. Agricultural Exports by Type of Commodity (billion dollars)

Commodity Group	1976/77	October/September Fiscal Years				Percentage of Total Exports	
		1980/81	1982/83	1983/84	1984/85	1983/84	1984/85
Feedgrains	5.39	10.40	6.50	8.13	6.78	21.4	21.8
Oilseeds	4.64	6.98	6.33	6.25	4.32	16.4	13.9
Oilseed meal	0.97	1.67	1.49	1.22	.85	3.3	2.7
Vegetable oils	0.77	1.10	.90	1.13	1.02	3.0	3.3
Wheat and wheat products	3.05	8.05	6.22	6.78	4.53	17.8	14.5
Rice	0.69	1.54	0.87	0.90	0.68	2.4	2.2
Meat and meat products	0.61	0.99	0.93	0.93	0.91	2.4	2.9
Hides and skins	0.80	1.00	1.00	1.32	1.32	3.5	4.2
Dairy products	0.17	0.24	0.35	0.39	0.41	1.0	1.3
Poultry and poultry products	0.30	0.77	0.39	0.41	0.39	0.9	1.3
Other animals and animal products	0.77	1.11	1.01	1.17	1.05	3.0	3.4
Cotton	1.54	2.23	1.68	2.39	1.95	6.3	6.3
Fruits, vegetables, and nuts	2.45	3.56	2.87	2.82	2.83	7.4	9.1
Tobacco	1.08	1.34	1.49	1.43	1.59	3.8	5.1
Others	0.78	1.63	2.75	2.84	2.56	7.5	8.2
Total[a]	24.01	42.61	34.77	38.03	31.19	100.1	100.2

Source: U.S. Department of Agriculture, Economic Research Service, *Foreign Agricultural Trade of the United States* (Washington, D.C.: USDA, Fiscal Year 1985 Supplement).

[a]Totals may not add due to rounding.

at about double the rate of complementary items (Table 1.10). The latter increase indicates that U.S. producers have lost some of their competitiveness in such products as fruits, vegetables, nuts, alcoholic beverages, tobacco, and dairy products. The high purchasing power of the dollar and rapid domestic economic recovery from the 1981 recession contributed to growing imports of both complementary and supplementary products.

The United States has been a major importer of selected meats and wines, primarily from developed countries. Fruits and vegetables, coffee, sugar, and cut flowers comprise most imports from developing countries, and some selected meats are imported from the CPEs. Of the total 1985 U.S. import value of $19.7 billion, $7.8 billion represented imports from the developed countries, $11.5 billion from the developing countries, and only $.5 billion from the CPEs (Table 1.11).

Since 1970, the United States and West Germany have ranked among the top three agricultural importers. The top ten importing countries accounted for $141 billion of the total $242 billion of world agricultural imports during the 1980–1984 period (Table 1.12). The United States holds large shares of the Mexican, Canadian, Taiwanese, and Japanese markets.

The Nature of the World Agricultural Market

In addition to reviewing the magnitude and causes of past trends, it is appropriate to describe those characteristics of world agricultural markets that play an important role in determining how these causal factors could affect future world agriculture and trade.

The Thinness of the World Market

Most international agricultural markets are relatively thin. Although interna-

Table 1.10   Value of U.S. Agricultural Imports by Commodity Groups (billion dollars)

Product	1975/76	1980/81	1982/83	1983/84	1984/85	Percentage of Change 1975/76 to 1984/85
Complementary imports						
Cocoa and chocolate	0.60	0.95	0.83	1.06	1.29	115
Coffee	2.39	3.08	2.83	3.09	3.05	28
Rubber	0.47	0.77	0.58	0.85	0.73	55
Tea	0.09	0.13	0.13	0.19	0.18	100
Bananas and plantains	0.26	0.53	0.59	0.63	0.71	173
Drugs	0.11	0.14	0.16	0.20	0.20	82
Others	0.28	0.32	0.35	0.68	0.62	121
Total complementary imports	4.21	5.92	5.47	6.68	6.78	61
Supplementary imports						
Dairy products	0.26	0.52	0.71	0.76	0.76	192
Hides and skins	0.20	0.28	0.19	0.22	0.24	20
Meat and meat products, excluding poultry	1.44	2.22	2.09	1.93	2.21	53
Poultry and poultry products, excluding eggs	0.09	0.10	0.09	0.12	0.09	0
Other animal products, and animals	0.33	0.61	0.78	0.89	0.85	158
Fruits, nuts, vegetables, and products	0.88	2.32	2.32	2.94	3.48	295
Sugar and products	1.35	2.42	1.13	1.35	1.15	−15
Alcoholic beverages	0.43	1.13	1.32	1.51	1.55	260
Oilseeds and products	0.54	0.91	0.49	0.80	0.78	44
Grains, grain products, and feed	0.23	0.41	0.45	0.53	0.60	161
Tobacco	0.28	0.37	0.73	0.56	0.56	100
Others	0.30	0.01	0.50	0.63	0.69	130
Total supplementary imports	6.31	11.30	10.80	12.24	12.96	105
Total agricultural imports[a]	10.51	17.22	16.27	18.92	19.74	88

Source: U.S. Department of Agriculture, Economic Research Service, *Foreign Agricultural Trade of the United States* (Washington, D.C.: USDA, Fiscal Year 1985 Supplement).

[a]Totals may not add due to rounding.

Table 1.11   U.S. Imports from Developed, Developing, and Centrally Planned Countries, 1975-1986 (billion dollars)

Fiscal Year	Developed	Developing	CPEs	World
Total Agriculture				
1975	2.8	6.4	0.2	9.4
1976	3.0	7.0	0.3	10.5
1977	3.4	9.5	0.4	13.4
1978	4.1	9.4	0.4	13.9
1979	5.1	10.6	0.5	16.2
1980	5.4	11.4	0.5	17.3
1981	5.9	10.7	0.6	17.2
1982	6.0	9.1	0.4	15.5
1983	6.5	9.4	0.4	16.3
1984	7.3	11.2	0.5	18.9
1985	7.8	11.5	0.5	19.7
1986[a]	7.9	11.7	0.5	20.0

Source: U.S. Department of Agriculture, Economic Research Service, *Foreign Agricultural Trade of the United States* (Washington, D.C.: USDA, Fiscal Year 1985 Supplement).

[a]Forecast.

tional trade has become increasingly important, only about 10 percent of world agricultural production was traded during the 1960s and early 1970s, and the proportion peaked at less than 20 percent in 1980. Thus, relatively minor changes in local production, if transmitted to world markets, produce large changes in world trade.

World markets are also thin with respect to the number of countries actually playing a significant role in international trade. In 1980, the top five exporting countries accounted for more than 90 percent of wheat, soybean, and corn exports. On the import side, the top seven importers accounted for more than 50 percent of wheat and corn imports, and the top two importers accounted for about 60 percent of soybean imports. International agricultural trade is conducted to a large extent by marketing firms and public marketing agents that exercise considerable oligopolistic, and in many cases, monopolistic marketing power within their domestic economies. Even in the United States, trade is conducted by a few large private sector firms. In all of the CPEs, many developing countries, and some developed market countries, imports and exports of agricultural commodities are handled by government agencies or by state-sanctioned monopolies.

World Market Variability

Another important characteristic of world markets is the variability of production and consumption and the actions that various countries take to manage this variability. There is some indication that production variability has increased since 1960 as new technology and more fragile lands have been brought into production. The growth of Soviet trade probably has increased

Table 1.12   Major World Agricultural Markets and U.S. Shares, 1980–1984 Average and Selected Years

Country Rank by 1980-84 Import Value	Agricultural Imports from (1980-84 average) (billion dollars)		Country Rank by Import Value (rank)				U.S. Share in Major Markets (percent)			
	World	United States	1970	1976	1980	1984	1970	1980	1984	1980–84
1. West Germany	22.00	1.53	2	1	1	2	8.4	7.3	5.2	6.9
2. Soviet Union	19.41	1.79	7	5	3	3	0.6	5.8	14.9	9.2
3. United States	18.18	—	1	2	2	1	—	—	—	—
4. Japan	17.79	6.25	4	3	4	4	29.3	34.3	36.4	35.1
5. United Kingdom	14.46	0.88	3	4	5	5	7.1	5.7	5.5	6.1
6. Italy	13.34	0.96	5	6	7	6	6.2	7.4	6.2	7.2
7. France	13.22	0.60	6	7	6	7	5.0	5.0	4.1	4.5
8. Netherlands	10.41	2.94	8	8	8	8	24.9	29.3	22.5	28.2
9. Belgium-Luxembourg	7.48	0.80	9	9	9	9	9.2	8.0	10.4	10.7
10. Saudi Arabia	4.91	0.45	38	26	13	10	12.4	8.9	9.0	9.2
Subtotal	141.43	16.20	—	—	—	—	14.2	12.4	13.6	13.2
11. Canada	4.65	1.89	10	10	11	11	64.7	40.3	39.3	40.7
12. China, Mainland	4.61	1.37	19	12	10	18	15.5	38.9	29.7	21.4
13. Spain	3.92	1.26	14	11	12	13	16.8	25.7	28.7	32.2
14. South Korea	3.48	1.77	21	23	14	15	51.5	54.5	48.1	51.0
15. Hong Kong	3.37	0.40	17	14	15	14	8.3	13.8	11.5	11.8
16. Egypt	3.19	0.88	42	22	22	12	12.5	32.8	24.6	27.6
17. Switzerland	2.85	0.31	11	13	16	20	10.1	8.5	11.0	10.9
18. Iran	2.68	0.06	52	19	26	16	21.5	0.4	0.1	2.2
19. Mexico	2.65	2.00	41	44	17	21	71.9	78.6	81.8	75.6
20. Taiwan	2.62	1.23	28	24	25	17	40.2	48.9	48.8	45.1
World Total	242.21	40.62	—	—	—	—	—	—	—	—

Sources: Trade Yearbook, 1984, Food and Agricultural Organization of the United Nations; *U.S. Foreign Agricultural Trade Statistics Calendar Years 1980–84*; Econ. Res. Serv. U.S. Dept. Agri., *Agricultural Trade Statistics of Taiwan*, Republic of China, Council of Agriculture. Assembled by Arthur Mackie, ERS, USDA.

world market variability because of that country's changing climatic conditions.

Demand also has become more variable as financial markets have become more integrated. As a result, changes in macroeconomic conditions and policies are transferred quickly from the domestic to the world economy. The move to floating exchange rates has made monetary exchange a major mechanism for transmitting macroeconomic changes and a major source of demand variability.

Price and Income Responsiveness of World Markets

Accurate projections of future world production, consumption, and trade depend on the assumptions made for both demand and supply elasticities with respect to prices and incomes. There is considerable evidence that suggests that demand and supply are relatively price responsive in world markets, at least more so than domestic demand and supply in individual country markets. It also is accepted generally that supply and demand elasticities increase as time allows for adjustment.

Demand responsiveness with respect to income varies greatly among countries with differing levels and distributions of income. Demand in the lower income countries is considerably more responsive to income changes than in the developed countries, but the capacity of developing countries to import food is often constrained by the availability of foreign exchange, even when domestic income increases. Some estimates place the income elasticity of demand for all food in the developing countries between .5 and 1.0; similar estimates are near zero for many of the more developed countries.

The Future World Food Situation

Future trade levels and patterns will depend on factors that affect domestic demand and supply of agricultural products in individual countries. Changes in income, population, tastes, and preferences will continue to be important demand determinants. Changes in the availability and utilization of land, water, technology, and other inputs and investment in physical and institutional infrastructure (research, extension, credit, etc.) will determine future supply conditions. Government interventions, changing exchange rates, and changing relative product and input prices (which will no doubt occur during the 1980s and 1990s) will affect both supply and demand.

Research conducted by the Economic Research Service at the U.S. Department of Agriculture offers some insight into the future world food and trade situation. Alternative levels of income growth and protectionism in world markets were considered in making projections. The baseline projections in the study assume that growth in incomes in all regions will continue at recent levels and that trade constraints will remain stable.

Preliminary baseline findings suggest that demand and, possibly, supply are very sensitive to population growth and the degree of urbanization in a country. Most of the world's population growth is centered in the developing countries. The two most populous countries, China and India, have experienced much of the total growth in consumption. The migration of rural people to the urban areas increases the market dependency of the country. In many cases, this has negatively affected production, and increased imports have been necessary to meet demand.

World population was projected to grow an average of 1.7 percent annually between 1980 and the year 2000, thereby reaching 6.27 billion by the turn of the century. In 1980, about 17 percent of the world's population lived in the developed countries. With an annual growth of only about .6 percent, the population of developed countries will fall to about 14 percent of world population by the year 2000. The CPEs, including China, comprised 32 percent of the world's population in 1980 but will likely grow at an annual rate of only 1.2 percent, thus reducing their share of world population to 29 percent by 2000. The developing countries are expected to grow at an annual rate of 2.27 percent, which will increase their share of world population from 51 percent in 1980 to 57 percent in 2000. The net result is an additional 1.3 billion people in developing countries with high-income elasticities for food, 0.1 billion in the developed countries, and 0.38 billion in the CPEs.

Alternative income growth rates were projected for various regions. The rate ranges from a low of 1.88 percent per year in the EEC to a high of 4.39 percent in the Middle East. Income, including both level and distribution, will be a particularly important factor to monitor because consumer purchasing power varies greatly among countries.

The study considered that long-term supply will depend on such factors as productivity, yields, new lands brought into cultivation, and relative real factor and product prices. Productive capacity is projected to increase at approximately trend rates but also is affected by changes in real product prices. Real product prices were used to balance demand and supply and to link the behavioral relationships that tie together the grains, oilseeds, and livestock subsectors.

These analyses can only partially account for the many unexpected changes in the institutional, political, and economic environment and the domestic and trade policies that countries employ to manage their domestic agriculture and trade. Changes in exchange rates, trade subsidies, foreign debts of importing countries, trade protectionism, and food security issues are treated implicitly in assumptions of economic growth and implied protection.

The major finding of the study, using the base assumptions, is that world supplies will be sufficient to satisfy the large projected increase in world demand caused by the large growth in population and the improved per capita consumption levels at reasonably stable real prices to the year 2000. From 1980 to 2000, world cereal supply-demand balance is projected to grow at an annual average of about 2 percent. For livestock, the projected annual growth rate is about 1.7 percent.

The projections for the major country groupings indicate several significant trends in economic relationships and in future macroeconomic and trade policy. The developed countries will become an even more important source of cereals supply for the developing countries and the CPEs by the end of the century. The prospect of continually stronger world economic growth combined with a fairly liberal trading environment for cereals would significantly boost world prices of both cereals and livestock products. This would dampen developing country consumption of cereals while increasing their domestic production. At the other extreme, a lower growth in income levels in many countries and increased protectionist policies designed to achieve greater self-sufficiency would depress real world prices.

According to these projections, the developed countries will increase the supply of cereals by 5 to 10 percent more than domestic demand. This would mean heavy accumulation of stocks, increased exports, and/or depressed prices. A growth in CPE demand for cereals of 15 or more percent during the 1980s and 1990s will not be balanced by increased domestic production. Thus, increased imports would be necessary to balance supply and demand at stable prices. For the developing countries, the demand for cereals will outpace domestic supply, thus requiring an increase in imports of more than 40 million metric tons by the end of the 1980s and an additional 35 million metric tons by the end of the 1990s. By the year 2000, these countries would have increased imports to 130 million metric tons per year, compared to less than 60 million metric tons in 1980.

For livestock, the developed countries will show a steady increase in supply and demand with net exports increasing slightly. The increase could amount to as much as 15 percent in each decade but will probably amount to less in the 1990s. The per capita animal product consumption in the CPEs will still be less than one-half that of the developed countries, but growth in supply and demand is expected to increase 15 percent annually by the year 2000. The developing countries will equal and could surpass the per capita consumption of the CPEs, with little need for increased imports.

In general, the world supply-demand projections imply compound growth rates between 1980 and 2000 of the following percentages: red meats, 1.4; poultry products, 2.4; wheat, 1.9; rice, 2.2; coarse grains, 1.8; oilseeds, 2.8; oilseed products, 2.8; dairy products, 2.0; cotton, 1.5; and sugar, 2.3.

In the world wheat market, the United States and other developed country producers remain major exporters to Asia, North Africa, and the Middle East. Although U.S. exports of wheat will increase by the year 2000, the U.S.

market share probably will decline.

Most of the increase in the demand for rice will occur in Asia, but the region will remain nearly self-sufficient. Increased rice imports are expected in Africa and the Middle East. However, the United States will face strong competition from other exporting countries, most notably Thailand. Projections for coarse grain exports suggest that the United States will continue as the dominant exporter. World trade in coarse grains by the year 2000 is expected to surpass the 1980 level by 100 percent.

Oilseeds and oilseed product markets will be dominated by the United States. In fact, projections are that the United States will increase its share of the market while Latin America will lose ground. Although the world market supply and demand growth is strong worldwide, developed countries will continue to be major importers.

Strong demand increases for cotton are projected in areas of the world with rapid population growth rates, primarily Asia and Latin America. The United States is considered the major exporter and will increase its share from about one-half to three-quarters of world cotton exports.

Projections in Perspective

These baseline projections are derived from a set of estimated and/or assumed relationships that explain the behavioral response of agricultural supply, demand, and trade. The functional relationships employed in making the projections are based upon observed behavior during a historical base period, 1960–1981. Different sets of assumptions and functional relationships estimated during different periods of time would yield different absolute estimates, but directional changes should be similar to those presented above.

The principal exogenous variables—population and income growth—are developed as extrapolations of trends between 1960 and 1981. However, it is clear from the trends in agricultural production and trade discussed earlier in this chapter that this period encompassed three different kinds of behavior. The late 1960s and early 1970s were years of relative stability in world agricultural prices with a relatively low and stable level of trade. The last half of the 1970s and into early 1980 was a period of explosive growth in agricultural trade accompanied by increasing variability in prices and quantities traded. Since 1980, there has been a reversal of these trends; world trade volumes and values have declined and prices have gotten lower.

A comparison of the prevailing economic and policy environment of the last half of the 1970s and the first half of the 1980s will help to explain the very different behavior of world agriculture during these two periods. Such a comparison also suggests some of the external factors that are likely to determine the performance of agriculture through the end of this century.

The 1970s, especially the latter half of the decade, were characterized by relatively rapid rates of economic growth worldwide. Most countries experienced high rates of inflation—even the United States experienced double-digit inflation. International reserves grew rapidly; given the actions of the Organization of Petroleum Exporting Countries (OPEC), these reserves were markedly redistributed from petroleum importing to petroleum exporting countries. The recycling of OPEC earnings made international credit readily available at low or negative real interest. Primary commodity prices in world markets were relatively high, and developing country export earnings were strong.

The combination of rapidly growing population, rising per capita incomes, policies that subsidized consumption and often taxed production, strong export earnings, and available and cheap credit in the 1970s quickly increased the willingness and ability of developing countries, especially the middle-income developing countries, to increase their dependence on imported agricultural products. The Soviet Union decided to improve the diet of its people, even if this meant importing food. This decision, combined with a series of relatively poor crops, made the Soviet Union a large net importer of both food and feed grains. China also engaged in more active trade relations with the rest of the world. All these global factors contributed to the rapid growth in world demand for agricultural products.

The United States participated more than proportionally in the growing market for two reasons. First, the United States allowed the dollar to float in world exchange markets. This resulted in a significant decline in the value of the dollar, thereby making U.S. agricultural commodities relatively more attractive to foreign purchasers. Second, the United States expanded production rapidly by bringing previously idled resources back into production. Thus, U.S. exports grew even more rapidly than did world exports.

The first half of the 1980s has seen an almost complete reversal of the 1970s economic environment. The world underwent a rather serious recession from which many countries still have not fully recovered. Credit became expensive with high real interest rates, and a number of low- and middle-income developing countries have serious debt service problems. Lower growth rates and lower export earnings in the developed countries significantly reduced their import demand. China's rapid growth in agricultural production coupled with foreign exchange problems also reduced its import dependence.

These factors have contributed to a slowing in the growth rate of world demand for agricultural imports. In addition, just as the depreciation of the dollar in the 1970s accentuated the effect on the United States of rapid growth in world demand for agricultural imports, the rising value of the dollar in the 1980s has accentuated the decline in world demand for U.S. agricultural exports and the increase in U.S. imports.

Whether the rest of the century will be more like the latter half of the 1970s or the first half of the 1980s will depend on the same economic determinants that differentiated these two historical periods. With a return to more rapid economic growth and resumed growth in world demand for the principal exports of the developing countries, their debt service problems will be reduced, and even higher rates of economic growth will be possible. Given continued rapid rates of population growth in the Third World and the relatively high income elasticities at prevailing income levels, higher rates of economic growth in developing countries and increased foreign exchange earnings would in all likelihood again result in increasing demand for imported food and feed grains. These two preconditions are dependent on sufficient economic growth in the developed economies to stimulate demand for developing country exports and on policies in the developed countries that allow them to open their markets to Third World exports. Current low levels of economic growth, however, make it very difficult for developing countries to overcome their serious debt service problems. The longer these low growth rates persist and the longer debt service requirements seriously constrain developing country investment, the more serious the long-term impact on future economic development is likely to be—and the longer it will be before developing countries again become an important source of growth in the demand for agricultural imports.

Although it may not be obvious that exchange rates are an important factor in determining the overall level of world demand for agricultural imports, they are a significant factor in determining trade patterns. The demand for U.S. agricultural exports will depend on whether the dollar continues to decline relative to other currencies and especially on whether it declines relative to currencies of countries that are competitors and customers for U.S. agricultural exports.

This chapter has not treated policy in any explicit way, but it is important to recognize that the domestic and trade policy environment will be as important as the economic environment in shaping the future of world agriculture and agricultural trade. Future agricultural trade will depend greatly on the success of the next round of the General Agreements on Tariffs and Trade (GATT) negotiations in relaxing policy constraints on trade, especially in dealing with domestic agricultural policies that both distort market signals and create barriers to trade.

Commentary

Barbara Insel

The authors of "Global Trends in Agricultural Production and Trade" are to be commended for a valiant, often successful effort to explain what has happened globally to agricultural trade since 1960 and to identify some signposts for the future. They make some very important points and give us some useful data. They also raise some major issues that deserve more exploration.

The first part of the chapter describes the trade patterns in evidence since 1960. The picture presented of the agricultural trade sector at the start of the 1970s and the complex interactions that produced the boom in that decade is a helpful one. The chapter is less effective in explaining the reversal of this pattern in the 1980s, although the authors seem to be aware of this weakness.

However, there are factual errors in the text and some generalizations that don't hold up under closer scrutiny. The contrasts between developed and developing, centrally planned and market economies become awkward when we realize that several of the developing countries don't fit their category (that divergence is exactly what makes them interesting) and that the principal change among developed countries was the emergence of the EEC as a new exporter. The relative importance of two long-term developed country exporters, Canada and Australia, actually declined in the period under examination. The authors' reluctance to name countries starts sounding like nonspeak. Similarly, by reducing their analysis to tables of generalized data and by extrapolating from such statistics, the authors sometimes miss the point. They tend to conclude that countries "chose" a result that was actually—and more often—the consequence of mistakes and oversight.

The authors also include a summary of a large grain market forecasting study whose projections are based on observable behavior during the base period 1960–1981. Thus, the forecasts don't account for the most interesting variables and scenarios or deal with the major changes that occurred during the 1980s. Although it may be interesting to see what might happen if the past repeated itself in simplified form, investing a great deal of intellectual effort in this direction is probably of limited benefit. I think the writers agree with this judgment.

The authors conclude that "world supplies will be sufficient to satisfy the large projected increase in world demand." Somehow, I do not think many of us had doubts about supply growth—although it might be a useful surprise to those who once again seem determined to rediscover Malthus. I in fact fear that the forecast underestimates supply growth by underestimating the pace and impact of technological change in the agricultural sector.

I am genuinely curious about the basis upon which a "large projected increase in world demand caused by the large growth in population and the improved per capita consumption levels at reasonably stable prices by the year 2000" was made. The last boom, as the authors note, was fueled not only by rapid internal growth and growing exports but by the availability of cheap foreign exchange in the form of bank credits at negative interest rates and rapid worldwide inflation, neither of which appear likely to become a factor in at least the near future, although such things do tend to be cyclical.

But then, as the authors note, a forecast is just a function of one's assumptions. However, the institutional, political, and technological changes that are excluded from the forecast have been critical in the past and will continue to determine the future. Much as I understand the difficulty of including such factors in a quantitative study, the value of the resulting forecast may be questioned. But I don't think anything is gained by trading assumptions and scenarios about the future—in that respect I am most sympathetic with the authors. It is far more interesting to think about what has changed and what is most likely to change. Understanding those changes and their roots is crucial to where the future might take us.

Major Issues

The foregoing critique notwithstanding, the authors make some valuable observations that enrich our understanding of the market and that deserve further comment. The chapter also recounts much of the conventional wisdom of recent agricultural policy debates. A second look at these issues also might help elucidate what is going on around us.

Growing Dependence
White, Overton, and Mathia clearly demonstrate the growing disparity between the haves and the havenots. I usually am tempted to say that rich coun-

tries have surpluses, poor countries have deficits. Yet to make it a rich country versus poor country, developed country versus developing country issue is really misleading. The exceptions to these categories prove that the developing countries that have succeeded in expanding production faster than population are among the poorest in the world. The ability to turn around agricultural performance, assuming the basic physical resources are available—and we often forget they are in a great number of countries—is almost entirely a function of public policies. (We used to say infrastructure investment as well, but perhaps the Chinese finally have proven that management and organization can more than make up for scarce capital, at least for a while.)

We all know what kind of policies are needed to ensure agricultural expansion. Thus, for a country with any agricultural potential to increase its agricultural dependence at this moment in history means that its government willfully has chosen to follow the wrong policies, and it is stunning to look at a broad picture of willful impoverishment. We also need to remember that the countries that have made this choice constitute some of the major U.S. markets. The food-exporting countries are the prime beneficiaries of the inappropriate domestic agricultural policies of the food importers.

The Thin Market

The authors have done a major service in showing how thin agricultural trading markets really are. Only a very small fraction of agricultural production actually moves into international trade, and the amount traded is also only a small fraction of total global consumption. However, at the same time, trade increasingly is concentrated among just a few major players. For most major commodities there are hardly more than four or five major exporters. Although there are a large number of individual importing countries for whom imports may constitute a major share of total food supplies, a relatively small number of importers dominates the market. Basically, a few countries have such large populations and production volumes that very small changes in their production or consumption have enormous impact on the international market.

Thus, during the course of a decade the market can be rocked by even relatively small changes in Soviet output or consumption or by output increases in a small number of large countries, such as France, Britain, China, India, or Brazil. To think of these changes happening in the same few years is to begin appreciating the massive structural changes that have occurred since 1960. The thinness of the market, along with the strong impact of policy on agricultural performance, makes all the players very vulnerable to each others' policy and politics, something we do not often invest enough of our efforts in understanding. Yet, relatively little of this is noted by the authors.

Policy, Politics, and Economic Behavior

The authors note that there have been occasions, even in the United States, when policy-determined domestic price signals did not reflect what was going on in the wider world market. They note that producers tend to respond to domestic prices, whatever may be happening in world markets. I appreciate seeing this explicitly stated—population-based market forecasts often fail to acknowledge the influence of these factors on supply and demand. We know U.S. policy is a function of domestic politics and economic relationships. However, our analysis too often seems to think all the other countries should be responding rationally to market economics, and we exhibit a well-practiced indignation when they do not.

Somehow I have lost my ability to understand why U.S. subsidies are inherently more moral or efficient than anyone else's. They are just different. Moralistic thinking about political and cultural solutions may inhibit a full appreciation of what is actually going on in different environments and cloud vision and effective policymaking. It should be clear to everyone that agricultural policy everywhere is about domestic politics.

Rapid Deterioration of U.S. Agriculture

The chapter's picture of the rapid deterioration of U.S. agriculture is persuasive. This sector entered the 1970s in superb shape and then proceeded to fall apart. The explanation provided for the decline is less effective: recession, high interest rates, debt service problems, reduced exports, reduced import dependency in China, the high dollar, and high U.S. prices. The weight of the authors' argument is placed on cyclical macroeconomic phenomena. That anything more fundamental or lasting also may be emerging is not considered. But then, as the chapter notes, one would not expect to find such factors included in an extrapolation of the past. Loyally, no mention is made of the role of U.S. policy in this debacle, beyond a quiet reference to the fact that U.S. prices did not decline with world market signals at the start of the 1980s. Actions such as passing a farm credit bill that authorized lending at 97 percent of land value are quietly excluded from the discussion.

This brings us to the second set of issues and some of the weaknesses of the chapter, which in a way reflect problems with which conventional analysis has not dealt very well.

The U.S. Price Umbrella

I agree that recent high U.S. prices made life a lot easier for all U.S. competitors. However, to conclude that the only reason those competitors are in the market is because of recent high U.S. prices and that merely lowering those prices will simply cut out those competitors is false. It does a disservice to the analysis and reflects a lack of appreciation of both the politics and the production economics of those competitors. Let us take two examples of our competitors' situations.

The EEC's Common Agricultural Policy (CAP) is more than two decades old and dates from a period of relatively low U.S. prices. It is, as most of us would agree, essentially an internal political creation and a political compromise among EEC members (to oversimplify, high price levels to satisfy its German constituents and a controlled system to satisfy the French). The guarantee of high stable prices, strong protection, and, in most cases, subsidized, generously available investment credit led inevitably to surpluses that had to be exported. The EEC quickly came to think of grain exports as, to mix metaphors, a sort of foreign exchange cash cow. The EEC discovered, as did everyone else, that it is cheaper to export than to keep stocks, even with export subsidies, and that those exports fit very well with various foreign policy priorities as well. That France and England would someday become exporters should not have surprised us. It is interesting to look at the production cost functions of some of the larger and more sophisticated French and English producers. We discover that although CAP prices may be needed to protect the tiny German part-time farmer and the surviving French peasants, many of the larger European producers could export at world market prices with very little change in their production techniques. What the U.S. price umbrella did do—and only in recent years—was to help the Europeans avoid the social costs of their policies and the social change that must come with agricultural modernization. That was indeed a very generous gesture.

Let's take another case, that of Brazil. The opening for Brazil's soya exports was indeed created by U.S. policies, but by the soya embargo, not high prices. Brazilians actually produce at farmgate prices that are less than U.S. farmers'. The United States is just lucky that Brazil has such an expensive, unreliable execution system, no grading system and unpredictable trade policies, or that country would have taken even more of the market from the United States.

The countries that are most dependent on high U.S. prices—Australia and Canada—are hardly mentioned. Both have allowed production to become so inefficient that they will have major problems competing with the new, lower U.S. prices. The EEC, conversely, can pay the financial cost sooner than it can the political cost (among farm voters) of ceasing to export. But for the larger grain producers in Britain and France who are responsible for the bulk of the exported crop, there is considerable room for improved efficiency and technology that would allow them to compete even if the EEC did not protect them and even if they at last were forced to improve the quality of their grain. U.S. policymakers underestimate the pace of productivity improvements and modernization among the modern producers in the EEC and, for that matter, in Brazil and Argentina, and do so at their own peril.

The Storage Issue

The authors repeat the commonly held assertion that other countries "chose" to let the United States pay the costs of storage for them. Although there is some validity to this argument, we need to put it in perspective. The planet is littered with storage facilities constructed during the last few decades by governments and government-sponsored cooperatives in the Third World and parts of Europe. Many of these facilities stand empty, closed, or in disrepair, monuments to the confused but dedicated "storage development" policies of many U.S. competitors and customers. We should be careful not to confuse the failure of these policies with an intent to tax the United States. (I don't mean to suggest that many of the policymakers would not have been happy to do so, but they seldom perceived that having the United States store their food supplies was actually in their interest.)

Governments have proven to be inefficient stockholders, and they still are unable to understand why the private sector doesn't assume this responsibility. Yet, at the same time, usually in the name of interseasonal "price stabilization" (what foolishness has been wrought in the name of those two terrible words), governments also have created policies under which only a completely imprudent investor—or a government-financed cooperative—would undertake the risk of holding stocks. Moreover, in much of the Third World, governments seemed to think the purpose of holding stocks was to have something to dump on domestic markets whenever there was a danger that domestic prices might actually reflect demand.

For a variety of highly rational reasons those policies never quite worked as they were intended. The United States was one of the few countries, along perhaps with Canada and Australia, that allowed a domestic pricing flexibility that rewarded stockholding risk. One has to be careful not to take for policy what is often the result of incompetence.

On the other side of the issue, it is impossible to be a major exporter without large carryover stocks, and even the EEC is beginning to realize this. The United States has an obligation to hold stock proportional to its share of the trading market if it is to be considered reliable. Such is the cost of doing business. The EEC is becoming the second largest stockholder as its exporting role grows. China also is beginning to build large stocks.

Elasticity of Demand and Supply

The authors certainly are correct in arguing for a significant price elasticity in both supply and demand. However, one cannot produce as evidence of price elasticity of demand the fact that importers facing a cross section of prices on one day for the same fungible commodity in an auction market will choose the lowest bid. Moreover, on the supply side, we must acknowledge the complexity of the calculation. The farmer is maximizing profits and guessing about future political decisions. If a farmer thinks productivity will increase more than prices will decline, or that the price decline will not be sustained, he or she still will make money by expanding output. In France, where productivity has been growing by more than 20 percent, only a price decline in excess of 20 percent will begin to have any income effect. If the farmer still makes more money by expanding rather than by reducing production, he or she will still go on producing. Less profit is better than none at all. So, as has been said for a very long time, the price decline has to be very large and sustained to have a supply impact. As long as there are many countries with very rapidly growing productivity and a potential for still further technological breakthroughs, the price elasticity of supply will be a very delicate issue.

In developing countries in particular food demand is certainly very price elastic. But the ability to convert that demand into increased imports is quite another issue, which the authors don't really face, or rather they explain it away by assuming a growth in export markets.

Sources of Demand

The authors state that demand and, possibly, supply are sensitive to population growth. Would it be impudent to suggest that access to foreign exchange may prove to be more important in the demand equation than population or even income growth, unless we want to exchange exports for naira? Access to foreign exchange means increased hard currency exports or expanded cheap credit. As there is not much of the latter around for the foreseeable future, the model depends on a worldwide trade boom far greater than that of the 1970s, as it will lack the stimulus of either cheap credit or high inflation.

The authors further comment that "migration of rural people to [urban areas] increased the market dependency of [developing countries]," thereby negatively affecting production and creating a net increase in demand. We are tripping over some gross generalizations here. Except for the Ghanas of the world, where aggressive antifarm policies quickly emptied the farms, such migration often accompanies agricultural modernization and expanded local production. One can cite innumerable examples, a fact that leaves me wondering what kind of data the authors were using.

Trade Monopoly

As one who has spent a great deal of time in developing countries hearing trading companies described as "monopolistic exploiters" by ideologues, I get more than a little uncomfortable reading about how grain exports are dominated by a few monopolists. Not only do we have more companies trading grain than selling cars or coffee, but I have seen the alternative, and it is definitely worse.

The more important point that should have been emphasized is how much trade is now dominated by governments, in which politics, long-term agreements (LTAs), and tender offers are more important than are service and efficiency. The United States as the high-quality, high-service exporter is at a disadvantage in that trade. We know that political, credit-based trade usually ignores actual price. In sum, this trend is not really in the U.S. interest, although even as we speak, the trend is changing slowly. Many developing countries do not have the resources to continue controlling grain procurement, and privatization is increasing. The wheat trade, however, which is always the most political, continues to be dominated by government and politics.

Exporting Variability

The authors restate another familiar argument—that Soviet production is subject to high variability at least for physical reasons and that by increasing Soviet dependence on U.S. imports the USSR has exported its variability to the U.S. market. I can't help but find this reasoning curiously backward, although familiar. Let me rephrase it—the Soviets have proven unable to manage their own variability, and this weakness has created a market for U.S. exports. If the United States is unable to manage this variability and to reflect that cost in U.S. margins, then the United States is proving itself less competent than it should be. It is a cost of making those sales. One should not expect to profit from a sales opportunity and then criticize its cause.

The Corn Market

White, Overton, and Mathia suggest that the United States will probably continue to lose market share in wheat, which is quite likely. But at the same time, they see the United States continuing its dominance of the feedgrain market. The authors note that while world wheat production burgeoned, corn output grew much more slowly. They seem to conclude that there is little capacity in the world for expanding such output. Oh, the folly of extrapolation! They should have talked to the hybrid seed companies. Very few countries even use hybrid corn seed. The potential for expansion of corn output is enormous, particularly in East Asia and Latin America. The U.S. hold on the world feedgrain market is tenuous at best. The slow growth of competition in the past is not an indicator of security but of risk and untapped opportunity.

Technology

We all know that there now exists the potential for significant technological developments that may dramatically change and shift both demand and supply curves and undermine extrapolations from the past. Much of that change will be in reducing the feedgrain requirements of livestock and increasing the yields and viability of wheat production still further. I also would wager that both demand and ease of testing and marketing regulation would lead to commercialization of those products first in Europe, then in the more advanced developing countries, and much later in the United States. This would have severe implications for the competitive position of U.S. exports. The writers, however, just barely acknowledge these potentially critical factors. Surely they deserve more attention.

Specific Issues

There are a few specific country references in the analysis that should be addressed. The authors note that the Brazilians recently have employed policies that favor the export of soymeal. What they do not explain is that Brazil exports soymeal instead of beans because the government subsidized the construction of an enormous crushing industry and now has to keep it in business, which is done by reserving for this industry a major share of domestic bean production. This reserve also subsidizes domestic soybean oil consumption, which is politically very attractive. Both policies are prohibitively expensive, and Brazil would profit from exporting the beans.

The authors suggest that EEC imports from the United States fell because of the recession, but the impact of both the levy policy and of feedgrain substitution policies is not mentioned. The substitution of surplus feedwheat plus proteins such as corn gluten feed for corn as a feedgrain in the EEC is a powerful trend and should not be treated merely as a cyclical phenomenon. Although I realize this is an unpopular position in U.S. agricultural circles, we also should be prepared to see this trend spread to Spain and Portugal, thereby reducing U.S. feedgrain exports to these countries.

Conclusion

We need to understand the world as a complex environment and agriculture as a changing, highly competitive, political, technologically driven industry. This volume's first chapter does not succeed at that task. To accept the authors' caveats at face value, it was never their intent to present or examine such a complex picture. However, the authors discuss the prospects for U.S. global trade by excluding most of the factors that are likely to influence such trade and by including factors whose influence probably will be thwarted—an analytical framework apparently forced by the exigencies of the authors' model.

part two

Agricultural Development and Trade: Case Studies

chapter two

Agricultural Development in Africa: Kenya and Tanzania

Cheryl Christensen
Michael Lofchie
Larry Witucki

Sub-Saharan Africa as a region has been characterized by severe food and economic crises since the mid-1970s. Food and agricultural production per capita has declined, export-oriented agricultural production has floundered, and real per capita Gross National Product (GNP) has decreased, thus threatening not only the longer-term growth prospects of the region, but the immediate survival of its economies and people. Yet the picture is not uniform. Differences in development strategies sometimes have made a significant difference in economic performance, even within the admittedly difficult economic niches available to exporters of primary products.

Our purpose in this chapter is to elaborate some of these differences by examining two countries—Kenya and Tanzania—that share important similarities, such as political stability, geographic proximity, population size, and status as primary exporters, but that, because of differences in economic strategy and development policies, also illuminate the impact of policy on economic performance. Both countries also have suffered considerably from external economic shocks such as the precipitous increases in the price of petroleum, rising interest rates that exacerbate debt, and a general tendency toward declining terms of trade for countries dependent upon the export of primary agricultural commodities.

In time it has become clear that the differing policy frameworks of these countries have equipped them very differently to deal with the effects of international economic forces. Previous analyses of selected developing countries have concluded that countries with relatively open economic systems, although more exposed to international economic shocks, also are better able to cope with them. Our comparison of Kenya—a more open economy—with Tanzania—a more closed economy—lends support to this thesis.

The economic differences between Kenya and Tanzania are striking.

During the decade following independence, Kenya's agricultural Gross Domestic Product (GDP) grew at a rate of more than 4.5 percent a year. It has slowed somewhat since the early 1970s but has continued to average better than 3 percent a year, even during a decade of severe economic shocks and generally declining prices for primary agricultural commodities. The remarkable feature of Kenya's contemporary agricultural performance is that it has been able to sustain positive growth despite powerful constraints, such as a limited area of arable land, a series of serious droughts, and an international environment that is demonstrably adverse to the economic prospects of countries dependent upon the export of agricultural products.

Tanzania has not performed nearly as well. Although observers frequently describe Tanzania as undergoing an economic "crisis," that term is perhaps inappropriate, for it conveys an impression that the country's situation is of a short-term nature. Tanzania's current economic predicament, however, is the culmination of nearly two decades of worsening economic performance. Despite the hopes of those who believe in the necessity of an immediate economic turnaround lest disaster occur, there is little hope for economic recovery unless the government abandons the economic policies and strategies that have produced the current state of affairs.

Thus, these countries are launched on entirely different economic trajectories. Kenya's economy has been consistently stronger than that of Tanzania. Its real per capita GDP was significantly higher than the Tanzanian GDP at independence and has increased significantly during most of the last two decades. Although drought and global recession have caused some fluctuation in per capita GDP since 1980, Kenya's per capita income today is substantially higher than it was in the 1960s. Tanzania, on the other hand, has experienced more anemic economic growth with intermittent periods of sharp economic decline.

The differences in GDP growth are only partially accounted for by agricultural growth. They also reflect considerable differences in the performance of the nonagricultural sector. Agriculture has historically comprised a smaller share of GDP in Kenya than in Tanzania. In 1965, for example, agriculture accounted for 32 percent of Kenya's GDP compared with 42 percent of Tanzania's. Because of the robust growth of its agricultural sector, Kenya has been able to allot significant economic resources for the expansion of the nonagricultural sectors of its economy. As a result, despite—or perhaps because of—strong agricultural performance, agriculture's share of total GDP has declined, falling to 27 percent in 1984. In Tanzania, the poor performance of the agricultural sector has placed a fundamental constraint on the allocation of resources elsewhere in the economy. As a result, weaker growth in nonagricultural sectors meant that there was an increase in agriculture's share of GDP to 44 percent in 1984, even though agricultural performance was relatively poor.

One of the most important benefits of recent agricultural growth in Kenya is the extent to which it has been able to achieve improvements in rural welfare. Here, too, the contrast between the two countries is significant. Although both countries had approximately equal levels of real per capita agricultural GDP in 1980, Tanzania's level had fallen to only 90 percent of Kenya's by 1984. Given the stronger performance of Kenyan export crops, per capita agricultural income has continued to grow more rapidly in Kenya than in Tanzania. In addition, Kenya's policy of "passing through" a larger proportion of increases in world prices to farmers has enabled farmers to gain substantially more from export crops than has been the case in Tanzania, where export crops have been more heavily taxed and/or where inefficiency and high operating margins in the marketing system often have meant less income for producers.

The different agricultural performances of these two countries also is reflected in their widely contrasting capacity to manage and service their external debt. Both countries have substantially increased their outstanding external debt in recent years, primarily in response to the financial crises of the 1970s and early 1980s. The pattern of growth in public debt was fairly similar, and by the end of 1984 both countries had roughly comparable debt levels—Kenya, $3.8 billion; Tanzania, $3.3 billion. The structure of their debt burdens is slightly different. Approximately 15 percent of Kenya's debt is private, compared with only about 2.3 percent of Tanzania's. As a result, Tanzania's debt burden as a whole has been contracted on slightly easier terms than has Kenya's. But this difference is not so great as to affect the magnitude of the annual debt burden in any substantial way.

The critical difference between the two countries is that Kenya has been able to service its debt burden in a timely manner. Its arrears on international debt at the end of 1984 were negligible, and its *ex ante* debt service ratio (debt owed as a percentage of export earnings), although high (approximately 32.5 percent), was well within the country's financial capacity. Indeed, thanks partly to its high foreign exchange earnings during the 1984 tea boom, Kenya was repaying some of its international debt before the date of maturity and enjoyed an *ex post* debt service ratio (debt payments as a percentage of export earnings) of about 37 percent. Tanzania, on the other hand, has been badly deficient in servicing its external debt. Its *ex ante* debt service ratio at the end of 1984 was close to 60 percent, but it was able to make payments on only about one-half the amount owed, which resulted in an *ex post* debt service ratio of about 35 percent. As a result of its inability to make prompt payments, Tanzania was in arrears on about 10 percent of its total international debt.

Despite a lower level of debt service, Tanzania has been experiencing a severe foreign exchange crisis. Its foreign exchange earnings have been in-

sufficient to allow the country to undertake the imports necessary for its industrial sector, which currently operates at only about 10 to 15 percent of
installed capacity. Indeed, Tanzania has recently been compelled to curtail
its imports even of vital necessities such as fuel.

Development Strategies and the Role of Agriculture

Kenya and Tanzania can be usefully compared because of the strikingly different development strategies they have pursued since independence.[1]
Such a comparison is further facilitated by the fact that in each country there
has been great continuity of policy since the mid-1960s. Neither country has
altered the broad political/ideological underpinnings of its development
strategy since the early years of the postindependence period. Kenya's development strategy features a mixed economy with substantial private sector involvement in both economic and agricultural development. In the agricultural sector, this has translated into a strong commitment to private
ownership of land, which provides freedom for market-based land transactions, and a heavy emphasis on transforming the basis of land ownership
from traditional, communal patterns to individual holdings with title deeds.

Tanzania has focused on creating a socialist economy, one in which the
operation of market forces has been constrained or eliminated in an attempt
to limit or reverse inequalities in assets and income. Indeed, the country's
developmental institutions were set up principally to administer growth in
such a way as to minimize socioeconomic disparities. Following the 1967
Arusha Declaration, major economic assets were nationalized, including all
land and key industries such as banking, insurance, and transportation. In
the agricultural sector, the commitment to a socialist development strategy
resulted in the creation of collective *ujamaa* villages in which production
was to be conducted along collectivist lines. Private farming has been systematically discouraged, and private farms sometimes have been
nationalized in order to create communal or parastatal farming operations.
Private transactions in land, like many other private economic transactions,
are officially forbidden.

Tanzania's stated development objectives have put much weight on
overcoming poverty and fostering equality.[2] During the 1960s and 1970s,
there was considerable investment in programs to improve living standards
and human potential, including expanded access to basic education, clean
water, and both curative and preventive health care. The emphasis on fostering social equality has been associated with an all-pervasive pattern of state
interventions intended to limit, and in most cases eliminate, private economic endeavors and/or accumulation. These interventions include the reduction of salary differentials through public sector practice and legislation,
the use of price controls, centrally financed investment to combat regional
inequality, and measures to reduce private economic activity.

Agriculture and the Industrial Sector

After independence, both Kenya and Tanzania, like many other newly independent African countries, adopted industrial strategies based on the principle of import substitution. Such strategies generally have disadvantaged agriculture by creating an antiexport bias and worsening domestic terms of trade. However, the two countries differed substantially in the manner in which they implemented import substitution. There were at least two critically important differences: the degree and duration of the antiexport bias and the role of the state in planning and undertaking production and investment.

As early as the mid-1970s, Kenyan officials began to acknowledge that trade and industrial policy overemphasized import substitution, and they began corrective measures.[3] With the Local Manufactures (Export Compensation) Act of 1974, the Kenyan government began a series of measures to reduce the import-substitution bias in favor of local industrial production. These included the introduction of a sales tax (to generate government revenue without encouraging additional production, which higher tariffs would do); tariff reform (designed to narrow the spread of tariff rates and thereby reduce levels of effective protection); and introduction of export subsidies. At the same time, an emphasis was placed on promoting agricultural exports, generally through favorable pricing policies, infrastructure development, and effective marketing. Kenya consistently reenforced these measures in subsequent years. In 1980, for example, the government increased the level of export subsidies and broadened their scope to include a number of manufactured goods as well as agricultural commodities. Perhaps most importantly, Kenya initiated a policy of flexible exchange rate devaluations, which was a more general and far more powerful way of promoting exports.

Kenya's success in promoting agricultural exports has been basic to its ability to continue an industrial program based partially on import substitution. Earnings from tea, coffee, and other agricultural products have enabled Kenya to continue developing industries that are oriented toward the production of consumer goods for domestic consumption.

Tanzania reaffirmed its commitment to import substitution in 1975 by introducing a new program called the Basic Industry Strategy.[4] The purpose of this strategy was to extend import substitution beyond the consumer goods sector and to begin the domestic production of more essential capital goods, such as agricultural implements and construction materials. The program's underlying assumption was that Tanzania's severe foreign exchange shortage ruled out the importation of even these economically vital inputs. Tanzanian planners had come to believe that the very survival of such key sectors as agriculture, construction, and transportation depended upon the development of an internal capacity to provide for their equipment and other needs. The difficulty confronting the Basic Industry Strategy, however, was precisely the same as that confronting the consumer goods industries based on import substitution—namely, that the launching of new industries, however foreign exchange-conserving their products might be in the long run, requires heavy initial inputs of foreign exchange and investment capital.

To be successful, then, the Basic Industry Strategy would have had to be accompanied by an agricultural strategy that generated sufficient foreign exchange earnings to finance the capital requirements of the new industries. Indeed, the Basic Industry Strategy was given a temporary economic boost by the commodities (especially beverages) boom of 1976 and 1977. That boom was brief, however, and only concealed the fact that Tanzania's agricultural policy during this period was not designed to provide for long-term increases in export earnings. Rather, as its principal reaction to the food crisis of 1973–1974, the Tanzanian government had committed itself to the goal of food self-sufficiency, a decision that manifested itself in increased producer price levels for food staples relative to exportable agricultural commodities. The goal of this policy, like the goal of the Basic Industry Strategy, was to conserve foreign exchange by boosting domestic production of essential goods that previously had been imported. But by raising the prices of food staples out of proportion to those for export crops, the government of Tanzania was setting the stage for a widespread tendency to favor food crops over export crop development and, thus, for a sharp reduction in export earnings.

The most destructive effect of Tanzanian import substitution, however, was its tendency to starve the agricultural sector of vital capital inputs. During the second half of the 1970s, there was a major shift away from agriculture in the country's total capital investment. By 1981/82, agriculture and livestock received only about 11.5 percent of capital resource allocations while industry received nearly 30 percent.[5] Expressed in real terms, this meant that while capital allocations to all sectors including industry increased by 33 percent, those to agriculture dropped by about 50 percent. Under these conditions, it is not surprising that Tanzania's agricultural economy has shown little growth. Indeed, given the impact of capital starvation in addition to other adverse policies, the only surprise is that this sector performed as well as it did, a testimony perhaps to the willingness of small landholders to continue their efforts even under the most difficult circumstances.

Domestic Agricultural Policies

Kenya and Tanzania, like most countries in sub-Saharan Africa, intervene heavily in their agricultural economies through government pricing policies, the operation of parastatals, and the provision of agricultural inputs. Tanzania also has intervened extensively to restructure agricultural production and marketing. Three policy areas are particularly important in accounting for the differences in the two countries' past agricultural performance: land policy, pricing policy, and exchange rate policy.

Land Policy

When Kenya gained its independence in late 1963, the administration of President Jomo Kenyatta made land policy the center of its approach to the rural sector. The fundamental cornerstone of this land policy was the principle that Africans should have full rights to acquire, possess, and cultivate land on a private freehold basis. For only in this way could Africans aspire to the same degree of agricultural prosperity that Europeans had enjoyed during the era of British rule. Although this principle has frequently been criticized as legitimizing large-scale land acquisition by members of Kenya's political elite and thus gross inequities in landownership, it has contributed enormously to the development of an African smallholder farming community and to the implementation of policies designed to ensure the economic stability of this social class.

The Kenyan government's commitment to the principle of private land-ownership as the basis of sustained agricultural growth has been so strong that the basic operational premises of its land policy have remained constant since independence. These premises are, first, that there should be minimum changes in the highly productive agricultural economy developed during the colonial period by the European settler community. Second, that insofar as possible the basic structure of this sector should be maintained while a gradual process of land transfer from European to African farmers is pursued. Third, that land transfers should be made on the basis of individually owned farms, not collective holdings; that these transfers should, insofar as possible, occur on a willing buyer–willing seller basis; and, that where European farms were being subdivided, any newly created African farms should be large enough to produce marketable surpluses of export and food crops. (Some European farms have been purchased by private African companies and by African cooperatives formed for that purpose.) Fourth, that a free market in land should be rigorously maintained so that efficient and productive farmers could expand their holdings and that government programs, such as loans from the Agricultural Finance Corporation, should encourage this process.

Tanzania's land policy since independence stands in sharp contrast to Kenya's. The Tanzanian government's attempt to implement a nationwide system of collectivized agriculture has been documented extensively. Between 1969 and 1975, Tanzania attempted to transform the socioeconomic basis of its entire rural economy. The purpose of this transformation was to replace existing patterns of largely individualized household production with a network of village communities in which land would be collectively held and production collectively organized. During this brief period of time more than five thousand new villages were created or existing villages were designated "socialist." Intensive efforts were undertaken to lay the basis for collective agricultural practices. Before the collectivization program began, less than 5 percent of Tanzanians lived in villages. By the end of 1975, more than 60 percent of the rural population lived in settled village communities that had embarked to varying degrees upon the implementation of collective farming.

The socialist village program contributed to the poor performance of Tanzania's agricultural sector. The process of implementation sometimes interfered directly with agricultural production, as in cases where peasants were forcibly moved between planting and harvesting seasons or during one or the other of these periods of peak labor needs. In some cases peasants were moved to districts and regions that were so environmentally different from their traditional areas of residence as to be wholly unsuitable for the crops they were accustomed to growing. Given that one of the key purposes of collective villagization was to promote social equality, villagization was sometimes accompanied by outright confiscation of the farmlands of the country's larger-scale farmers. Inasmuch as this stratum of farmers had accounted for a very large proportion of the country's marketed agricultural surplus, the land seizures caused a severe reduction in the available food supply. Although the Tanzanian government has eliminated its insistence on collective production since 1975, it has never fully regained the confidence or trust of its peasant population.

Pricing Policy

Export Crops   Like most countries in sub-Saharan Africa, both Kenya and Tanzania have strong government involvement in agricultural pricing, and in both countries these pricing interventions are the subject of heated dialogue with development assistance agencies such as the World Bank and the U.S. Agency for International Development (AID), which advocate less governmental control of the pricing and marketing of agricultural commodities. As in the case of land policy, however, the differences between the two countries are important. Their widely contrasting approaches to agricultural pricing policy help account for the wide variance in the economic performance of their agricultural sectors. The differences between the two are particularly striking with regard to export crops, where Kenya's pricing policies have escaped the pitfalls that characterize so much of the rest of sub-Saharan Africa.

Kenya's agrarian success has been shaped by an export pricing policy that gives producers incentives to grow and market an increasing volume of their crops. This is most conspicuously the case with respect to the country's principal agricultural exports, coffee and tea, whose marketed volumes have grown steadily since the mid-1970s. Kenya's pricing policy for these two crops differs fundamentally from that of virtually every other independent African country in that the government does not set producer prices for these commodities. Rather, it allows their prices to be determined by and vary with the world market price. Its export pricing policy for coffee and tea has been referred to as a "throughput" system—that is, the world market prices for these crops are passed on to the growers after a modest percentage has been deducted to cover the operating costs of the parastatal corporations that handle the purchasing, transportation, and marketing of these crops.[6]

Tanzania controls the price of its export crops and, like the vast majority of African countries, sets prices well below world market levels.[7] Until recently, the government also had taxed export crops as a means of generating revenue, thereby further lowering the net return to producers. The suppression of export crop prices has been so great that it largely accounts for the drop in export volumes of key commodities. Between 1969/70 and 1980/81, the real producer price of coffee dropped by 45 percent and tea by 49 percent. Other export crops also suffered badly from official underpricing. During this period, for example, the real producer price of cashew nuts fell by 27 percent.[8] This sort of price suppression has resulted in a disastrous drop in the country's marketed production of major agricultural exports. By the mid-1980s, coffee production was only about 90 percent of its previous peak; tea production, despite heavy donor assistance, was about equal its previous peak; cotton production was less than 70 percent of its former level; and the production of cashew nuts, which in the mid-1970s had briefly emerged as the country's largest foreign exchange earner, was less than one-fourth its peak.

Food Crops   Both Kenya and Tanzania have sought self-sufficiency in basic food grains—that is, they have sought to minimize imports of maize, wheat, and rice without setting prices so high that they might generate surpluses that would need to be exported. There are sharp differences in food pricing policies in the two countries, however. In Kenya, cereal pricing has been the focus of extensive public debate, and the government has developed a pricing policy that provides adequate incentives for the country's maize producers (see Figure 2.1). At least part of the reason for the debate has been the influence Kenya's large- and medium-sized farmers have wielded as a pressure group. Indeed, because large numbers of Kenya's civil servants and political leaders own agricultural land and engage in the cultivation of maize as well as export crops, the country's political establishment is responding to its own self-interest in formulating an overall pricing strategy that offers attractive prices for all the country's agricultural commodi-

Figure 2.1   Corn Producer Prices in Kenya and Tanzania, 1966–1985 (with world price comparison)

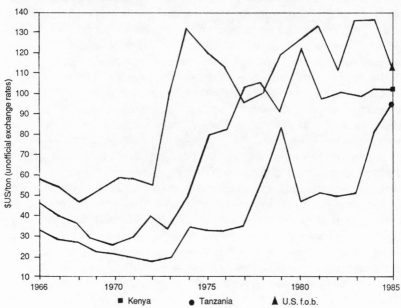

ties. Because the political elite has a direct stake in the economic well-being of the countryside, Kenya is a major exception to the tendencies toward urban bias that are so all-pervasive an influence on the pricing policies of other countries throughout sub-Saharan Africa.

Tanzania is closer to the African norm. Until the mid-1970s, pricing policy for agricultural commodities was not viewed as the basic means for stimulating economic growth in the rural sector, but, rather, as a part of the country's effort to build a socialist political and economic system. Indeed, the country's commitment to socialism imparted a decidedly antiagricultural bias to its pricing policy. As an additional component of Tanzania's socialist strategy, political leaders and civil servants were not permitted to have secondary sources of income and, thus, could not invest in agricultural land. As a result, Tanzania's political elite did not have a direct stake in the economic well-being of the countryside. The antifarmer bias inherent in the country's socialist philosophy has been further reenforced by the urban life-style and political base of the governing political elite.

To achieve a balance between domestic supply and demand, Kenyans have chosen to set maize prices at or slightly below import parity. The assumptions underlying this pricing strategy are fairly straightforward. If the official price were above import parity, it could be expected to encourage maize imports, either legally or illegally, and the result would be a maize glut. If the maize price were set substantially below import parity—that is, closer to export parity—it would result in a price level so close to or so far below the cost of production that maize producers would either shift to other crops or withhold their crop from the market. The result of pricing maize at close to export parity would be a serious shortfall in domestic production, the inevitable growth of a massive informal market in maize, and an increased need for imports. The Kenyans have had considerable success in setting official producer prices at import parity, and this policy has yielded a strong record of national food self-sufficiency.

Tanzania's annual production of marketed food crops has been adversely affected by pricing policies that have lowered the real return to the agricultural producer. De Wilde's figures show that the real producer price levels of Tanzania's three major food crops—maize, wheat, and rice—fell measurably between the mid-1970s and 1980.[9] During the latter half of the 1970s, the Tanzanian government did attempt to implement a strategy of food self-sufficiency by offering farmers dramatic increases in the nominal price of foodgrains, including maize. As a result, marketed production of maize did increase during this period and reached a peak of about 225,000 tons in 1978/79. Since that time, however, the continuing trend of falling real prices has had a powerful effect; by the mid-1980s, marketed maize production fell to approximately 70,000 tons or only about 30 percent of its recent peak level.

Exchange Rate Policy

Tanzania and Kenya have had strikingly different exchange rate regimes in recent years. Beginning in 1981, Kenya took measures to devalue its currency and has sought to keep the official exchange rate for the Kenyan shilling close to the market-determined rate. Tanzania, on the other hand, has been reluctant to undertake systematic currency devaluation. As a result, high rates of inflation have steadily widened the gap between the official exchange rate and the real market value of the Tanzanian shilling (Figure 2.2).[10]

An overvalued currency is, in effect, a hidden form of taxation on the agricultural producer and, as such, has as much of a disincentive effect as do low commodity prices. Overvaluation directly affects the producers of export crops because the farmgate price levels for these commodities are, to a large extent, a function of the ratio at which the international price is converted into units of local currency. It has indirect but equally consequential effects on the producers of locally marketed food staples because governments that involve themselves in the determination of prices for agricultural commodities cannot allow the ratios between export crop prices and food staples to vary randomly. Low real prices for exportable commodities have to be sustained partially by low real prices for food staples lest there be an

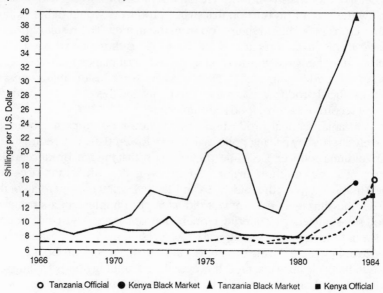

Figure 2.2   Kenyan and Tanzanian Exchange Rates, 1966–1984 (official and black market)

○ Tanzania Official   ● Kenya Black Market   ▲ Tanzania Black Market   ■ Kenya Official

incentive to shift between the two.

Tanzania's export farmers, like others throughout Africa, are paid for their crops in their national currency, and the prices they receive are calculated, as elsewhere, on the basis of the official exchange rate. The precipitous decline in Tanzania's production of exportable commodities is a direct function of the diminishing real purchasing power of the currency the country's farmers are receiving in payment for their crops. Overvaluation also has had a negative impact on the marketed production levels of local food staples. This is partially a consequence of the need to maintain some sort of ratio between export and food crop prices; but it also results from the fact that currency overvaluation has cheapened the cost of food imports, thus making them more attractive than locally produced foods, especially in the large cities. Overvaluation also may have affected Tanzania's ability to provide locally produced food grains by lowering producer prices in comparison to nearby countries and, thereby, encouraging an illegal, but highly lucrative, cross-border trade in maize.[11]

It would be a gross oversimplification to suggest that devaluation alone would stimulate a recovery in Tanzania's agricultural productivity. For the real prices received by Tanzanian farmers are affected by a variety of factors including direct governmental controls, the level of taxation, the operating margins of the agricultural parastatals, and the amount of subsidy provided for agricultural inputs. Exchange rate policy is thus only one of a number of policies that determine whether or not there is sufficient incentive for farmers to produce a marketable agricultural surplus. When overvaluation exceeds 500 percent, however, its effects are considerable. By discouraging exports and encouraging imports of grains that could be locally produced, overvaluation has contributed directly to Tanzania's foreign exchange crisis and, thereby, to the country's overall economic malaise. It would be unrealistic to think that an economic recovery could begin without a major devaluation.

Patterns of International Agricultural Trade

Both Kenya and Tanzania import substantial quantities of food grains (Figures 2.3 and 2.4). But their import patterns differ substantially. Tanzania's imports of maize, wheat, and rice are of a long-term nature and reflect ongoing structural deficits that arise from inappropriate agricultural policies. Kenya's heaviest grain imports are of maize, and these are generally of a short-term nature and arise out of climatic emergencies such as the 1984 drought. Both countries have come to rely heavily on food aid.

Kenya's maize imports have almost invariably coincided with periods of adverse weather. But it has been suggested that these imports also may have roots in policy. Robert Bates, for example, has argued that there is a policy-induced maize cycle triggered by the fact that import parity pricing tends to generate periodic surpluses.[12] When this occurs, the government must respond by lowering the maize price in order to reduce inventories and avoid the need for exports. If the timing of the lowered price should happen to coincide with a period of poor climate, the result would be a serious shortfall. Thus, for example, the Kenyan government set a particularly

Figure 2.3   Kenyan Total Grain Imports, 1966–1985

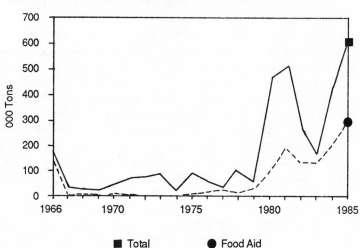

■ Total   ● Food Aid

Figure 2.4   Tanzanian Total Grain Imports, 1966–1985

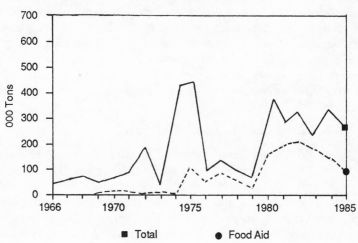

low price for maize for the 1979 harvest as a means of coping with large carryover stocks from the 1977 and 1978 harvests. That a year of serious drought would begin in late 1979 could not have been anticipated, but the combination of poor climate and low prices resulted in a need for substantial imports in 1980/81, only two years after the country had been forced to export its surplus.

Kenya was also a heavy maize importer in 1984/85, following the extraordinarily severe drought of early 1984, one that, according to most observers, may well have been the worst in the region in this century. Total maize production dropped by about 40 percent from an anticipated 2.2 million tons, which necessitated imports of approximately 600,000 tons to compensate for the shortfall in the domestically marketed surplus. Kenya's 1984/85 imports ended early in 1985 as soon as the country's rainfall pattern returned to normal. Indeed, the recovery of Kenya's maize sector was so strong that in the early months of 1986, the government had to reexport some of its imported maize in order to provide storage for the large domestic crop. Importantly, Kenya's maize imports during the crisis for the most part were obtained on the basis of direct commercial transactions rather than as food aid. Kenya's ability to afford heavy maize imports was made possible by the country's success as an exporter of tea and coffee and ability to take advantage of favorable world prices for beverages.

Kenya's wheat imports show a different pattern (Figure 2.5). These increased from negligible levels in 1970 to 300,000 tons in 1985 and exceeded domestic production. Until the mid-1970s, imports were exclusively commercial, and they remained predominantly commercial throughout the rest of the decade. During the 1980s, however, Kenya has imported heavily (sometimes exclusively) on commercial terms. The United States, the European Economic Community (EEC), and Australia all provided wheat food aid; the United States was the major donor. Although high levels of imports in 1985 reflect to some extent the shortfall in maize production, Kenya's steadily rising wheat imports indicate a structural import requirement. Recent field analyses by AID and the U.S. Department of Agriculture (USDA) suggest a consumption shift to wheat, especially in urban areas.

Tanzania has had consistently high levels of grain imports since the early 1970s. Despite this pattern, many observers in the international donor community believe that Tanzania, given normal weather, produces sufficient grain to feed its entire population, an assertion that, if true, only reenforces the inappropriateness of the country's exchange rate, pricing, and marketing policies. Among many of Tanzania's donors, there is a strong suspicion that grain imports are necessitated by the fact that some of Tanzania's annual grain production finds its way across the country's borders to Malawi, Zambia, Zaire, and, occasionally, Kenya.

Differences in real producer prices between Tanzania and its neighbors tend to support this analysis. Tanzania's principal maize-growing areas, such as Arusha-Moshi in the north-central part of the country and the vast plains area of the southern highlands along Lake Tanganyika, are physically located in border regions directly adjacent to countries that have harder currencies, better supplies of consumer goods, and higher real producer prices. Because of infrastructural deterioration, southwestern Tanzanina is virtually

Figure 2.5   Kenyan Wheat Imports, 1966–1985

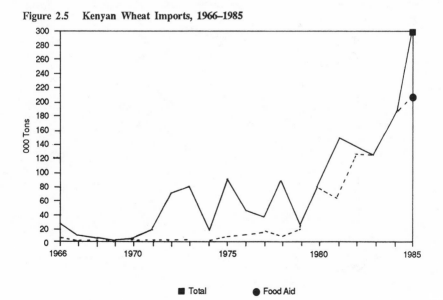

cut off from the country's principal maize markets in Dar es Salaam and Tanga. It is impossible to determine exactly the amount of Tanzanian grain traded informally across its borders, but because Tanzania's grain-producing regions have the capacity to produce large surpluses, the view that Tanzania's annual production is, in fact, equal to its annual consumption is highly persuasive.

Tanzania's maize imports were comparatively small until 1974, when there was a sharp increase due to a serious food crisis (see Figure 2.6). Food imports declined during the period 1976–1978 due to strenuous efforts to increase the producer price for maize. But by the end of the 1970s, it was clear that Tanzania had developed a structural import gap resulting from the government's growing inability to procure adequate supplies from local producers. Food aid provided the bulk of Tanzanian imports until 1984–1985 but has since dropped sharply, thereby forcing the government to rely upon commercial imports.[13] There are several factors responsible for the fall in food assistance to Tanzania. Food aid requirements for countries elsewhere in sub-Saharan Africa escalated in 1983/84 and peaked in 1984/85 in response to the drought across much of the continent and dire emergencies in Ethiopia, Sudan, Mozambique, and Kenya. In this context, Tanzania's needs had a relatively lower priority. Some donors had become disillusioned with the country's policies and, as a result, responded more slowly to Tanzania's food aid requests.

Tanzania has had a structural import requirement for wheat since 1975. Although the country's import levels are less than one-third those of Kenya, they are nearly equal to domestic production levels. Food aid, mostly from

Figure 2.6   Tanzanian Corn Imports, 1966–1985

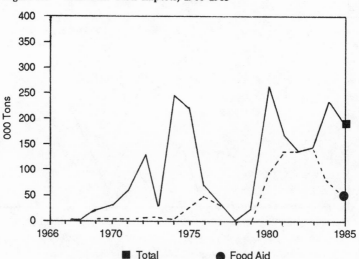

the United States, has provided the majority of Tanzania's wheat imports. Tanzania also has a structural import requirement for rice, with imports double those of Kenya and equal to nearly 25 percent of domestic production in 1984. Since 1984, the bulk of Tanzania's rice imports have come through food aid provided principally by Japan and the United States.

Conclusion: Policy Implications

This comparison of Kenya and Tanzania suggests a number of conclusions, some well defined and some not. The most striking difference between the two countries is their trade performance and the links between economic growth and trade strategies. Despite the very real limitations imposed by primary commodity markets and the prevalence of international economic shocks, Kenya's export-oriented strategy overwhelmingly outperformed Tanzania's more extreme import-substitution strategy. Because the two countries participated in similar agricultural commodity markets, it is difficult to associate these differential results with differences in their international export environments. Kenya's gains resulted far more from its domestic policies than from a more favorable natural endowment and, in this case, demonstrate quite conclusively the long-term payoff from a continued support of a sound, adequately maintained institutional and infrastructural base. Effective production incentives, adequate marketing infrastructure, and the ability to take advantage of short-lived increases in commodity prices contributed substantially to Kenya's growth.

Having said this, it is important to recognize the serious constraints on export-led growth facing low-income countries dependent upon the export of primary agricultural commodities. Kenya's performance, although impressive when measured against the rest of sub-Saharan Africa, is not impressive by global standards. Diversification provides a measure of protection against commodity market variability but does not escape the growth limitations inherent in many tropical agricultural markets. The fact that Kenya did better than expected in 1984 and 1985, for example, has more to do with short-term forces (the ban on Indian tea exports in 1984; drought in Brazil in late 1985), than on the nature of the markets themselves. Kenya's ability to move quickly to exploit short-lived opportunities represents a skillful implementation of trade strategy, not a generalizable feature of the strategy itself.

Kenya's export-oriented agricultural strategy by and large has not come at the expense of domestic food production. In Tanzania, on the other hand, attempts to increase food self-sufficiency involved a clear tradeoff between cash crops and food crops (which in part was a result of policy and the pervasive poor performance of state institutions). The question now is whether Kenya can continue to pursue food self-sufficiency and an aggressive export-oriented agriculture during the next decade. Barring a major technological breakthrough, production increases will depend on narrowing the yield gap between smallholders and larger farms and estates. Achieving this, in turn, will require sustained investment in the agricultural sector, especially in extension and research. Current constraints on inflows of capital make funding for such activities more problematic, although this may improve if interest rates continue to moderate in a noninflationary environment.

Despite very significant differences in agricultural policies and performance, Kenya and Tanzania's food and cereal import patterns did not differ dramatically. Increases in imports in both countries came from food aid, although substantially less so in the case of maize in Kenya. Given the variability of production and the region's repeated food emergencies, this trend can be explained in part by the international response to food emergencies. Underlying the international response, however, is the tendency toward chronic food aid that characterizes many countries in sub-Saharan Africa. In most instances, this tendency reflects stagnant or declining per capita food production (as in Kenya) and a limited ability to finance additional food imports without further sacrificing development prospects. Rather considerable economic recovery, in many instances based in turn on improvements in the agricultural sector itself, will be needed to finance increased food imports. If income and foreign exchange earnings were to rise substantially, diversification away from cereal- and starch-dominated diets almost certainly would lead to increased food imports. Yet, both countries are still far from "graduating" into this stage of development.

Despite significant policy differences, "food security" in both Kenya and Tanzania depends heavily upon international trade. Production variability figures significantly in both countries' trade patterns and is more significant than economic factors in explaining grain trade patterns since the mid-1960s. In both cases, however, the longer time frame obscures the dramatic increase in import levels in recent years. More research of the kind in Chapter 7 of this book on the role of food aid, its relationship to agricultural policy, and its impact on commercial imports is needed.

Notes

1. See, for example, Joel Barkan, ed., *Politics and Public Policy in Kenya and Tanzania,* rev. ed. (New York: Praeger, 1984).

2. See, for example, Bismarck U. Mwansasu and Cranford Pratt, eds., *Towards Socialism in Tanzania* (Toronto: Toronto University Press, 1979).

3. This discussion follows Patrick Low, "Export Subsidies and Trade Policy: The Experience of Kenya," *World Development* 10, no. 4 (April 1982):293–304.

4. For a full discussion of this strategy, see C. George Kahama, T. L. Maliyamkono, and Stuart Wells, *The Challenge for Tanzania's Economy* (London: Heinemann and James Currey, 1986), 76–78.

5. Alberto Ruiz de Gamboa, "Resource Allocation and the Agricultural Sector" (Dar es Salaam: no date, unpublished ms.), Table 1.

6. The Kenyan government does impose a fixed export tax on coffee and tea, but this comes into effect only when the world market price rises above a certain level.

7. The classic study of agricultural producer pricing in Tanzania is Frank Ellis, "Agricultural Price Policy in Tanzania," *World Development,* vol. 10, no. 10 (1982):263–283. Also see his article "Relative Agricultural Prices and the Urban Bias Model," *Journal of Development Studies* 20 (April 1984):28–51; and John C. de Wilde, *Agriculture, Marketing and Pricing in Sub-Saharan Africa* (Los Angeles: African Studies Center and African Studies Association, 1984), Chapter 3.

8. De Wilde, ibid., Table 3.3.

9. Ibid.

10. It is difficult to measure the extent of overvaluation in either Kenya or Tanzania because there is no legal free market in their currencies, and figures for unofficial conversions therefore are problematic. In this analysis, we have used the unofficial prices as reported in *Picks Currency Yearbook.* Visitors to Tanzania have suggested that this source somewhat underestimates the extent of overvaluation in Tanzania.

11. For an outstanding cautionary statement on the benefits of devaluation, see Delphin G. Rwegasira, "Exchange Rates and the Management of the External Sector in Sub-Saharan Africa," *Journal of Modern African Studies* 22, no. 3 (September 1984):451–457.

12. Robert Bates, "The Maize Crisis of 1979–80: A Case Study and Update" (1985, unpublished ms.).

13. Some of Tanzania's "commercial" imports, about 40,000 tons per year, have come from Uganda as repayments of debts to Tanzania associated with Tanzania's military intervention to remove Idi Amin from power in 1979. Tanzania also has been able to purchase cheap maize from Thailand.

chapter three

Agricultural Development and Trade in Latin America: Prospects for Reform

Alberto Valdés

The first part of this chapter presents an overview of the trends in consumption, production, and trade of food and nonfood agricultural products in Latin America since 1960. I discuss the dynamics of agricultural growth and analyze diverse problems in a food security strategy for the region.

This is followed by an attempt to characterize the two principal policy instruments governments use for agriculture: government expenditures and incentives policies. These two sets of policies are used extensively to influence agricultural performance, and they represent the "revealed" development strategies toward agriculture. I also present a quantitative description of the level and impact of government expenditure policies on agricultural growth in nine Latin American countries from 1950 to 1980.

The last part of the chapter examines agricultural production incentive policies for selected South American countries from 1960 to 1983. I end my discussion with an examination of the long-run effects of incentives on the performance of agriculture in Argentina and Chile since 1960.

Food Consumption in Latin America, 1960–1980

Developments in Food Consumption and Nutrition
Food consumption in Latin America since 1960 has grown at an annual rate of 2.8 percent, about the same rate as population growth.[1] During the same period, total animal feed use of grain grew at close to 5.4 percent a year due to the rapid increase in the consumption of meat and dairy products. Total livestock production during the 1970s rose 3.6 percent annually, a rate higher than that of food consumption as a whole.

It is risky to specify what aggregated figures such as these imply in terms of welfare and nutrition; I identify only general trends here. Some analysts maintain that the nutritional state of the lowest income groups in Latin America has worsened.[2] Many support that view with estimates of the extent of malnutrition arrived at after comparing caloric requirements and supply at certain points in time.[3] This is a critical subject on which there is substantial disagreement.

A very brief overview suggests the following—at an aggregate level, the average caloric intake in Latin America has risen moderately since 1960. Between 1961–1965 and 1979–1981, it increased from 2,432 to 2,591 calories per capita a day; calories originating from animal sources increased from 403 to 455 calories per capita a day. The rate of protein intake in the region has been quite stable, and the average protein supply per capita has been greater than the minimum recommended level in each of the countries in the region.[4] The regional average (around 65 grams a day) is close to the world average, although considerably less than the average for developed nations.[5]

These averages do not necessarily indicate that the lowest income groups have maintained their portion of total consumption. One might deduce that the number of people with nutritional problems has increased to the extent that the present income distribution is less balanced than before. Nevertheless, available information on shifts in income distribution does not definitively answer whether income distribution is in fact less balanced than before. Instead (and as an illustration), it is useful to cite results of three recent studies that rigorously examine some indicators of nutrition.

Mohan, Wagner, and Garcia estimated the extent of malnutrition in two Colombian cities for 1973 and 1978 and concluded that in 1978 the ratio of population with a food intake below the required level in Colombia had declined since 1973.[6] Miguel Urrutia examined the evolution of family income and expenditures of the lowest income groups in the Cali region of Colombia in 1970, 1974, 1976, and 1980.[7] He found that the family income of these groups increased substantially in real terms between 1970 and 1980 and that the budget share spent on food declined from 79 percent in 1970 to 51 percent in 1980. At the same time, Urrutia found that real wages of the lowest income groups in Cali (farm workers and noncontract female workers) rose more rapidly than the national income per capita in the 1970s. Finally, a study by Castaneda in Chile found a constant and dramatic decline in that country's infant mortality rate between 1955 and 1983.[8] Mortality for children less than one year old dropped from 116.5 per 1,000 live births in 1955 to 21.0 per 1,000 in 1983, in spite of the increase in urban unemployment between 1975/76 and 1982/83.

It is difficult to reconcile these findings in Colombia and Chile with the opinion that the nutritional state of the lowest income groups in these countries has worsened. Measuring the deficit in caloric supply in middle-income countries at a certain point in time can be misleading. Recent analyses are critical of the estimates of the nutrition gap based on aggregate caloric supply and requirements.[9] Indeed, it seems that we can learn more about nutrition by examining trends in food consumption, family expenditure, and other, indirect indicators.

The fact that malnutrition seems to be diminishing in Latin America does not mean it has disappeared. Malnutrition does exist, and to a large extent its existence is contingent on the purchasing power of the poorest families. Agricultural development can contribute directly to solving malnutrition in rural areas by raising the family incomes of small farmers and rural wage earners. Agricultural growth also plays a significant albeit declining role in overall economic growth, which in the long-run is the principal solution to poverty in Latin America.

Changes in Food Consumption Patterns
In addition to the changes in total calorie and protein consumption in Latin America that were pointed out above, there has been a significant modification in the composition of the region's diet. Indeed, Latin America is gradually developing the diet patterns of more developed nations. There has been an increase in wheat and rice consumption per capita, but direct human consumption of maize and other indigenous cereals typical of the traditional regional diet has gone down significantly. (Cereals as a whole continue to account for approximately 40 percent of total calories.) In addition, the consumption per capita of vegetable oils has greatly accelerated. Vegetable and fruit consumption also has risen. Furthermore, the consumption per capita of roots and tubers (cassava, potatoes) and dry legumes (beans), typical staples of the traditional Latin American diet, has decreased substantially. Finally, there has been an increase in per capita consumption of meats (especially poultry), eggs, and dairy products.

The fact that diet has recently diversified to include a more ample variety of staples containing more protein and vitamins confirms the view that the measurement of caloric intake exclusively is not appropriate in assessing the trends in food consumption and nutrition in Latin America. Reasons for these changes in the diet of the average Latin American are various. They include rural-urban migration, income growth, the growing participation of women in formal labor markets, and relative price changes resulting from technological change and price policies.

The pronounced rural-urban migration in most Latin American countries has indeed brought about substantial changes in dietary habits.[10] Urbanization favors the consumption of more storable processed foods, such as wheat derivatives, rice, and vegetables, which take less time to prepare; urbanization disfavors the consumption of typical foods like cassava, potatoes, quinoa (for Andean countries), and dry legumes. Also, the growing participation of women in formal labor markets suggests that food preparation time at the household level is very important in determining consumption. Although the deeply rural population continues to follow more traditional habits, these urban consumption patterns are spreading slowly to outlying rural areas as the number of wage earners who must buy a large portion of their food increases.

Income growth also has played a large role in changing consumption patterns in Latin America. It is to be expected that as per capita income rises, the consumption of foods with high income elasticity of demand will increase. Because most of the demand comes from middle- and higher-income groups, the supply of products they demand will expand. Conversely, low-income elasticity products will diminish in relative importance, especially among middle- and high-income groups.

The modification of relative prices as a result of technological changes and price policies also has affected consumption. An example of the impact of technological change is the large increase in the consumption of poultry in many Latin American countries. It has been suggested that this could be a consequence of the fall in poultry prices due to the adoption of modern cost-saving, marketing-improving technology. Another example is rice. In Colombia and other countries the spread of modern rice varieties led to a substantial increase in rice production and, given export restrictions, reduced its relative price to consumers.

With regard to price policy, one of the permanent concerns of Latin American governments is keeping food prices stable and, when necessary, low. Because of the importance of certain staples in the consumer basket (as reflected in the Consumer Price Index, or CPI), especially in middle- and low-income urban areas, controlling food prices is often a convenient way to regulate wages and inflation. The variety of mechanisms used to control food prices include direct price controls, differential tariffs, export quotas and taxes, and exchange rate policy. The dominant group of commodities in the CPI in several Latin American countries is meats and meat derivatives, followed by cereals and cereal derivatives. In individual products, wheat and wheat derivatives fluctuate between 3.2 and 7 percent of the total CPI, with rice and maize lower. Beef ranges from 3.2 percent (Peru) to 15 percent (Paraguay), and accounts for about 6 percent of the CPI in other countries. Milk ranks after wheat and beef, but beans, cassava, and pork have less weight. High-share CPI items are attractive targets for price controls in urban areas; price controls thus reinforce high-share item consumption as well as the prevailing consumption pattern.

Food and Agricultural Production, 1960–1980

Food Production

Between 1961 and the middle of the 1970s, food production in Latin America grew at an annual rate of 3.2 percent, 0.5 percent faster than population growth in the region. This was the fastest food production growth rate in the developing world. During the same period Asia's food production growth rate was 2.6 percent, North Africa and the Middle East's were 2.5 percent, and sub-Saharan Africa's was only 1.5 percent. Among Latin American subregions, the Mexican, Central American, and Caribbean subregion had the highest growth rates in food production, followed closely by tropical South America. The southern cone of the continent had the lowest growth rate, but in all three subregions, food production rose at a faster pace than did population.

The situation changed in the second half of the 1970s. During this period food production in the Third World as a whole accelerated, while in Latin America it diminished sharply from an average of 4.2 percent annually for 1961–1970 to only 1.7 percent for 1971–1980. This was true for all three subregions. (To a large extent this decline could have resulted from the fall in the real exchange rate during the last decade after the massive flow of foreign credit to the region, a hypothesis I develop later.)

The main reason for the increase in Latin American food production during the 1960s and 1970s was the expansion in cultivated area. During the 1960s, cultivated area expanded at an annual rate of 2.7 percent, while yields increased 1.5 percent. In the 1970s, the increase in cultivated area diminished to 0.6 percent a year, and the rise in yields went down slightly to around 1 percent a year. The contribution of expanded cultivated land to the rise in food production decreased from 65 percent in the 1960s to 37 percent in the 1970s. The relative contribution of expanded farm area and yield increases varies with each subregion. Mexico, Central America, and the Caribbean maintained high rates of yield increases (more than 2 percent), and yield increases for the southern cone rose from 0.9 percent in the 1960s to 2 percent in the 1970s. Yield increases in tropical and subtropical South America decreased from 0.8 percent in the 1960s to 0 in the 1970s; the expansion of cultivated land diminished drastically from 3.7 percent to 1.8 percent annually. In sum, temperate and subtropical zones in Latin America have increased their yield per hectare, while tropical Latin America has not.

It is no surprise then that the growth of farm output in Latin America varied greatly during the 1970s. Four countries (Brazil, Colombia, Guatemala, and Paraguay) had annual farm growth rates greater than 4 percent. Five others, on the other hand (Haiti, Honduras, Panama, Peru, and Uruguay), had growth rates lower than 2 percent. On average, the gross value of agricultural production per capita in Latin America went up 0.8 percent annually during this period.

It is useful to point out the disparity in the growth rates of different groups of farm products. During the 1970s, production growth was greatest in livestock products, poultry, hogs, eggs, and milk, followed by oilseeds (particularly soybeans), vegetables, and fruits.[11] The growth rates of cereals,[12] beverages, dry legumes, and beef were lower. A third group of products (including roots, tubers, and vegetable fibers, but not cotton) had a negative growth rate. This disparity in growth rates is closely related to the diverse growth of export markets and, of course, of domestic demand. For example, domestic demand and exports of soybeans rose markedly during this period. Fruits, citrus, and apple production also expanded rapidly, but bananas did not.

In some countries (Brazil, Argentina, Paraguay), the expansion in farmland was largely in the area planted to soybeans. Land devoted to cereals (not less than 50 percent of total cultivated land) expanded at a much lower rate (0.7 percent). Other crops that showed higher than average rates of land expansion were sugar cane, vegetables, and tobacco. It is also important to note that there were negative growth rates in yields for cassava, dry legumes, and vegetable fibers.

Crop production (food and industrial crops) continued to rise as a result of the expansion of cultivated land. Nevertheless, the relative contribution of yield to this increase went up in the 1970s. In the 1960s, one-third of crop production growth was a result of yield increases, compared to two-fifths in the 1970s.[13]

Livestock production rose at a faster pace than crop production (around 3.3 percent annually), and the production of poultry and eggs was the most dynamic. Beef production had the slowest growth rate (2.1 percent annually), lower than the population growth rate. The low relative price of beef has made the intensive use of advanced inputs less profitable than in the United States and Europe. In Latin America it has been more profitable to raise cattle production by expanding pasture area than by increasing the carrying capacity per hectare.[14]

Area Expansion Versus Yield Increases
The increase in productivity in Latin America can be associated with more extensive use of fertilizers and pesticides, and increased planting of new crop varieties. In contrast, machinery tends to substitute for labor and promotes expanded cultivation. The region increased its use of both tractors and fertilizers during the 1950s and 1960s but not in the late 1970s. (Although there is no hard data to support this thesis, the cutback in the use of fertilizers and tractors during this period might be explained by the increase in the relative price of oil derivatives, especially after 1973 and again in 1979. Some countries—Brazil and Venezuela—did establish subsidies to compensate for the rise in costs. In addition, during the late 1970s and early 1980s the real exchange rate aggravated the squeeze in profitability in agricultural production in several Latin American countries.)

Although on the surface, Latin America appears to have an elastic supply of land but a less elastic supply of labor, this perception is oversimplified.

With few exceptions, Latin American countries have increased the productivity of land as well as labor. For example, the use of fertilizers and pesticides before the late 1970s rose more rapidly than did the use of machinery (this would seem not to have happened if land was in surplus).

Some observers believe that this inconsistency may be more apparent than real and that the simultaneous increase in area and productivity is probably due to the heterogeneous nature of Latin American agriculture.[15] The current costs of expanding cultivated lands in most tropical countries of the region is high and not as profitable as raising the productivity of the land already in use. The uneven distribution of farmlands is another problem, for the small farmer can only raise production by means of raising yields per hectare. In contrast, larger farms that have greater area and that hire labor invest more in machinery to substitute for labor, which suggests a dualism in land and labor markets.

Land expansion, mechanization, labor substitution, and, in general, the decisions affecting the relative use of productive factors in agriculture are not really independent of established economic policies and institutional factors. Some policies unintentionally have favored overvaluation, and minimum wage legislation has brought about implicit subsidies for the use of machinery and a rise in the price of labor. What is the final impact of economic policies on the input mix? Do they favor more intensive use of labor or of land? These are questions that bear further investigation. At any rate, production elasticities of land and labor vary greatly from one country to another.[16] This strengthens the hypothesis that it might be inappropriate to generalize on the best ways to expand production.

Finally, it should be noted that the composition of domestic and foreign demand will affect the (derived) demand for purchased inputs, land, and labor. It is possible that there is a surplus of land that is potentially advantageous for the production of crops with very limited domestic and foreign demand. This is the case, for example, for cassava. But this is an area for which there is no hard evidence.

Food Security

Stabilization of food supplies (especially cereals in urban areas) is a basic food security concern in Latin America. This concern derives, in part, from the risk associated with dependence on foreign supplies to cover part of domestic consumption. Experience shows that this risk has not proved problematic in wheat, but the situation is different for rice and white maize, which have "thin" international markets, are dependent on only a few suppliers, and are subject to delay and interruption in shipment.

The second cause for concern is the short-term instability of international prices. These do not offer a reliable base for planning imports or for establishing a long-term policy for domestic production. Fluctuations in the world price of cereals increased drastically during the 1970s in comparison with the 1960s—much more than could be explained by the modest increase in the variability of world production.

The third reason Latin American countries worry about supply is financial insecurity—that is, the capacity of each country to finance growing and fluctuating food imports in the face of an unstable supply of foreign exchange. To what extent could the current economic crisis in Latin America seriously limit its capacity to finance food imports in the near future? The ratio of the dollar value of food imports to total export revenues from goods and services is a reasonable measure of the pressure food imports exert on the balance of payments.

Estimates of the average food import/export revenue ratio in six Latin American countries were computed for various periods between 1965 and 1981. These estimates were made for two alternative definitions of food. In the first definition, food includes cereals only. The second definition of food is much broader and includes vegetable oils, dairy products, fruits, vegetables, and sugar, which are all significant imports. If the restricted definition is used, the average ratio in these countries is relatively low and rises to a maximum of 10 percent in Brazil and Peru in exceptionally unfavorable years. Estimates for Asian and African countries indicate that, at least in cereals, foreign exchange constraints are more serious in other regions, where several countries average import/export revenue ratios of more than 10 percent.[17]

Using the wider definition of food, including noncereals, the food import bill goes up significantly. Chile and Peru were the countries with the steepest food import bills, with average ratios of 11 and 12 percent respectively. Even so, these figures are much lower than comparable estimates for African and Asian countries, several of which had averages greater than 45 percent. As for long-term tendencies, there are no clear indications that financial pressure intensified before 1980/81. Nevertheless, these estimates should be reassessed to take into account the foreign debt situation and current restrictions on the supply of foreign exchange.

Another point to consider is that for a few countries, imported food accounts for a high proportion of total domestic food supply. This is sometimes considered risky. Calculations for Peru illustrate how much that country depends on imports to satisfy domestic consumption of certain staples.[18] Since 1960, Peru's imports of edible oils and cereals (maize, wheat, and rice) have increased dramatically and now account for more than 80 percent of domestic consumption!

Export Potential and Import Demand
Agricultural exports still account for more than 50 percent of total foreign exchange revenues (exports of goods and services) in Argentina, Brazil, Co-

lombia, Costa Rica, El Salvador, Guatemala, and the Dominican Republic. This ratio varies between 25 and 48 percent in Ecuador, Mexico, and Peru.[19] Thus, changing conditions in world markets and in domestic supply and demand of exportable agricultural products have macroeconomic repercussions in these countries and make price policy management much more complex.

From 1972 to 1979, the most dynamic Latin American farm exports were vegetable oils, fats, processed foods, and alcoholic beverages (wine). At the other end of the spectrum, exports of sugar, furs, hides, rubber, oil, processed fats, livestock, meat, textile fibers, and animal oils and fats decreased in absolute value. More than 70 percent of all Latin American farm exports are sold to industrialized countries, and only 7 to 9 percent are exported to other nations of the region.

The agricultural export potential of Latin America is good. World markets for oilseeds, vegetable oils, poultry, meat, tobacco, beverages, fruits, and vegetables are among the most dynamic, and it would be profitable to stimulate their export. Given that Latin America's share in world exports in these commodities is small (except for coffee), the continent can maintain its share in the most dynamic international markets without affecting world prices.

As for imports, approximately 70 percent of total agricultural and livestock imports in Latin America come from industrialized nations, and another 26 to 28 percent come from the region itself. This last share has not varied in a long time. The region as a whole is largely self-sufficient in coffee, tea, sugar, fruits, vegetables, fibers, and meats.[20] Cereals have been dominant in total regional imports; wheat ranks first, then maize and cereal preparations. Other significant food imports to or through the region are, in order of diminishing importance, fruits and vegetables, dairy products, and vegetable oils. There was a marked increase in oilseeds and vegetable oil imports between 1962 and 1979.

Government Policies as a Determinant of Agricultural Growth

Governments act principally through expenditures and related incentives policies to affect agriculture. Victor Elias examined government expenditures for Argentina, Bolivia, Brazil, Chile, Colombia, Costa Rica, Mexico, Peru, and Venezuela for the period 1950 to 1978.[21] All expenditures directed toward the rural sector were considered, including research and extension, irrigation, marketing, transportation, education, health, administration, and some transfer payments. In addition, various levels of government spending were included—central and state governments and decentralized government agencies—although the state government and decentralized agency figures are less complete.

Figure 3.1 shows that government expenditures climbed steadily in real terms for all countries except Argentina, which maintained a low but stable growth rate. There was an upward surge in the trend for many countries around 1964. When the averages for the nine countries are taken together, the aggregate average rate of growth per year is 8 percent in real terms. These graphs, however, show the wide variation from Argentina's almost stable 2.5 percent growth rate to Bolivia's startling rise in government spending of 18.7 percent. In 1970 the nine countries together spent a total of $6.3 billion in 1980 dollars. This is about 15 percent of what the U.S. government spends annually on agriculture (transfer payments included).

How significant are government expenditures on agriculture in these Latin American economies? By examining the degree of variation in agricultural expenditures from year to year we can tell how much they are subject to changes in government policies. By comparing such expenditures with the value added of agriculture, we can tell the extent to which fluctuations in expenditures influence agricultural output. Finally, by comparing them with Gross Domestic Product (GDP) we can judge how strongly governments in each country emphasize agriculture.

As shown in Table 3.1, the 5 percent average share of government expenditures on agriculture in the total government budgets of the major Latin American economies is a much smaller share than that of the education, health, or transport and communications sectors. This ratio also varies to a greater extent from country to country than do other expenditures. However, this ratio also varies widely in other countries, such as the United States, possibly because of transfer payments.

Table 3.2 shows government expenditures on agriculture relative to total government expenditure (GA/G), to value added of agriculture (GA/A), and to gross domestic product (GA/Y) from 1950 to 1978 for nine Latin American countries. The variability in the ratio of government expenditures on agriculture to the GDP from year to year appears to be explained largely by fluctuations in the share of government expenditures on agriculture in the total government budget. This could indicate that government expenditure policies are extremely active in Latin America.

To complement his aggregate analysis, Elias also examined variations in the major components of government expenditures on agriculture—research and extension, irrigation, education, and health. Although the percentage of total government expenditures on agriculture by each country in each category varies greatly, education and irrigation appear to receive more funds than the others.

The effects of government expenditure policies on agriculture in the same nine countries of Latin America were examined in a more recent study by Elias.[22] He found that the contribution of government expenditure to agriculture (GEA) was high in countries where GEA per hectare was high. On

Figure 3.1   Indexes of Government Expenditures in Latin America, 1950–1978 (in real terms)

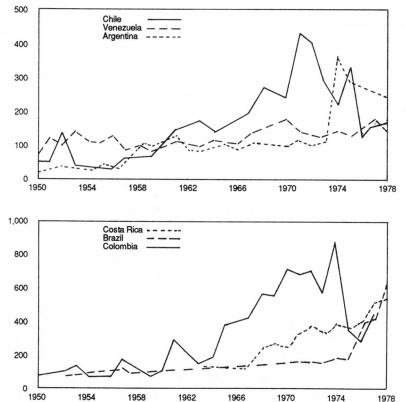

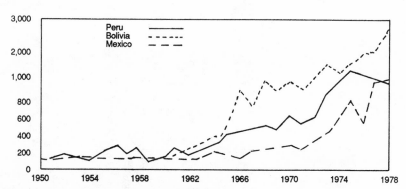

Although real government spending varied widely between countries and from time to time, the trend is upward for all except Argentina, which is stable. To find expenditures in real terms, figures in current prices are deflated to 1960 dollars by the Gross Domestic Price index and, for the most recent years, by the wholesale price index.

Source: V. Elias, *Government Expenditures on Agriculture in Latin America*, Research Report no. 23 (Washington, D.C.: IFPRI, May 1981).

Table 3.1   Shares of Various Components of Central Government Expenditures, 1950, 1960, 1975 (in percentage)

Country	Agriculture			Education			Health			Transport and Other[a]		
	1950	1960	1975	1950	1960	1975	1950	1960	1975	1950	1960	1975
Argentina	2.9	2.5	1.5	10.4	10.9	15.7[b]	5.3	5.8	6.0[b]	14.5	23.9	16.6[b]
Bolivia	n.a.[c]	4.2	23.3[b]	n.a.	n.a.	16.4[b]	n.a.	n.a.	7.4[b]	n.a.	n.a.	8.5[b]
Brazil	4.6	3.9	1.1	n.a.	6.8	6.2[b]	n.a.	4.0	1.6[b]	n.a.	21.6	16.4[b]
Chile	3.3	4.0	5.5[b]	n.a.	12.1	12.6	n.a.	10.2	8.1	n.a.	17.6	14.5
Colombia	4.9	4.5	5.6	5.6	n.a.	19.8	4.6	n.a.	9.3	46.5	n.a.	32.7[b]
Costa Rica	n.a.	1.8	2.9	n.a.	n.a.	22.0	n.a.	n.a.	2.1	n.a.	n.a.	16.7
Mexico	16.6	4.5	10.1	6.4	9.5	15.7	3.1	2.4	3.8	10.8	8.0	15.1
Peru	5.9	2.6	8.5	n.a.	n.a.	21.4	n.a.	n.a.	5.3	n.a.	n.a.	4.3
Venezuela	5.5	7.0	8.6	5.9	7.5	21.3[b]	6.3	6.7	13.3	34.3	23.3	21.3

Source: Victor Elias, *Government Expenditures on Agriculture in Latin America*, Research Report no. 23 (Washington, D.C.: IFPRI, May 1981).

[a] Includes transport, communications, and public works.
[b] Refers to 1970.
[c] Not available.

Table 3.2 Arithmetic Means, Standard Deviations, and Coefficients of Variation of the Ratios GA/G, GA/A, and GA/Y, 1950–1978[a] (in percentage)

Ratios	Argentina	Bolivia	Brazil	Chile	Colombia	Costa Rica	Mexico	Peru	Venezuela
GA/G									
Mean	2.82	18.80	2.96	3.82	8.33	2.34	8.03	6.26	6.58
Standard deviation	0.63	7.70	1.53	1.61	3.89	0.60	2.79	2.32	1.41
Coefficient of variation	0.22	0.41	0.52	0.42	0.47	0.26	0.35	0.37	0.21
GA/A									
Mean	3.58	10.44	3.07	11.74	14.33	1.79	9.48	6.68	24.00
Standard deviation	0.74	6.91	0.56	7.14	4.95	0.69	6.73	4.31	12.56
Coefficient of variation	0.21	0.66	0.18	0.61	0.35	0.39	0.71	0.64	0.52
GA/Y									
Mean	0.57	1.97	0.70	0.98	3.90	0.38	1.12	1.07	1.53
Standard deviation	0.15	1.10	0.16	0.46	1.14	0.12	0.51	0.53	0.60
Coefficient of variation	0.25	0.56	0.23	0.47	0.29	0.32	0.46	0.50	0.39

Source: Victor Elias, *Government Expenditures on Agriculture in Latin America*, Research Report no. 23 (Washington, D.C.: IFPRI, May 1981).

[a] GA/G = share of government expenditures on agriculture in total government expenditures;
GA/A = share of government expenditures on agriculture in the value added of agriculture;
GA/Y = share of government expenditures on agriculture in the Gross Domestic Product.

the average, GEA contributed almost 8 percent of the growth of total agricultural output. This is comparable to the contribution of modern inputs. The rest is explained both by the growth of traditional inputs and by the residual. In countries where the rate of growth of agricultural output was lower, GEA's contribution was smaller. The contribution of GEA to agricultural growth was found to be higher as the share of the irrigation or the research and extension components of GEA increased.

The components of GEA also were associated with the growth of private inputs. Positive correlations were found between research and extension expenditures and the use of fertilizers and between land reform expenditures and the use of irrigation. A small negative association was found between education and health expenditures and the use of labor. Also, the contention that public investment crowds out private investment seemed to be true only when public investment accelerated rapidly.

Approximately 60 percent of the growth of agricultural output is explained by the growth of traditional inputs—land, labor, and capital. These inputs increased at an average annual rate of slightly more than 2 percent. In most countries, the amount of agricultural land increased, on average, about 2 percent annually. The number of people in the agricultural labor force increased about 1 percent annually, and the amount of capital—agricultural equipment, farm construction, and land improvements—increased about 1 percent annually.

In three of the four countries with the lowest rates of farm output growth (Argentina, Bolivia, and Peru) the contribution of capital to growth was the largest. In contrast, in the countries with the highest rates of growth (Brazil, Costa Rica, and Venezuela) the 40 percent of that growth unexplained by traditional factors of production made the largest contribution. This 40 percent residual can be accounted for, in part, by the growth of GEA and by the growth of such private modern inputs as tractors, fertilizers, and irrigation. Modern inputs and GEA each accounted for almost 20 percent of the growth of the residual in the nine countries. This added between 0.1 and 0.7 percent to annual growth rates. On the whole, modern inputs grew faster than capital, but their contributions to growth were small because, according to the elasticities estimated from production functions, output increases only a fraction of any increase in modern inputs in Latin America. Modern inputs contributed the most to agricultural growth in Brazil, Colombia, and Costa Rica. The size of the residual was positively associated with the rate of growth of capital. Because the residual includes most technological changes, this implies a positive relationship between capital accumulation and technological change.

All these components are of course a part of expenditure policy. An analysis of GEA should include estimates of expenditures on price policies as well, but the information needed for such estimates (transfer payments, including food subsidies) is not available. However, estimates of credit subsidies made for Argentina, Brazil, Chile, Colombia, Mexico, and Venezuela show the subsidies to have been highly variable, perhaps because the size of the subsidies depends mainly on the real rate of interest. This in turn depends on the difference between the nominal rate of interest and the actual rate of inflation, which was itself variable in Latin America.

Agricultural Trade and Macroeconomic Policies

Agricultural growth interacts very closely with developments in other sectors of the economy, particularly with trade and macroeconomic policies. Intervention in agricultural markets is widespread in Latin America. Direct price intervention policies include agricultural trade restrictions (import tariffs, export subsidies or taxes, import or export licensing) and price support and price fixing in input and output markets.

There are other policies involving the macroeconomic management of the economy that affect nominal exchange rates, government spending, wages, international capital flows, and industrial protection that have special significance for agriculture in Latin America, in part because the agricultural sector is a highly tradable one. The consequences of these policies can reinforce or neutralize policies directed solely at agriculture. In several Latin American countries import-substitution-based industrial growth pursued through tariffs and other import restrictions appear to have had a strong bias against agriculture, which has resulted in a structure of incentives that could have had deleterious effects on long-term agricultural production. In small, open economies, including most of Latin America, it could well happen that trade and macroeconomic policies may have a stronger and even opposite effect on agricultural prices than policies designed specifically to benefit agriculture.

The real exchange rate, defined as the ratio of the price of tradables to nontradables (or home goods, as they are called), plays a central role in the profitability of agricultural tradables—both import competing (such as cereals) and exportables. Indeed, it is mostly through the real exchange rate that macroeconomic management of the economy affects agriculture. The distinction between home goods and services and tradables becomes crucial where the prices of tradables are exogenously determined by foreign prices, nominal exchange rates, and trade policy. In contrast, the prices of home goods will clear domestically and could be influenced indirectly by macroeconomic and trade policies.

The tradable component in agriculture is larger than it is in other sectors of the Latin American economy. Tradables represent more than two-thirds of the agricultural sector in Argentina, Colombia, and Chile. In contrast, the nonagricultural sectors in most countries are characterized by a much larger proportion of nontradables. In Colombia it is estimated that more than 50 percent of nonagricultural production is derived from non-tradables such as commerce, public services, transportation, construction, housing, and banking.[23]

Sustained overall sectoral growth involves resource flows between sectors, such as labor and capital that adjust to the relative opportunities between those flows. Thus, in analyzing the long-run effects of incentives on production, we must have an economywide view of returns to these factors. The real exchange rate approach is applied because it is relevant in studying such sectoral movements resulting from trade and macroeconomic policies. Unfortunately, although some realize that the macroeconomic setting is important to agricultural performance, so far macroeconomics has remained outside the scope of an appropriate strategy for agricultural development in Latin America.

Since the late 1970s and early 1980s, Latin American countries have faced complex issues of adjustment and growth. Their economic difficulties have been attributed to both the international economic environment and domestic economic policies. Although international economic conditions —such as lower export prices for several products and higher real interest rates in the early 1980s—are crucial to understanding the current economic setting, I have thus far chosen to emphasize economic policies. The domestic policy environment has simply not been adequate for stimulating agricultural growth in Latin America.

Current external and macroeconomic conditions should not be ignored—they may offer an opportunity to revitalize the agricultural sector in Latin America. Export diversification and expansion may constitute the principal structural change that many countries in the region need to make. The success of such change could depend on agricultural growth. One thing is certain—correct real exchange rate alignment is crucial for taking advantage of the growth opportunities offered by international trade for agriculture in Latin America.

Measuring the Agricultural Terms of Trade
For an analysis at the sectoral level, it is useful to compare the effects of what can be called "direct price" intervention, which results from explicit agricultural price policies including trade policies, relative to the effect of "indirect" or economywide policies affecting the sector's relative prices. The results of a comparison of the level of price intervention on representative products in three countries—Argentina, Chile, and Colombia—are presented in Figures 3.2, 3.3, and 3.4.

In Argentina between 1960 and 1984, both agricultural and economy-wide policies have taxed the production of wheat and beef (Figure 3.2). This could have been anticipated given the existence of an explicit export tax on

Figure 3.2   Argentina: Direct and Indirect Interventions in Wheat

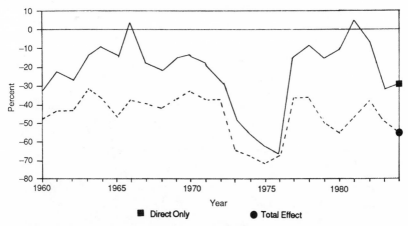

Argentina: Direct and Indirect Interventions in Beef

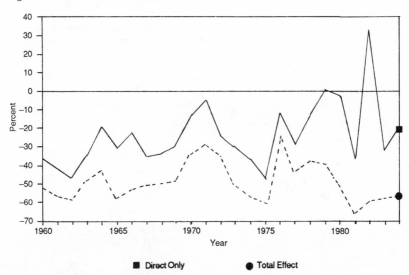

agricultural exports (the highest of which was applied during years of high world prices, such as 1974/75). Direct price interventions reduced the domestic price between 12 and 42 percent for wheat and between 11 and 35 percent for beef. Economywide (indirect) interventions added substantially to the total taxation of the production of these goods. For example, during the period 1981–1984, the effect of economywide price interventions added 29.2 and 39.5 percent to the total tax on wheat and beef respectively over and above the direct (sectoral) taxation of 17.3 and 13.8 percent. On the other hand, a subsidy occurs with respect to domestic consumers in Argen-

Figure 3.3   **Chile: Direct and Indirect Interventions in Wheat**

Chile: Direct and Indirect Interventions in Milk

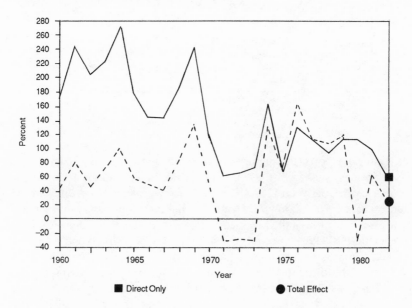

Figure 3.4   Colombia: Direct and Indirect Interventions in Wheat

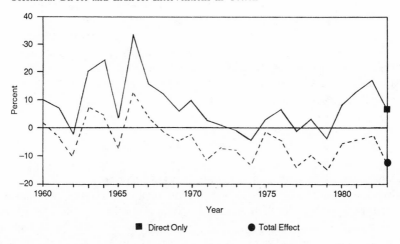

Year

■ Direct Only   ● Total Effect

Colombia: Direct and Indirect Interventions in Cotton

Year

■ Direct Only   ● Total Effect

tina. As a result of direct taxation to exports, and aside from other possible price interventions applied at actual levels, prices to domestic consumers during 1960–1984 were subsidized between 12 and 42 percent for wheat and 11 and 35 percent for beef. Fiscal revenue objectives and a cheap food policy for urban consumers were undoubtedly very strong forces behind the taxation of agricultural exports.

The situation in Chile (Figure 3.3) indicates a relatively stronger effect of economywide policies on incentives to farmers. Wheat growers received slightly positive nominal protection (except during 1971–1975, a period coinciding with two years of high world prices), and dairy farmers received a very substantial level of nominal protection during the entire period. Economywide intervention substantially reduced the net level of protection of milk production (with a net effect of taxation in 1971–1975) but nonetheless left that sector with levels of protection of around 25.3 to 93.0 percent through the period 1960–1980. For wheat, on the other hand, the slightly positive direct protection is overwhelmed by substantial indirect taxation, resulting in an overall taxation for the period 1960–1975. Positive protection of 20.8 percent prevailed in 1976–1980.

In Colombia, coffee producers were taxed consistently throughout the 1960–1983 period. However, there is a real question as to how much of this export tax was applied to improve coffee prices as part of an international commodity agreement between large coffee exporters. Wheat and cotton in Colombia (Figure 3.4) present the opposite case—that of an import-competing product and an exportable, respectively, with substantial nominal protection for wheat production (except 1971–1975) and lower protection (positive) for cotton. Adjustment for economywide interventions substantially reduces real protection for wheat and cotton production. In fact, there was negative (total) protection for wheat and cotton between 1971 and 1980 and negative protection for cotton, except during 1966–1970.

As can be observed for all three countries, the effect on agriculture's relative prices attributable to economywide policies in most cases has been equal to or greater than the effect of sector-specific (direct) price policies. This measured economywide effect represents in essence the impact of the real exchange rate on the region's trade, fiscal, and monetary policies.

Agriculture's Output Response

Much of the Latin American literature on development strategies during the 1940–1970 period assumed that agriculture was destined for a static role technologically; industry, on the other hand, was supposed to be dynamic. This reasoning implied that although individual crop output responds to price movements, the aggregate supply of agricultural products from the sector as a whole was quite unresponsive to incentives—the so-called (aggregate) supply inelasticity of agriculture in Latin America. If that really were the case, then the social cost of viewing agriculture as a tax base for economic development would be low. Agricultural taxation here meant not land or income taxes, but an implicit tax affecting agricultural terms of trade vis-à-vis the rest of the economy.

This assumption is highly questionable. If we examine the conventional arguments for the subsidization of infant industries, we can establish easily that these same arguments are as relevant for agriculture as they are for industry because technological change can and has occurred as much, if not more, in agriculture as in industry. One expects the aggregate supply response to price movements to be lower than that of individual crop output because the cost of switching resources between sectors, required for aggregate supply response, is higher than it is for switching resources between crops. But the usual prescription that has discriminated in favor of industry on the grounds of agriculture's static technology and low price responsiveness is a bad one.[24]

Recent work on aggregate agricultural supply response in Latin America—which measures supply response through a much fuller specification of rural-urban linkages in the labor and capital markets—is beginning to challenge the pessimistic view of the supply response of the agricultural sector. Some of the best technical work on this question has been done at the International Food Policy Research Institute (IFPRI) by Cavallo and Mundlak on Argentina,[25] and Coeymans and Mundlak on Chile.[26]

In their analysis of Argentina during the 1950–1971 period, Cavallo and Mundlak simulated two alternative policies—one, which liberalized trade, eliminated the tax on agricultural exports and the tariff on nonagricultural imports. Results indicated that the elimination of the export tax would have led to a substantial expansion of agricultural output. However, the resulting decline in real exchange rates diluted the effect of the tax reduction on agricultural growth. This, together with the elimination of tariffs on imports, resulted in a decrease in the per capita output of the nonagriculture sector that was more than the corresponding per capita increase in the agricultural sector.

The alternative was to keep the real exchange rate from falling in response to liberalized trade. In the simulation, the combination of liberalized trade and managed real exchange rates produced impressive increases in both agricultural and nonagricultural per capita output. But trade liberalization caused the price of food to increase more than nominal nonagricultural wages. (This suggests that it might be useful to examine the use of food subsidies to compensate wage earners for the improved economic environment for agriculture.)

A follow-up study by Cavallo for Argentina showed that agricultural output response to permanent changes in relative prices converged gradually to an elasticity close to 1.0—that is, a 10 percent increase in relative agricultural prices generates a 10 percent increase in aggregate output. Cavallo observed a high elasticity for capital with respect to price. Trade liberalization scenarios for Argentina show an impressive increase in capital utilization in agriculture. Despite a relatively low response of labor to prices and with an elasticity of cultivated land with respect to prices of 0.4, this high response of capital and significant response of land results in a strong overall agricultural output response to relative prices in Argentina.

In the Chilean study, the economy was divided into five sectors linked by an input-output matrix for the period 1962–1982. Coeymans and Mundlak showed that a permanent increase of 10 percent in agricultural (relative to nonagricultural) prices generates an increase in output of 20 percent, implying an implicit long-run elasticity of about 2.0.[27]

These values are not consistent with the unresponsiveness of agricultural output to prices presumed by the structuralist view of inflation and growth in the 1950s and 1960s in South America. These results suggest that the cost to agricultural as well as overall growth can be substantial. Indeed, the benefits might not have justified the costs.

Notes

1. The definition of food used here includes cereals, vegetables, roots, tubers, plantains, and bananas; noncereals were converted to their equivalent in wheat according to basic caloric content. This estimate takes into account the consumption of livestock, poultry products, fruits, and vegetables. Consumption is determined as production plus imports less exports.

2. J. M. Caballero and H. Maletta, "Estilos de desarrollo y políticas agroalimentarias: Tendencias y dilemas an América Latina," CEPAL/FAO. (Santiago, Chile: Consulta de Expertos Sobre Estilos de Desarrollo y Políticas Agrícolas, November 1983): 137.

3. See S. Reutlinger and M. Selowsky, *Poverty and Malnutrition* (Baltimore, Md.: Johns Hopkins University Press, 1976).

4. See C. Seré and L. Rivas, "Some Thoughts About Nutrition and Animal Protein Consumption in Latin America," *Trends in CIAT Commodities* (Cali, Colombia: CIAT, March 1983).

5. Seré has classified countries of the region in three levels according to their protein intake: Group 1 (greater than 80 grams per person, per day) includes Argentina, Paraguay, and Uruguay, countries with comparable advantages in cattle production; Group 2 (less than 80 grams and greater than 60 grams) includes Brazil, Chile, Cuba, Guyana, Jamaica, Mexico, Nicaragua, Trinidad and Tobago, and Venezuela; and Group 3 (less than 60 grams) includes Bolivia, Colombia, Costa Rica, Dominican Republic, Ecuador, El Salvador, Guatemala, Haiti, Honduras, Panama, and Peru.

6. R. Mohan, J. Garcia, and M. Wagner, *Measuring Urban Malnutrition and Poverty: A Case Study of Bogota and Cali, Colombia,* Staff Working Paper no. 447 (Washington, D.C.: World Bank, April 1981).

7. M. Urrutia, *Winners and Losers in Colombia's Recent Growth Experience* (Baltimore, Md.: Johns Hopkins University Press for the World Bank, 1985).

8. T. Castaneda, "Determinantes de la reducción de la mortalidad infantil en Chile, 1955–83," *Cuadernos de Economia* (August 1985).

9. T. Poleman, "World Hunger, Extent, Cause and Cures," and T. N. Srinivasan, "Hunger: Defining It, Estimating Its Global Incidence, and Alleviating It," in D. Gale Johnson and G. Edward Schuh, eds., *The Role of Markets in the World Economy* (Boulder, Colo.: Westview Press, 1983).

10. During the period 1970–1976, rural population grew at an annual rate of 0.91 percent while urban population rose 3.71 percent annually.

11. L. López Cordovez, "Trends and Recent Changes in the Latin American Food and Agriculture Situation," *CEPAL Review* (April 1982):7–41.

12. Maize production rose at a slower pace than other cereals, and the ratio destined for human consumption diminished.

13. Cordovez, "Trends and Recent Changes."

14. L. Jarvis, "Latin American Livestock Development: Issues and Prospects" (Paper prepared for the World Bank, Washington, D.C., April 1984).

15. See John Lynman, "Agricultural Production in Latin America: Performance, Growth Components, and Rural-Urban Migration," (Cali, Colombia: CIAT, September 1980). Mimeo.

16. Production elasticity is defined as the proportionate change in production caused by proportionate change in inputs.

17. See A. Siamwalla and A. Valdés, "Food Insecurity in Developing Countries," *Food Policy* 5, no. 4 (November 1980):258–272.

18. See A. Valdés and E. Alvares, *Government Policy and Food Supply Management in Peru: 1950–1981* (Washington, D.C.: IFPRI, March 1984).

19. A. Valdés, "Latin America's Food Situation and Perspective Within a Global Context" (Paper presented to the Club of Rome, Budapest Conference, September 1983.

20. Ibid.

21. V. Elías, *Government Expenditures on Agriculture in Latin America,* Research Report no. 23 (Washington, D.C.: IFPRI, May 1981).

22. V. Elías, "Government Expenditures on Agriculture and Agricultural Growth in Latin American Countries" (Paper presented at IFPRI Seminar, Washington, D.C., February 1984).

23. See J. Garcia and G. Montes, *Foreign Trade Regimes and Incentives to Agriculture in Colombia* (Washington, D.C.: IFPRI, forthcoming).

24. There are, of course, other possible arguments for taxing agriculture. There are essentially two. One is to trade taxes in order to help finance government. The second, the distributive argument, concerns cheap food policy and a presumed lower demand for labor.

25. D. Cavallo and Y. Mundlak, *Agriculture and Economic Growth in an Open Economy: The Case of Argentina,* Research Report no. 36 (Washington, D.C.: IFPRI, December 1982).

26. J. Coeymans and Y. Mundlak, *Agricultural Growth and Real Exchange Policy: The Case of Chile, 1960–1982* (Washington, D.C.: IFPRI, forthcoming).

27. These values are consistent with estimates of the aggregate long-run supply elasticity for agriculture for the United States by Griliches (1959), who obtained a value of about 1.2; Tweeten and Quance (1969) obtained values of about 1.5; for Australia, Pandey (1982) obtained values close to 1.0.

chapter four

Chinese Agricultural Development Strategy Since 1979

Charles Y. Liu

Agriculture always has served as the mainstay of the Chinese economy. But with a large population, limited cultivable land, frequent drought and flooding, backward technology, and little attention to agricultural development by its former ruling classes, China always has had difficulty feeding and clothing its people.

With 80 percent of the population still classified as rural, the same pattern continued after the founding of the People's Republic of China (PRC) in 1949 and culminated during the Cultural Revolution (1966–1976). It was not until after Mao's death in 1976 and the advent of a new leadership in 1978 that a pragmatic, planned development strategy was attempted. The results are reflected in China's current, much heralded agricultural success, an achievement that can be described as spectacular, both in comparison with the past and with the performance of other developing countries.

What strategies and policies led to China's recent success? Can they be adopted by other developing countries? In order to answer these questions the presentation here intends the following:

1. To delineate the five groups of factors that an economy must manage successfully in order to achieve notable, sustained growth in agriculture; draw the basic parameters for various stages of agricultural development; and explain how these relate to the foregoing factors as well as to this general framework.
2. To illustrate the political and economic strategies used by China to achieve advances in agriculture after 1978, particularly those strategies included in the Sixth Five-Year Plan (FYP) period of 1981–1985.
3. To explain the proposed strategies in the Seventh Five-Year Plan (1986–1990) as well as the issues raised in China's Year 2000 Study

and based on these make a tentative assessment about the likely performance in 1986–1990.

4. To assess briefly the adoptability of the "China model" in other developing countries.

Agricultural Development

In any economy, primitive or advanced, decisionmakers in the public and private sectors, in order to strive for maximum aggregate economic welfare within given constraints, must seek answers to six fundamental questions. They are for whom to produce, what to produce, how much to produce, where to produce, when to produce, and what method to use in production.

Factors in Agricultural Development

There are a number of factors that must be considered when making such decisions. For discussion purposes, these can be arranged into five groups. The first group of factors involves cultural, social, political, and institutional conditions within the nation and relations between that nation and others. The general macroeconomic environment comprises the second group of factors, which include the systems and policies of aggregate economic factors and the various kinds and degrees of direct or indirect participation in economic activities by the public sector as well as population growth, ecology, and so on. Sectoral linkages form the third group of factors. They include the basic manufacturing industries supplying necessary materials and inputs for farm production, such as energy, petrochemicals, and steel, as well as service industries involved in transportation, finance, and the like. The fourth group of factors consists of those agribusinesses that support the flow of farm products from farmgate to consumer. This group encompasses an entire range of marketing functions such as storage, processing, wholesaling, transfer, distribution, retailing, information, and public and private agricultural research. The fifth group comprises factors related to agricultural production, such as natural endowments, the structure of the rural economy, the level of agricultural technology and farm management, and specific agricultural policies. These factors most directly affect the quantity and quality of farm goods produced.

Stages of Agricultural Development

Policymakers also must consider the relative importance of these factors in the context of the particular stage of a country's agricultural development. Generally, if it is at a primitive stage of development, the agricultural economy will strive only for local self-sufficiency. In this case, answers to the six fundamental questions are rather simple, as producers and consumers are usually one and the same. They live at a very basic subsistence level and do not produce much, if any, surplus. Their objective only is to maximize food production, not revenue, profits, or aggregate economic welfare.

At this stage the agricultural economy only will utilize local resources as inputs. There will be relatively few steps between production and consumption. Product flow will be short, and the product itself will incur very few form changes before consumption. Agribusiness infrastructure will be very limited as there will be little need for complicated pricing and large-scale storage, processing, distribution, or marketing. More importantly, production will have very limited, if any, linkages with other products and other sectors of the economy.

As an agricultural economy shifts to more advanced stages, economic activity will be influenced by and will itself influence an increasing number of factors. Developing linkages and interdependencies will reach an optimum state in which every economic activity receives support from and in turn supports other activities, either directly or indirectly. At this stage, the nature and process of addressing our six fundamental questions become vastly more complicated.

The successful management of and support among the entire spectrum of political and economic factors listed previously are preconditions for successful agricultural development. When the agricultural economy advances, factors in the second through fourth groups join the first to lend support as needed. In an advanced agricultural economy, these factors usually are taken for granted. But they are lacking in primitive agricultural economies, and without these factors the fifth group—the basic factors of agricultural production—cannot be utilized fully for sustained growth.

Political Reform as a Development Strategy

In light of these basic factors and stages in agricultural development, where and how does the Chinese experience fit in? In order to answer these questions, the focus must be on the first group of factors and on the political and institutional reforms that have occurred in China since 1979.

Generally, the extent to which economics is allowed to play a role in any country's economic development depends entirely on the degree of dominance held by politics. The post-1978 leadership in China recognized the need to downplay political considerations in economic planning, such as those that characterized the Cultural Revolution. The Third Plenary Session of the Eleventh Central Committee of the Communist party of China (CPC) met in December 1978 to reconfirm the goals of the four modernizations, which stressed the development of agriculture, industry, national defense, and science and technology. These first were announced in 1976.[1]

To demonstrate their determination and sincere belief that change would not be fleeting, party leaders issued a document in June 1981 at the

Sixth Plenary Session of the Eleventh Central Committee of the CPC titled "Resolution on Some Historical Issues Regarding the Party Since the Founding of the People's Republic."[2] This was a bold document in which past mistakes made by the party, especially during the Cultural Revolution, were admitted openly, and in that and subsequent documents, the future course of the nation and party was charted. As a result, these basic changes in the political arena were made:

- The party reasserted its control of the government and the military apparatus, thereby replacing Revolutionary Committees usually headed by military personnel.
- The government bureaucracy was resurrected to implement party policies.
- Leftists in the party hierarchy who opposed reforms were purged.
- The government established an open door policy to the West, thereby relinquishing the past isolationist policy of literal self-reliance.
- A decentralization of administrative authority occurred—provincial level officials participated in foreign trade without the total involvement of the central government in Peking; increased interprovincial trade and economic cooperation was conducted without central directives; and the provinces had more freedom to make economic planning decisions funded by local sources.
- Most of all, Mao's basic ideological dogma of perpetual class struggle, which caused endless turmoil in the past, was renounced.

The party also revamped the party and government personnel system, retired aged cadres to advisory roles, and promoted younger, more educated personnel to key positions.[3] By 1984, this had been accomplished not only at the central level but all the way down to the county level.

Agricultural Reform as a Development Strategy

The reforms of the post-1978 period had a tremendous impact on China's agricultural economy. This is readily reflected in the changes in China's gross value of agricultural output (GVAO), agricultural production, per capita farm income, and per capita consumption of farm products from 1978 to 1984 (see Table 4.1). In this period, the GVAO increased 52 percent, and per capita rural income rose by 166 percent. Within the GVAO, livestock increased by 71 percent and crops by 45 percent. Of the crops, wheat increased 63 percent; cotton, 180 percent; and oilseeds, 127 percent.

An important reason for much higher per capita rural income in China is the slowing rate of population growth. Unlike the period from 1949 to 1978, when population growth was high and unchecked and agricultural production growth slow, total population in 1978–1984 increased only 7.5

Table 4.1   PRC: Progress in Agricultural Sector, 1978–1984

	1978	1984	Percentage Increase
Population[a] (million)	962.6	1,034.75	7.5
Agricultural Output Value (percent)			
Total output	100	152	52
Crops	100	145	45
Livestock	100	171	71
Forestry	100	160	60
Fishery	100	150	50
Sidelines	100	195	95
Commodity Output[a] (million tons)			
Total grain	304.8	407.3	33.6
Wheat	53.8	87.7	62.9
Rice	136.9	178.1	30.1
Corn	56.0	72.3	29.3
Cotton	2.2	6.1	180.6
Oilseeds	5.2	11.9	127.1
Meat	8.6	15.4	79.8
Per Capita Income (yuan)			
Urban	614.0	974.0	58.6
Rural[a]	133.6	355.3	165.9
Per Capita Consumption (kilograms)			
Grains	200.00	250.00	25.0
Edible oil	1.60	4.70	193.8
Pork	7.70	13.00	68.8
Beef and lamb	0.75	1.25	66.7
Poultry	0.44	1.35	206.8
Eggs	2.00	3.90	95.0
Fishery	3.50	4.35	24.3

Sources: Agricultural Statistics of the People's Republic of China, 1949–82, Statistical Bulletin 714 (Washington, D.C.: ERS, USDA, October 1984); *China: Outlook and Situation Report* (Washington, D.C.: ERS, USDA, July 1985), RS-85-5; *China: A Statistical Survey in 1985* (State Statistical Bureau, 1985).

[a] "SSB 1985 Communique," *People's Daily*, March 1, 1986, 2; population, 1,046.4 million; total grains, 379.0 million tons (mt); cotton, 4.2 mt; oilseeds, 15.78 mt; meat, 17.61 mt; per capita rural income, 397.6 yuan.

percent. The results, with agricultural production increasing rapidly, were reflected in higher per capita rural incomes and more farm products available for consumption.

Chinese agricultural production has progressed so rapidly that many of the original targets set in the Sixth Five-Year Plan (1981–85) for agriculture were surpassed in 1984 (for example, GVAO by 36 percent).[4] According to the official statistics for 1985, although grain output was about 5 percent less than the record year of 1984, other indicators, such as GVAO, per capita rural income, and output of almost all other farm products, reached a new record again. Presently, all indications point to another bumper year for 1986.[5]

In addition to the post-1978 political reforms, the CPC put forth a number of general and agriculturally specific policies designed to improve Chinese agriculture by being more pragmatic and less ideological.[6] These policies included

- a reintroduction of profit incentives;
- an emphasis on science and technology and deemphasis on ideological purity;
- an emphasis on attracting foreign capital and technology to rapidly accelerate economic growth and to narrow the technological gap;
- a focus on economic efficiency in resource allocation and usage;
- a more balanced attention to the agriculture sector instead of a single focus on heavy industry expansion;
- an emphasis on overall, balanced agricultural development instead of an emphasis on grains alone;
- the encouragement of specialization in regional agriculture and production and more interregional linkage and regionally balanced GVAO; and
- the decentralization of decisionmaking in farming.

In essence, these policies rejected the development model copied from the Soviet Union in the early 1950s and radically modified by Mao.[7] Three specific programs were implemented. All of them drastically veered away from or totally reversed Maoist policies.

Production Responsibility System

The first of these programs was the agricultural production responsibility system.[8] Under this system, the basic production unit was shifted from the production team of the commune to the individual household. Commune-owned farmland was assigned to the household for as long as fifteen years. A contract was negotiated between the production team and household specifying each party's obligations. Once sales were delivered and required payments made, the household was free to dispose of the remaining output as it saw fit. Under this system, the household incurred gains commensurate with its success, an incentive that released the previously absent initiative and energy of the peasants. Of course, this new relationship also transferred the risk to the household, which must suffer losses if the farm is mismanaged. Despite the presence of risk, the program was met with such enthusiasm that by the end of 1983, conversion to this system was nearly 100 percent.

Further modification of the responsibility system allowed households to specialize and concentrate, for example, on raising hogs without having to worry about producing grain. By the end of 1984, 26 million, or 14 percent, of China's 188 million rural households were registered as specialized households.[9]

To further enhance this program, communes were reorganized to concentrate on economic functions and to relinquish their administrative responsibility to newly reinstituted township governments. The commune system, which had played such an influential role in rural life since its establishment in 1958, in essence was dismantled.[10]

Price Incentives

The second program comprised the use of price adjustments to regulate production levels. In early 1979, government quota and above quota prices in the procurement of twenty-two basic agricultural products were increased by an average of 24 percent.[11] These and subsequent increases in the procurement price of cotton and soybeans have given producers added incentives and have contributed greatly to China's transformation from an importer to a net exporter of many farm products. Indeed, the cotton and tobacco programs were so successful that restricted procurement quotas and reduced procurement prices had to be imposed in order to induce producers to switch to other crops.

In 1985, the thirty-five-year-old quota system came to an end.[12] Although the government continues to plan and dictate procurement needs, Chinese farmers are expected to depend on contracts and the market to determine what and how much crops to produce. This is a marked, profound shift from the mandatory government directives of the past.

The Opening of the Private Sector

The third program, which was a logical extension of the first two, expanded the role of the private sector in some economic activities, such as transportation and marketing, that were previously largely or wholly performed by the government. Rural and urban free markets, where the rural households market their farm surplus and sideline products—specialized crops and/or handicrafts—expanded from zero in the Cultural Revolution years to 33,300 in 1978 and to 56,500 in 1984.[13] The government monopoly in shipping and selling farm products across county boundaries also was eased.[14] In addition, rural surplus labor now was allowed to leave the village and move to towns and cities in order to establish or to be employed in small business. As a result, about 60 million people had migrated by mid-1985.[15]

Foreign Trade as a Development Strategy

As a part of the open-door policy, the new leadership pushed hard to use foreign trade as part of its development strategy. To generate foreign reserves for purchases of foreign equipment and technology, emphasis was placed on exporting agricultural products and light industry goods such as textiles and handicrafts. In 1985, the volume of two-way foreign trade reached $59.2 billion, an increase of 189 percent from $20.5 billion in 1978.[16]

China always maintained a basic foreign trade policy of self-reliance in strategic products including food. But during 1978–1984, in order to promote agricultural growth and better living standards for both its rural and urban populations, the government temporarily put aside this long-standing policy and adopted a two-tier import policy for agricultural products.[17] Not only were long-term grain purchase agreements renewed with traditional suppliers such as Canada and Australia, but agreements were signed with new suppliers, such as Argentina, the European Economic Community, and the United States, to purchase an unprecedented amount of grains, oilseeds, and edible oils, which resulted in a record deficit trade balance for the PRC.

The large grain imports primarily were used to increase the food supply of the large, populated, coastal urban areas from Shanghai to Peking. The new grain imports enabled the rural population to keep more grain; the policy's purpose was to encourage growth in agriculture, thus reversing the policy of using peasants as grain suppliers to urban people and as support for the industrial sector.[18]

In addition, this policy also allowed the government to guarantee grain rations to producers of economic crops so that all suitable and more fertile land in economic crop areas would be planted with these crops and not be diverted for grain production. The success of this strategy is reflected in the huge increases in economic crop output since 1978, particularly in cotton and tobacco.

The Current Status of China's Agricultural Development

Where have China's post-1978 advances in agriculture brought the sector? During the years before 1978, unchecked population growth, political upheaval, and general economic and agricultural mismanagement greatly handicapped agriculture. The sector was primitive and largely isolated from the influence of Western modernization and technology; agriculture underutilized a huge pool of industrious people. Post-1978 policies radically changed all this. There is no question that the progress made after 1978 was the direct result of policy reform that allowed peasant households to utilize vastly greater, improved farm inputs. But if significant changes had not been made in the ideological and institutional structures that serve as the very foundation of policy, these reforms and resulting advances would not have been at all possible. Indeed, these larger fundamental changes created the environment in which Chinese peasants could make giant strides. Therefore, of the previously elaborated five groups of factors in agricultural development, only the first and fifth can claim most of the credit for the advances made in agriculture after 1978; the second through fourth groups lent limited or no assistance.

For thousands of years, traditional Chinese concepts associated agriculture with activities that went no further than the farmgate. When agricultural reform was initiated, the aim was simply to maximize production, and Chinese peasants were not given many resources. It is true that farm structures were reorganized, more fertilizer was supplied, and government subsidies in support of farm income were raised. But investment in agriculture from the central government's annual budget was not increased significantly.[19] Basically, farmers were expected to fend for themselves and increase production by using only local resources and initiatives.

Chinese policymakers were quite surprised by the degree of success in agricultural production. They were even more surprised by what happened to demand. After being denied for so long, consumers reacted to production increases with an insatiable appetite for more, higher quality farm products. The government, which was in charge of handling the flow of farm products from farmgate to consumption, was totally unprepared to take care of the rush. These activities involve what was regarded previously as the fourth group of factors: storage, processing, distribution, wholesaling, and retailing of farm products. At the same time, the government also was unable to improve and provide the required support from the second and third groups of factors: the macroeconomic environment and the other sectors of the economy.

China's agricultural economy cannot remain in the primitive stage of pre-1978. It now is poised to enter the more modern stage of economic development, and the boundary of the agriculture sector will no longer be confined just to farm production. That boundary will extend beyond the farmgate all the way to consumption. Unfortunately at this moment, neither the second, the third, nor the fourth group of factors can support adequately the modern farm economy that China hopes to develop.

Looking Toward the Future

One hardly needs a crystal ball to predict that Chinese agriculture will make advances from now to 1990. But it is difficult to predict how much and with what speed progress will be made. This will depend, to a large degree, on the pace and orientation of political and economic reforms, on the economy's ability to provide synchronized support for agriculture, and on advances in agribusiness itself. Based on preliminary observation, China's agriculture will grow at a much slower rate in the 1986–1990 period.

Fortunately, one of the benefits of China's open-door policy has been the increasing flow to the West of information and data on the agricultural sector, including detailed policy discussions. Information about the Seventh

Table 4.2   PRC: 1984 Agricultural Output and 1990 and 2000 Targets (million metric tons)

	1984	Year 1990			Year 2000				
		Target	Percentage over 1984 Total	Annual	Target	Percentage over 1984 Total	Annual	Percentage over 1990 Total	Annual
GVAO[a] (million yuan)	337.7	491.5	45.5	6.5	1,010.0	199.1	7.1	105.5	4.6
Total Grains	407.3	450.0	10.5	1.4	520–535	27.7–31.4	1.5–1.7	15.6–18.9	1.5–1.7
Cotton[b]	6.1	4.3	−30.3	−5.0	5.1–5.3	(16.1–13.7)	(1.3–1.1)	20.0–24.7	1.8–2.2
Oilseeds	11.9	18.3	53.4	6.3	21.3–21.8	79.7–83.9	3.7–3.9	16.7–19.5	1.6–1.8
Meat	15.4	22.8	48.1	5.8	27.8–30.0	80.5–94.8	3.8–4.3	21.9–31.6	2.0–2.8
Poultry/eggs	4.3	8.8	104.7	10.8	10.2–16.0	137.2–272.1	5.5–8.6	15.9–81.8	1.5–6.2
Aquatic Products	6.2				11.0	77.4	3.6		
Per capita rural income (yuan)	355.3	550.0	54.8	6.4	700.0	97.0	4.3	27.3	2.4

Sources: China: A Statistical Survey in 1985 (State Statistical Bureau, 1985); *China Agricultural Yearbook 1985* (Agricultural Publishers, 1985); *People's Daily*, January 9, 1986, 1; *Economic Daily*, November 9, 1985, 3; *China: Outlook and Situation Report* (Washington, D.C.: ERS, USDA, July 1986), RS-86-8.

[a]Gross Value of Agricultural Output (GVAO) is in constant prices and includes village-run industries.
[b]Figures in parentheses are negative numbers.

Five-Year Plan and the Year 2000 Study allows Western observers to gain un-precedented insights into the course China has set for its agriculture.

Issues in the Seventh Five-Year Plan
In light of the success experienced in 1979–1984, particularly in 1982–1984, the Chinese leadership unveiled the Seventh Five-Year Plan for 1986–1990 with a confident outlook that was absent in the Sixth Five-Year Plan. At the Twelfth CPC National Congress in September 1985 and the Fourth Plenary Session of the Sixth National People's Congress in March 1986, the proposal presented by Premier Zhao Ziyang on the Seventh Five-Year Plan was adopted.[20] It sets the guidelines for China's economic development for 1986–1990 and beyond. The essence of the plan is to reconfirm and strengthen recent agricultural policies, such as ensuring a stable grain supply and increased grain production; systematically improving and diversifying crops, livestock, forestry, fishery, and village and township enterprises; and further loosening the rural structure, farm prices, and private enterprises. The only quantitative target set for agriculture in the proposal is a 4 percent growth rate for GVAO (6 percent if village enterprises are included—see Table 4.2).

Vice Premier Tian Jiyun, in a speech to the National Conference on Rural Works, further discussed issues critical to Chinese agriculture in 1986–1990.[21] He pointed out that the economy faces serious problems that, if not addressed, will negate the progress made in 1981–1985 and greatly reduce the likelihood of reaching the targets set for 1990. He proposed policies to combat corruption among party and government officials; to further reform the price and wage systems and macroeconomic and microeconomic structures; and to address the widening gap between high- and low-income groups.

Speaking specifically on agriculture, Tian indicated that the government will seek to

- emphasize grain production while encouraging diversified agricultural development;
- further decentralize interprovincial grain transfers;
- gradually reduce government procurement of agricultural products and improve the procurement contract system;
- support strongly the development and expansion of rural industry in small cities and townships;
- strengthen farmland management; and
- grant more authority to township government in administering its revenue and expenditure so that more capital and resources generated in other sectors of the township economy can be channeled to agriculture.

Issues in Year 2000 Study

The Chinese government also commissioned a study that sought to outline China's economic issues in the century's remaining years. Agriculture is one of the study's twelve topics.[22] In published excerpts, the study envisions the agricultural scenario in the year 2000. The GVAO and per capita rural income will reach the level presented in Table 4.2; food grains, which are roughly 60 percent of total grains, will consist mainly of wheat and rice, and coarse grains will be used as feedstuff; the proportion of crops in GVAO will decrease as subsectors of livestock, forestry, aquatic products, and sideline enterprises experience greater growth rates. The proportion of sown areas for grains, economic crops and other crops will be 74, 15, and 11 percent respectively.

In addressing policy, the study stresses that the development of the agricultural sector must be balanced and synchronized with other sectors of the economy. The production, consumption, and distribution of farm products should be well coordinated at the aggregate level. Special attention should be directed to the conflict between population growth and ever decreasing farmland and to proper land management, conservation, and development. Sources of capital for investment in agriculture should be broadened vastly, and efficiency in the use of capital should be increased. Finally, a greater emphasis should be placed on promoting scientific research and on training agricultural scientists.

Problems for Agricultural Performance in 1986–1990

It is clear that China's policymakers have recognized the development problems in 1986–1990 and have sought to address them. Given that Chinese agriculture emerged successfully from the primitive development stage and is about to enter a more advanced one, it will depend increasingly on the first through the fourth groups of factors—the performance of the political and social environment, the macroeconomic economy, the nonfarm sectors of the economy, and agribusiness—to lend the necessary and adequate support. However, the key question still remains. How much effective support will these factors provide? All indications point to a monumental, difficult road ahead.

Problems in the Political and Social Arena

It almost goes without saying that in order for the enunciated policies to succeed, the basic political and economic philosophy that has prevailed since 1978 must continue and must serve as the foundation of future policies and programs. In addition, political and social reforms at all levels must continue.[23]

Although the leadership has shown determination to do so, serious problems still remain, including whether the present reformist policy will continue after the death of Deng Xiaoping. Currently, the most urgent problem is to eradicate widespread corruption in the party and government; all high party and government leaders at the National Conference for Party and Government Cadres spoke to this issue. However, recent reports from China indicate that the party has encountered serious difficulties in its effort to slow the tide of corruption.

Problems in Macroeconomics

China no doubt will continue to manage its economy with central planning, but it also will continue to rely increasingly on the market to determine supply and demand. But when dealing with macroeconomic issues, such as population, the balance between central planning and the market, the ownership of economic means, growth of the private sector, taxation and price systems, pollution, and so on, the problems are complicated and their impact on agriculture far-reaching.

A pressing question is how to reform the current practice in order to establish a price system that can

- reflect the true values of inputs, products, and services;
- convey messages on economic needs;
- regulate market imbalance;
- address imbalance among regions;
- resolve policy contradictions among different constituencies;
- lessen the impact of variable income distribution yet not impede economic incentives;
- stimulate economic growth and retard economic inefficiency; and
- at the same time be consistent with political and social ideology and goals.

The current system clearly does not fit the bill, and modifying the system only when problems arise is obviously an inadequate approach.

There is also a more fundamental question—how freely will publicly or privately owned inputs and products, including labor, be allowed to move within the economy? Within the context of the current system of ownership, how freely can an economic entity, public or private, exit the economy when unable to survive the competition? Likewise, how freely can a new entity enter the economy when that sector of the economy needs to grow?

Recent policy allowing rural excess labor to move to neighboring small cities and towns marks the beginning of labor market mobility. A legislative proposal on bankruptcy under consideration by the National People's Congress also is a step in the right direction.[24]

However, an overwhelming proportion of Chinese labor is employed by the government. Almost all resources are under state and collective ownership, and all manufacturing and service enterprises are owned and operated by the government, except for a few family businesses. As there is no quick cure for the lack of incentive and efficiency in publicly owned and operated entities and their tendency to depend perpetually on government funding, these problems will continue to adversely affect agricultural sector performance in the immediate future.

Problems of Support from Other Industries
The same basic problems that plague the general economy also have stifled the industrial sector and its ability to support agricultural production. Transportation and energy are two notable problems in this regard. Currently, reform of the sector has begun, and a preliminary industrywide census survey recently has been completed. Given the sector's immense size and complexity, it will be a long time before it can claim the same victory as agriculture. More and more reports from China reflect grave concerns about the stagnation of industrial reform. This lack of progress in reform eventually will limit badly needed support to agriculture and agribusiness.

Problems Between the Farmgate and Consumption
Before 1978, the government apparatus monopolized the handling of farm products between farmgate and consumption. As a result of the antiquity of that apparatus, it was unprepared to carry out its task in the post-1978 period of effectively handling rising farm production and growing consumer demand. The most severe problems are in storage, processing, and the lack of timely and accurate market information.

For example, the state-owned Chinese flour milling industry in the recent past only produced about 25 million tons of mainly "standard" grade flour, with a milling rate of 75 percent. Milling equipment in these plants was made mostly in the 1950s from designs of the 1930s and 1940s. The system aimed only to supply flour for an urban population of about 200 million. It was working at full capacity and could not be geared for more production.

Before 1979, China's 1 billion rural people had to fend for themselves. After that year urban residents began to demand more and higher-grade flour, which the existing facilities were not capable of producing. In the meantime, rural people, who sometimes made more money than their city cousins, were no longer content to grind their own flour; they, too, wanted higher-quality flour. It is not hard to imagine the problem that arose.[25]

Policymakers in China have ambitious plans for the food-processing sector during the 1986–1990 period. These include huge investments and large tax incentives.[26] But the problems the sector faces cannot be readily solved in just five years. Because of foreign trade mismanagement and a reported $15 billion trade deficit in 1985, the government slowed down payments for already signed contracts and virtually ceased purchasing equipment, except equipment that could generate future exports. In the longer run, growing dissatisfaction among foreign businesses with China's bureaucracy also will erode flows of foreign capital and technology that are needed badly in China's push to modernize.

Problems in Agricultural Production
Agricultural production in China will continue to face many old problems and many more new ones. First, there is the age-old problem of limited fertile farm land, frequent drought and flooding, and depletion of ground water. The utilization of existing cultivable land already is highly intensive with the multiple crop index (sown to cultivable acreage) hovering around 1.5. Prospects for opening up new frontiers in agriculture are slim at best. Chronic loss of farmland to other uses has been and will continue to be a serious problem. Total cultivable area for crops was reduced 13 million hectares in 1957–1984 and 5.9 million in 1978–1984. Unfortunately, the lost areas usually were more fertile, better developed farmland because they were located in more populated, industrialized regions where the needs for land acquisition were and are most acute. The Law of Land Use recently passed by the National People's Congress is a step in the right direction but hardly is sufficient to solve the problem.

Given the continued emphasis on grain production, serious difficulty will arise if continued rapid agricultural production has to come from crop yields; yields per sown hectare for most of the crops are already at or are greater than the world average. The law of diminishing returns suggests that to increase yields further would require much larger infusions of farm inputs and capital, which are both in severe shortage. Although there is room to raise yields for corn and soybeans (they are about 60 percent of the U.S. average), doing so would require extensive research for new varieties and local adaptation.

Pressure from the demand side to change the composition of grain production is also a problem. As per capita income rises, demand for finer grains and more animal products also will increase. Eventually, demand for wheat and feedgrains will surpass that for other grains, including rice. The problem is the limitation of regional cropping patterns. Wheat competes with other crops in the north—mostly with corn and soybeans—for limited farmland areas, as winter wheat is not harvested until June. Meanwhile, land in the south is most suitable for rice throughout the year and would be too wet for winter wheat. The same is true for corn, but to a lesser degree.

These problems are serious, but the biggest hurdle for Chinese agriculture is the lack of support from those in the first through fourth groups of factors that together determine China's future agricultural development—the political environment, macroeconomy, nonfarm industrial sectors, and agribusiness. Without the support of these groups, eventually there will be an insufficient market for production, and producers will lose the incentive to grow.

The Chinese Experience as a Model for Third World Development

Given the tremendous strides that Chinese agriculture has made in recent years, can the Chinese approach, or ones similar to it, be adopted successfully by other developing nations? Unfortunately, the answer is no and for obvious reasons. Economic development models cannot function without the support and synchronization of all segments of a nation's cultural, social, political, and economic resources. Indeed, the thesis here has been that only when favorable conditions exist in and among all supporting factors can lasting advances in agriculture be achieved.

Since World War II, there has been notable economic success made possible by massive U.S. aid in Western Europe, Japan, Taiwan, and South Korea. However, stable and long-term economic advances built on assistance from abroad are the exception rather than the rule. Despite massive U.S. economic aid to the developing world as well as aid from other donor nations and international organizations, the path to economic development is littered with skeletons.

The post–World War II philosophy for Third World development held that the road to successful development was the U.S. path to industrialization. That philosophy then shifted radically to emphasize the importance of native cultural and social values in development. Both philosophies failed for good reasons. The former approach ignored the fact that despite the presence of capital, advanced equipment, and technology, local economies still lacked the necessary supports that were taken for granted in the United States—namely, the physical and intellectual infrastructure that serves as the foundation for industry. The latter approach failed because native cultural and social values often caused or perpetuated economic backwardness.

This is also precisely why the next phase of Chinese agricultural development is going to be far more difficult and slower than the previous one. Those supports from the first and fifth groups of factors that served China well in its post-1978 phase no longer will be sufficient if the second through fourth group of factors lag far behind and are not able to lend proper assistance. Whether applied to China or to any other developing country in which there are intricately intertwined economic problems, the situation is clearcut—any single problem cannot be solved in isolation.

Conclusion

The performance of Chinese agriculture since 1978 is impressive by any measure. There is little doubt that its success is a result, in large part, of reforms made in the country's political and social environment and concomitant advances in peasant production. Now China's agricultural sector is at a threshold; it is emerging from a primitive stage of economic development into one that requires the active, effective participation of a more modern, complex economic structure. Until that structure is developed, it will be difficult to project long-term opportunities for Chinese agriculture.

Notes

1. For details, see various chapters in *China's Economy Looks Toward the Year 2000,* vols. 1 and 2 (Washington, D.C.: Joint Economic Committee, May 1986).

2. *People's Daily,* July 1, 1981, 1.

3. See *China's Economy.*

4. *Economic Daily,* November 12, 1985, 2.

5. For 1985, see Economic Research Service (ERS), *China: Outlook and Situation Report,* RS-86-8 (Washington, D.C.: Economic Research Service, U.S. Department of Agriculture, July 1986); for 1986 estimates, see monthly forecasts by China Section, ERS, USDA.

6. For a detailed analysis of agricultural policy since 1978, see Surls, F., "Widening Scope of Agricultural Reforms," ERS, *China: Outlook and Situation Report,* RS-85-8 (Washington, D.C.: ERS, USDA, July 1985), 5–7; Stone, B., "The Basis for Chinese Agricultural Growth in the 1980's and A Comment on Document Number 1, 1984," *China Quarterly* (March 1985):114–121; various chapters in *China's Economy.*

7. Dernberger, R., "The Chinese Search for the Path of Self-Sustained Growth in the 1980's: An Assessment," *China Under Four Modernizations, Part I* (Washington, D.C.: JEC, August 1982), 19–76.

8. Crook, F., "The Reform of the Commune System and the Rise of Township-Collective-Household System," in *China's Economy.*

9. Surls, F., "Widening Scope," 6.

10. Crook, "The Reform of the Commune System."

11. "Decision of CPC Central Committee Regarding Some Issues on the Acceleration of Agricultural Development," *Chinese Agricultural Yearbook, 1980* (Agriculture Publishers, November 1981), 58.

12. *China Daily,* January 28, 1985, 4.

13. *China: A Statistic Survey in 1985* (State Statistical Bureau, 1985), 84.

14. *China Daily,* October 5, 1985, 1.

15. *People's Daily,* September 27, 1985, 1.

16. *People's Daily,* January 23, 1986, 1.

17. Surls, F., "China's Grain Imports," *China Under Four Modernizations, Part II* (Washington, D.C.: JEC, December 1982), 127–136.

18. The quantity of per capita grain available, 319 kg, in 1978 was virtually the same as the 306 kg figure in 1957. During the same period, under Mao's policy of total emphasis on grain production, output of cotton and other oilseed crops dropped way below the high levels achieved in the 1950s; soybeans gained only slightly during the same period. See *China: A Statistic Survey in 1985,* 36.

19. A large portion of the government's annual budget is allocated to make up the difference between procurement and retail prices, which are kept low as an income subsidy to urban areas.

20. *People's Daily,* September 26, 1985, 1; and *People's Daily,* April 14, 1986, 1.

21. *People's Daily,* December 31, 1985, 1.

22. *Economic Daily,* November 9, 1985, 3.

23. "Notification from Party Consolidation Work Advisory Commission of CPC Central Committee on Plans for Rural Consolidation Work," *Economic Daily,* November 25, 1985, 1.

24. *China Daily,* January 22, 1986, 1.

25. Talks with Ministry of Commerce officials, February 11, 1985.

26. *Economic Daily,* September 9, 1985, 1.

chapter five

Economic Policy and Agricultural Development in the Philippines: Anatomy of Stagnation

Ramon L. Clarete
James A. Roumasset

There is little doubt that the recent political upheaval in the Philippines was induced, in part, by economic failure. Was the country's poor economic performance the result of idiosyncratic episodes and singular greed, or are there some general lessons to be learned? In particular, the Philippine agricultural sector has failed to propel economic development despite the fact that the country is relatively rich in agricultural resources. In what ways have agricultural development strategies in the Philippines contributed to economic stagnation?

Agricultural Development in Asia

Asian countries have the best economic performance record in the developing world. Since 1960, East and Southeast Asian economies have had annual average growth rates of about 7.5 percent, a performance unmatched by any other region in the world in recent history.[1] South Asia likewise has grown rapidly. Between 1960 and 1983, its annual growth rate averaged 4.5 percent, which is slightly above the world average growth rate of 3.9 percent for the same period.[2] Despite their rapid growth, Asian countries generally continue to have low levels of Gross National Products (GNPs) per capita. South Asia (Bangladesh, Burma, India, Nepal, Pakistan, and Sri Lanka) has the poorest average income within Asia, ranging between $130 and $380 in 1984 (Table 5.1). Southeast Asia (Indonesia, Malaysia, Philippines, Thailand, and Singapore) is relatively better off, with an average income between $540 and $7,260. Hong Kong, South Korea, and Taiwan, which together with Singapore comprise the newly industrialized countries (NICs), have the highest per capita incomes in Asia.

Agriculture is a relatively large sector in Asian economies. In South Asia, agriculture's value added ranges from 24 to 56 percent of Gross Domestic

Table 5.1   Some Economic Indicators of Asian Countries, 1984

Country	Population (million)	Area (thousands of square kilometers)	Gross National Product Per Capita (dollar)	Gross Domestic Product Distribution (%)		
				Agriculture	Industry	Services
South Asia						
Bangladesh	98.1	144	130	48	12	39
Burma	36.1	677	180	48	13	39
India	749.2	3,288	260	35	27	38
Nepal	16.1	141	160	56	12	32
Pakistan	92.4	804	380	24	29	47
Sri Lanka	15.9	66	360	28	26	46
Southeast Asia						
Indonesia	158.9	1,919	540	26	40	34
Malaysia	15.3	330	1,980	21	35	44
Philippines	53.4	300	660	25	34	41
Thailand	50.0	514	860	20	28	52
Singapore	2.5	1	7,260	1	39	60
East Asia						
Hong Kong	5.4	1	6,330	1	22	78
Korea, Republic of	40.1	98	2,110	14	40	47
Taiwan	18.8	36	3,060	7	42	51

Sources: World Bank, *World Development Report 1986* (New York: Oxford University Press, 1986); Asian Development Bank, *Key Indicators of Developing Member Countries of ADB 16* (Manila, 1985).

Product (GDP). The figure for poorer countries such as Bangladesh is closer to 50 percent. Southeast and East Asia are also fairly agricultural, with the sector contributing about 25 percent of GDP. On the other hand, the small city-states of Singapore and Hong Kong have agricultural sectors that contribute only about 1 percent of GDP.

The growth structure of Asian economies between 1960 and 1984 shows that growth rates peaked for most of Asia in the 1970s (Table 5.2). South Asian growth rates, however, were lower, ranging from 2.5 to 4.7 percent annually during that period—a sluggish performance compared to that of Southeast and East Asian countries. Now, South Asia appears to be gaining the momentum for growth, while East and Southeast Asia both seem to be slowing down. Interestingly, the largest drop in growth rates occurred in the Philippines. There, the growth rate fell from 6.3 percent in the 1970s to 1.8 percent in the early 1980s.

Industrial growth rates have outpaced growth rates of GDP in Asian countries, with only few exceptions. This implies that a structural transformation has been underway, with progressively lower shares of income and employment being generated from the agricultural sector. This was espe-

Table 5.2 Average Annual Real Growth Rates of Asian Countries, 1960–1984 (in percentage)

Country	Gross Domestic Product			Agriculture			Industry		
	1960–1970	1970–1980	1980–1984	1960–1970	1970–1980	1980–1984	1960–1970	1970–1980	1980–1984
South Asia									
Bangladesh	3.7	3.9	3.2	2.7	2.2	3.0	8.0	9.5	2.9
Burma	2.6	4.6	6.1	4.1	4.3	7.5[a]	3.1	5.2	8.0
India	3.4	3.6	5.1	1.9	1.9	3.7[b]	5.4	4.5	3.9[b]
Nepal	2.5	2.5	3.2	[d]	0.5	3.1	—	4.2[c]	3.4[c]
Pakistan	6.7	4.7	6.7	4.9	2.3	2.6	10.0	5.2	5.2
Sri Lanka	4.6	4.1	5.1	3.0	2.8	4.5[a]	6.6	4.0	5.3
Southeast Asia									
Indonesia	3.9	7.6	5.8	2.7	3.8	4.3[a]	5.2	11.1	6.8[b]
Malaysia	6.5	7.8	6.7	—	5.1	3.4	—	9.7	7.8
Philippines	5.1	6.3	1.8	4.3	4.9	2.1	6.0	8.7	0.1
Thailand	8.4	7.2	5.6	5.6	4.7	3.4	11.9	10.0	5.4
Singapore	8.8	8.5	8.7	5.0	1.8	-1.3[a]	12.5	8.8	9.2
East Asia									
Hong Kong	10.0	9.3	7.6	-0.9	-0.1	—	—	7.8	4.0[a]
Korea, Republic of	8.6	9.5	5.3	4.4	3.2	3.3[a]	17.2	15.4	16.8
Taiwan	9.3	9.8	6.3	—	1.6	0.4	16.4	12.3	17.9

Sources: Asian Development Bank, *Key Indicators of Developing Member Countries of ADB 16* (Manila, 1985); James, W. E., Naya, S., and Myers, G., "Comparative Studies of Asian Economic Development" (Honolulu: East-West Center, 1986), mimeo; Mark, S., and Morrison, C., Macroeconomic Performance of Developing Countries in the Asia-Pacific Region (Honolulu: East-West Center, 1985), World Bank, *World Development Report 1982* (New York: Oxford University Press, 1982).

[a]1980–1983 only.
[b]1980–1982 only.
[c]Includes services.
[d]No data available.

cially true in the 1970s despite the high cost of energy-related inputs in that period. It is interesting to note that Philippine industrial growth in the 1980s is a clear exception to the trend toward industrialization in Asia. Philippine industry grew at the rate of only 0.1 percent in the early 1980s—a very disappointing performance relative to the region as a whole and a sharp contrast to the country's 8.7 percent industrial growth rate in the 1970s.

Agricultural growth in Asia also has been impressive. In the 1960s, South Asian countries, with the exception of India, had quite high agricultural growth rates. Although somewhat diminished in the 1970s, agricultural growth in South Asia recovered in the early 1980s. Agricultural growth rates in Southeast Asia also have been high. Hong Kong and Singapore, which have fairly insignificant agricultural sectors, were exceptions, as was Taiwan, which experienced rapid industrialization. Although an NIC, South Korea has had high agricultural growth rates, partly as a result of domestic policies that protect Korean agricultural producers. The most interesting exception to the overall picture of vigorous agricultural growth in Asia is, again, the Philippines. Philippine agriculture grew only 2.1 percent from 1980 to 1984, which was a sharp drop from the 4.9 percent growth rate it achieved in the 1970s.

Asia's superior economic performance seems correlated with impressive gains in overall agricultural development in the region. The region as a whole moved toward greater self-sufficiency in food despite high population growth rates. In addition, production of agricultural exports increased, particularly in Southeast Asia.

Cereal production increased tremendously in South and Southeast Asia, and grain imports to the region fell. Annual rice production expanded from 140 million to 190 million tons between the early 1970s and the early 1980s, resulting in a substantial rice surplus. Wheat production in South Asia grew by nearly 110 percent between 1973 and 1984. During the 1970s, maize production increased by 30 percent. With rapid gains in cereal production, the Philippines achieved self-sufficiency in rice by the late 1970s, and Indonesia, a large rice importer, did likewise in 1984. Under normal weather conditions, India, formerly a larger grain importer, now produces surpluses of rice and wheat. Exporting countries, especially Thailand and Burma, also achieved rapid growth in grain production. Rice imports into South and Southeast Asia fell from almost 9 million tons in 1973–1975 to less than 1 million tons in 1981/82.

With the exception of Thailand, the growth in cereal production was associated with the intensification of agricultural production, with growth of agricultural employment substantially exceeding the expansion in cultivated area. James, Naya, and Myers attribute the rapid growth in cereal production to three primary components of intensification: rapid adoption of modern (land-saving) seed varieties, increased use of chemical fertilizer, and expanded coverage of irrigation, in that order.[3]

Southeast Asia achieved impressive gains in producing noncereal export crops. Thailand increased its production of cassava, bananas, pineapples, and sugar, largely through area expansion. Indonesia expanded cassava and coconut production and initiated government programs to develop the palm oil sector. Malaysia had rapid productivity growth in rubber and palm oil and also encouraged further area expansion in palm oil. From 1973 to 1982 in the Philippines, growth rates in the privately controlled pineapple, banana, coffee, and cassava sectors grew at average rates of between 10 and 20 percent a year.

The rapid growth in incomes in Southeast Asia has brought with it a rapid growth in consumption of meat and dairy products. This has led to increased imports in both livestock products and feed. As the domestic pork and poultry industries have grown behind the wall of tariff protection, the importation of feed grains and mixed feeds also has increased.

As mentioned previously, although economic growth rates are generally high in Asia, the Philippines stands out as a clear exception to the trend. Philippine GDP grew at an average of 4 percent from 1955 to 1980.[4] The GDP growth figures in Table 5.2 for 1980–1984 suggest that the country has "dropped out of the pack." The output of the industrial sectors declined, and the growth rate of agricultural production was exceptionally low. From 1980 to 1984, the growth rate slowed to an average of .9–1.6 percent.[5] Since 1984, the growth rate has been negative. Moreover, the export to GNP ratio only grew from 13 to 20 percent from 1955 to 1980, which pales in comparison to the sixfold increase of the ratio in South Korea during the same period.

Agricultural performance in the Philippines since 1980 has been no better. The hard-earned self-sufficiency in rice was lost in the 1980s when the country again began to import rice. Production of coconut and sugar, two of the country's leading cash crops, fell, resulting in a considerable loss of foreign exchange and a substantial decline in farm incomes. Indonesia displaced the Philippines as the world's top coconut producer in 1984, and Philippine sugar producers are discouraged by low world sugar prices due to competition by sugar substitutes.

The Philippines' economic performance, the worst in the Association of Southeast Asian Nations (ASEAN) and certainly one of the most disappointing in Asia, is a direct result of the country's economic policies. These policies promoted import substitutes at the expense of agriculture-based, export-oriented sectors.

Poor agricultural policies accompanied this thrust, thereby further retarding agricultural growth. It does not appear, however, that the patterns and level of protection alone accounted for the agricultural growth differentials between the Philippines and other Asian countries. Asian countries have typically been "provisionist" with respect to staple foods, especially rice, by providing consumers with at least limited access to food at controlled prices. Agricultural exports have had typically negative protection rates, especially in comparison to nonagricultural products. Capital-intensive, agricultural import substitutes such as pork and poultry have enjoyed positive protection rates.

Because the patterns and level of agricultural protection were not drastically different in the Philippines and in other countries, it is useful to examine the whole range of Philippine agricultural policies. To do so, it is necessary to first describe the Philippine agricultural sector.

An Overview of Philippine Agriculture

The Rural Household Sector

The majority of Filipinos live in rural areas. In 1982, the rural population was 31.5 million, about 62 percent of the total population. The proportion of rural residents, however, has declined steadily. Rural residents accounted for 73 percent of total population in 1948, 70.2 percent in 1960, 67.1 percent in 1970, 68.4 percent in 1975, and 62.7 percent in 1980. In absolute terms, however, the rural population continued to grow at an average annual rate of 1.5 percent between 1975 and 1980.

About 85 percent of the people employed in rural areas are engaged in activities involving the production of crops, livestock, and poultry as well as fishing and forestry. Off-farm occupations in the rural sector mostly involve agricultural services such as transportation and retailing. In fact, about one-third the entire Philippine service sector is in rural areas.[6] Mining and quarrying as well as cottage and other small-scale industries in rural areas provide alternative employment.

Family incomes are low and distributed unevenly in the Philippines. This is especially true in rural areas. Table 5.3 shows income distribution in both the Philippines as a whole and in the country's rural areas in 1975. The average income of rural families was P 4,745 ($655), roughly 65 percent of the mean family income for the entire country. Close to 40 percent of the 4,764 rural households received incomes no greater than P 3,000 ($414). Together, these families accounted for only 16 percent of the total rural income of P 23 billion ($3 billion). Almost 90 percent of rural families had incomes below P 8,000 ($1,104) and shared about one-half the total rural income. The corresponding statistics for the country as a whole show a slightly less uneven income distribution.

Food, housing, clothing, fuel, and water are the major commodities purchased by rural households. In 1975, these goods accounted for roughly 75 percent of total rural family expenditures. Expenditures on food were

Table 5.3   Distribution of Families and Income by Income Class for
Philippines and Rural Areas, 1975

Income Class (in pesos)	Philippines[a] (percentage)	Rural Areas[b] (percentage)
1–3,000	32.3	38.3
	(11.2)[c]	(16.1)
3,001–5,000	30.6	31.1
	(20.3)	(25.6)
5,001–8,000	20.4	18.9
	(21.6)	(24.5)
8,001–10,000	5.9	5.0
	(9.1)	(9.3)
10,001–15,000	5.9	4.0
	(12.1)	(10.0)
15,000+	4.9	2.7
	(25.7)	(14.5)

Source: National Census and Statistics Office, *Philippine Statistical Yearbook 1984*
(Quezon City: NEDA-APO Production Unit, 1984).

[a] Total number of Philippine families in 1975 was 6,859 households; total income in
   1975 was 50.9 billion pesos.
[b] Total number of rural families in 1975 was 4,764 households; total rural income was
   22.6 billion pesos.
[c] Percentage of total (Philippines or rural areas) is described by upper-level numbers,
   and percentage of total income (Philippines or rural areas) is described by lower-
   level numbers.

especially large, comprising 56 percent of the rural family budget. This underscores the importance of food policies to rural households.

Agricultural Sectors
Crop production is the dominant activity in Philippine agriculture. Of the total gross value added (GVA) in agriculture in 1982, about 58 percent originated from the crop sector (Table 5.4). Fisheries was the second largest sector and contributed about 20 percent of agricultural output. Livestock and poultry together contributed about 14 percent, and forestry accounted for the remaining 8 percent. A similar distribution of value added across agricultural sectors occurred in most previous years.

The major agricultural crops are palay (rough rice), corn, coconut, sugar cane, and bananas. The output of palay was 27 percent of total crop production in 1982 (Table 5.5). Coconut, the second largest crop, contributed 13 percent of total crop output. Corn and sugar cane each contributed about 10 percent to total output. Other crops, including mangos, pineapple, rootcrops, citrus, vegetables, coffee, cacao, beans, peas, peanuts, tobacco, abaca, ramie, rubber, and maguey, accounted for 37 percent of the country's crop production. In terms of land use, the palay, corn, and coconut subsec-

Table 5.4   Value Added in Agriculture by Sector, 1970–1982 (in percentage)

Commodity	1970	1975	1980	1982
Total Agriculture[a]	100.0	100.0	100.0	100.0
Crops	54.7	62.4	58.9	58.3
Livestock/poultry	15.1	11.6	12.1	13.7
Fishery	15.8	17.0	18.1	20.1
Forestry	13.9	8.8	10.9	7.9

Source: Bautista, L., and Duremdes, E., "An Overview of Structural Change in the Philippines, 1950–82," in National Economic Development Authority, *Towards a Balanced Agro-Industrial Development: A NEDA Workshop on Development Planning* (Manila, 1984).

[a]Totals are approximate.

tors each utilized about 27 percent of the total area harvested in 1983, or about 11.7 million hectares (Table 5.6). Sugar cane and bananas accounted for 6 percent, while all other crops utilized 11.3 percent of the total area harvested.

The Role of Agriculture

A significant part of the country's total GDP comes from agriculture. As shown in Table 5.1, in 1984, agricultural value added was 25 percent of GDP.

Table 5.5   Agricultural Production, 1982 (in thousand metric tons)

Commodity	Amount	Percent
Total Crops	29,712	100.0
Food Crops	22,264	74.9
Palay	8,108	27.3
Corn	3,290	11.1
Others	10,866	36.5
Commercial Crops	7,448	25.1
Coconut	3,785	12.7
Sugar	3,403	11.4
Others	260	1.0
Livestock[a]	12,346	100.0
Poultry[a]	58,121	100.0
Fishery	1,829	100.0
Forestry[b]	4,514	100.0

Source: Bautista, L., and Duremdes, E., "An Overview of Structural Change in the Philippines, 1950–82," in National Economic Development Authority, *Towards a Balanced Agro-Industrial Development: A NEDA Workshop on Development Planning* (Manila, 1984).

[a]In thousand heads.
[b]In thousand cubic meters.

Table 5.6   Agricultural Area Harvested by Crops, 1983
(in thousand hectares)

Crops	Area	Percent
Total Area	11,656	100.0
Palay	3,240	27.8
Corn	3,157	27.1
Banana	315	2.7
Coconut	3,209	27.5
Sugar cane	424	3.6
Other crops	1,311	11.3

Source: National Census and Statistics Office, *Philippine Statistical Yearbook 1984*
(Quezon City: NEDA-APO Production Unit, 1984).

However, agriculture's importance has declined steadily. Its value added fell from 29 percent of GDP in 1970 to 26 percent in 1982 (Table 5.7). Agriculture's contribution was much higher before 1970.[7]

Agriculture is the largest source of employment in the Philippine economy. Between 1970 and 1982, an average of about 50 percent of the total labor force was employed in agriculture. By comparison, the average employment rate was only 31 percent in the service sector and 15 percent in the industrial sector during the same period.

Philippine exports comprise primary agricultural products and agriculturally based processed commodities. Since 1950, the country's ten principal exports have been copra, sugar, bananas, lumber, dessicated coconut, coconut oil, canned pineapples, gold, unmanufactured abaca, and copper concentrates. Agricultural exports accounted for more than 60 percent of total exports in the 1970s (Table 5.8). In 1982, the share of agricultural ex-

Table 5.7   Gross Domestic Product and Employment by Sector,
1970–1982 (in percentage)

Sector	1970	1975	1980	1982
Agriculture	28.9	26.6	25.6	25.6
	(46.0) [a]	(49.8)	(49.7)	(49.1)
Industry	29.5	33.2	36.1	26.1
	(16.0)	(15.0)	(14.3)	(14.5)
Services	41.6	40.2	38.3	38.3
	(32.7)	(30.5)	(30.7)	(31.2)
Gross Domestic Product	100.0	100.0	100.0	100.0
Labor force	(100.0)	(100.0)	(100.0)	(100.0)

Source: Bautista, L., and Duremdes, E., "An Overview of Structural Change in the Philippines, 1950–82," in National Economic Development Authority, *Towards a Balanced Agro-Industrial Development: A NEDA Workshop on Development Planning* (Manila, 1984).

[a]Gross Domestic Product distribution is described by upper-level numbers and employment distribution by lower-level numbers. Remaining percentage of labor force is in other, undefined sectors.

Table 5.8   Agricultural Exports and Imports, 1950–1982
(F.O.B. value in million U.S. dollars)

Year	Amount	Exports (percent)	Amount	Imports (percent)
1970	708.2	62.0	99.7	8.6
1975	1,546.5	67.4	280.2	8.1
1980	2,442.4	42.2	363.2	4.7
1982	1,922.9	38.3	506.0	6.6

Sources: Bautista, L., and Duremdes, E., "An Overview of Structural Change in the Philippines, 1950–82," in National Economic Development Authority, *Towards a Balanced Agro-Industrial Development: A NEDA Workshop on Development Planning* (Manila, 1984); National Census and Statistics Office, *Philippine Statistical Yearbook 1984* (Quezon City: NEDA-APO Production Unit, 1984).

ports in the total dropped to about 38 percent (the share was 67 percent in 1957), due to the growth of manufactured exports.

Agriculture has generated substantial foreign exchange. Between 1970 and 1982, the foreign exchange value of Philippine agricultural exports averaged $1.6 billion, while only $0.3 billion was required by the sector to purchase its imported inputs. Thus, the average net foreign exchange generated by the sector was $1.3 billion.

The sector is also a major source of capital in the Philippine economy. De Leon has traced positive capital flows out of agriculture to nonagricultural sectors beginning in the 1950s.[8] This trend was interrupted only in the 1970s when the government invested heavily in agriculture. The trade surplus in agriculture always has been positive and grew at an average annual rate of 6.1 percent from 1955 to 1965 and at 3.8 percent from 1969 to 1978.

Trade and Industrial Policies Affecting Agriculture

The main thrust of postwar trade and industrial policies in the Philippines has been the promotion of import-competing sectors at the expense of agricultural-based, export-oriented industries. Trade policies protecting import substitutes include restrictions on imports and foreign exchange in the 1950s, tariffs since the 1960s, and export taxes during the 1970s. Incentives granted to industrial investors since 1967 have supplemented the protection afforded by trade policies to import substitutes. Although trade liberalizing policies were put into effect in the 1960s and 1970s, they had limited success in promoting exports. In 1962, tariffs replaced import quotas and neutralized the export-promotion effect of devaluing the peso. Export taxes blunted the liberalizing impact of a floating exchange rate and export subsidies in 1970.

Tariffs were imposed in 1957 for the purpose of raising revenue. The prevailing system at that time of import and foreign exchange controls made them redundant.[9] But in 1962, the tariffs became binding, and the tariff structure preserved the bias in favor of import substitutes and against agriculturally based exportables. On average, the tariff rates ranged from 15 percent on highly essential commodities to about 50 percent on nonessential consumer goods.[10] This escalating tariff structure reinforced the bias in favor of import substitutes.[11]

The Investment Incentives Act of 1967 likewise discriminated against agriculture by granting a package of fiscal incentives to preferred industries. Initiated to accelerate Philippine industrialization, the Incentives Act allowed accelerated depreciation as well as deductions of organizational and preoperating expenses from taxable income, granted tax credits on domestic capital equipment, and exempted beneficiaries from paying taxes on imported capital equipment. These incentives effectively subsidized the cost of using capital and in effect attracted new firms to the capital-intensive manufacturing sector.

The Philippines devalued its currency and embarked upon a floating exchange rate system in 1970, thus abandoning the fixed-exchange rate policy of previous years. Under this regime, the peso was allowed to fluctuate within a given range. Another policy reform, the Export Incentives Act of 1970, was initiated to encourage exports and offset the discrimination against exports in the tariff system. The package of incentives included tax credits for duties paid on imported materials as well as double deduction of shipping costs and promotional expenses. In addition to these benefits, investments in export industries also were entitled to the incentives offered by the Investment Incentives Act of 1967. Nontraditional exports consisting mainly of manufactured products such as clothing, textile and garments, electric machinery and appliances, and cement and other nonmetallic mineral products clearly benefited from the program.

Despite these reforms, existing policies remained and new laws were decreed that continued import substitution and the discrimination of agriculturally based exportables. The extra income of agricultural producers from the devaluation of the peso was taxed under the Stabilization Tax Law of 1970. Enacted to cushion the inflationary impact of devaluing the peso and to finance the fiscal deficit,[12] this law explicitly taxed exports for the first time.

The Tariff Code of 1973 simplified the prevailing tariff schedule and incorporated export taxes. A basic tariff rate of 10 percent was imposed on all imports for revenue purposes. A five-level schedule of discriminatory rates ranging up to a maximum of 100 percent was added to the 10 percent revenue rate to promote import-substituting industries. A basic rate of 4 percent was levied on all exports. Additional rates of up to 10 percent were required on top of 4 percent to promote the domestic processing of agricultural products like copra.

Nontariff trade barriers also have been part of the protectionist trend. The importation of nonessential and unclassified consumer goods now requires the approval of the central bank. Of about 3,500 goods in the tariff schedule, 1,304 nonessential consumer imports are subject to some form of import restriction. A few intermediate goods that are mostly used as inputs in producing exportables also require import licenses. Like tariffs, nontariff barriers create wedges between world and domestic prices and thus subsidize domestic producers of import substitutes.

Major Agricultural Policies

Agricultural policies have complemented trade and industrial policies in retarding agricultural growth. Price controls, production taxes, and marketing policies in agriculturally related industries have been disincentives to agricultural producers. Important agricultural industries such as rice, sugar, and coconut have been subjected to price controls, production taxes, and state trading. In addition to these interventions, the government also has protected producers of crucial agricultural inputs by raising the prices farmers pay for them.

Rice

Despite the growing demand for rice due to a high population growth rate (2.5 percent annually), the Philippines stopped importing rice and even became a marginal rice exporter in the second half of the 1970s. This good production record was primarily the result of the government's efforts, through credit, input subsidies, and extension programs, to propagate the use of high-yield rice varieties from the International Rice Research Institute. In addition to increasing yields in rice farming at the rate of 5.2 percent annually, these varieties, like the IR36 or IR50, tend to mature faster, resist more disease, and tolerate more moisture.[13]

Price subsidies also helped to increase rice production. The government has set floor producer prices that it defends with production subsidies. The National Food Authority (NFA) was set up solely to handle the local rice trade and enforce the price policy. Although it is a rice monopoly in principle, the NFA's limited budget allows it to cover only about 10 percent of total rice output. Other rice traders buy and sell rice at the lower market price.

In addition to price subsidies, the government subsidizes the use of critical rice inputs, which complement the modern rice varieties. The government has invested heavily in irrigation and has subsidized close to 90 percent of the operating costs of installed irrigation systems. Until 1976, inorganic fertilizers had been available to rice producers at roughly one-half the world price.[14] To promote the use of high-yield rice varieties, the government launched Masagana-99, a program subsidizing the credit used for purchasing fertilizers and pesticides required in planting high-yield rice varieties.[15]

Another of the government's goals is to provide rice locally at low consumer prices. With the current glut of rice in the world market, enforcing the cheap rice policy is not really a problem.

It is interesting to find out how the government actually managed to have price supports and ceilings on rice simultaneously through the years. When the country was importing rice in the 1950s and 1960s, the ceiling on consumer prices could not be enforced. Foreign exchange constraints led to the rationing of rice on the local market. Domestic retail prices were above world or ceiling prices depending upon the availability of foreign exchange. However, official producer prices prevailed, and rice producers received subsidies. Where rationing was severe, rents also accrued to importers.

However, when the country became a rice exporter, the low retail price policy was easy to implement. The export restriction, in this case, was caused primarily by the NFA's monopoly of the rice export trade. With a limited budget, the NFA could only handle a portion of the local rice surplus. The rest was dumped into the local market, thus keeping local retail prices lower than the world price. Hence, rice farmers, prevented from selling freely on the world market, ended up subsidizing rice consumption.

Accordingly, domestic retail prices during importing years were above ceiling or world prices, while actual producer prices in the current exporting period are lower than floor or world prices.[16] Thus, rice farmers who received protection in earlier importing years are now penalized by the marketing policy. Furthermore, policies that protect producers of important agricultural inputs also lower effective protection for rice farmers. The effective protection in the Philippine rice industry is now negative.

Sugar
Sugar accounts for about 10 percent of Philippine merchandise exports and represents about 5 percent of the world trade in sugar. The sugar industry became important to the Philippine economy during the colonial period, when the United States imported most of the country's sugar at above world prices. This preferential agreement continued after Philippine independence through a bilateral quota agreement under which the United States was required to purchase the Philippine sugar quota at premium prices. This caused substantial resources to be invested in the industry. The benefits to sugar producers increased further when the United States eliminated the Cuban sugar quota and gave part of it to the Philippines in 1963.

The preferential trading agreement expired in 1974. Fortunately enough for the country and particularly for sugar producers, world sugar prices rose sharply in 1974, thereby cushioning the adjustment effects of the expiration. The Philippines has since started to diversify its sugar market by trading with the centrally planned economies.

In 1974, the government supported sugar prices in order to encourage production. This became an extremely costly program. Between 1977 and 1979, the government borrowed $370 million abroad for subsidy purposes. But during the same period, sugar exports amounted to only 67 percent of the borrowed amount.[17]

During that period, a sugar marketing board, the National Sugar Trading Company (NASUTRA), was created, and it effectively monopolized the sugar trade. Locally, the agency paid sugar producers a composite price calculated as a weighted average of world and domestic retail prices, with the world price given the weight of 54 percent. The composite price was updated to reflect changes in the world price.

Discrimination against the sugar industry began with the imposition of an export tax in 1970 at the rate of 4 percent *ad valorem.* The tax was followed by an export ban in 1974, when sugar prices increased sharply in that year. Although the ban benefited consumers, it meant lower sugar prices for producers. The discrimination intensified with the monopolization of sugar trade by NASUTRA. In 1979, NASUTRA updated the composite sugar price by only 50 percent of the increase in world prices that year in order to pay the loans it borrowed to subsidize producers between 1977 and 1979.[18]

That move appeared to be part of an industry-financed stabilization program in the sugar industry. Although it was well intentioned, the program was both arbitrary and easily abused.

Coconut
A similar pattern of discrimination against agricultural producers occurred in the coconut industry. The main difference in the coconut case was that huge rents were involved, and their extraction was hidden behind ostensibly innocent development objectives. The government sought to increase the productivity of coconut trees and encourage coconut farmers to move into the other sectors of the industry (trading, milling, and banking) to improve the farmers' welfare.

As in the sugar case, discrimination against coconut farmers started in 1970 with taxes on exports. The rates were then 10 percent for copra and 8 percent for processed coconut products. When world coconut prices increased drastically in 1973, the government began to subsidize the domestic consumption of cooking oil and collected the coconut levy from coconut farmers to pay for the program. With revenue from the levy the government moved to replant the country's coconut trees in 1975 with a hybrid variety, amidst optimistic promises of a fivefold increase in yield. The development and marketing of the coconut variety was monopolized by a quasipublic corporation.

In the same year, the government, on behalf of the coconut farmers, purchased the United Coconut Planters Bank (UCPB), which became the pivotal institution for vertically integrating the industry. The UCPB bought coconut oil mills and formed the United Coconut Oil Mills (UNICOM) in 1979. In that year, UNICOM controlled about 67 percent of the country's copra-crushing capacity. The government allowed the formation of UNICOM and fully supported it by prohibiting entry into the oil milling industry and by granting exclusive right to UNICOM to export coconut products. The monopolization of trading and milling in the industry appeared to lower the prices received by coconut farmers. Based on available coconut price data, producers received about 5 percent less than competitive prices in 1980 and 1981.[19]

Funding for these initiatives came from a coconut levy, which taxed coconut production at the rate of 20 percent *ad valorem*. Because coconut oil is highly substitutable and constitutes less than 10 percent of the world market of fats and oils, including soybean and palm oil, the country is unable to affect world coconut prices. Hence, the tax was borne primarily by coconut producers. The average annual yield of the levy was about P 1 billion. However, the coconut producers did not benefit significantly from these programs. Many believe that the coconut programs merely transferred income from coconut farmers to nonfarmers, the main beneficiary being the controlling owner of the UCPB, the same person who owned the coconut hybrid monopoly franchise.

Livestock

The livestock industry mainly produces hogs and poultry. Cattle tends to be limited to extensive production where marginal grazing land has a low opportunity cost in other uses. The output of hogs and poultry grew rapidly in the 1970s due to improved technology and protectionist policies. Meat imports were taxed at the rate of 100 percent *ad valorem* and were subject to licensing. In addition, the lower tariff rates on feeds increased the effective protection accorded to the industry.

Promoting the livestock industry has been costly. Feed imports account for 70 percent of the value added in the industry and cost more than the meat imports that the country would have purchased under a liberalized meat import policy.[20] The government, in its concern, has promoted yellow corn production with credit subsidies. Yellow corn accounts for about 60 percent of the total cost of producing animals feeds.[21]

Agricultural Inputs

Agricultural inputs generally have positive protection rates. The estimated implicit tariff rates for important agricultural inputs are positive, except for irrigation (Table 5.9). Imports of farm equipment had tariffs of 24 percent.

Table 5.9   Implicit Tariffs on Agricultural Inputs, 1980–1981 (in percentage)

Inputs	Tariff
Irrigation (NIA gravity)[a]	–86
(NIA communal)	–92
Irrigation pumps[b]	30
Hand tractors[b]	33
Four-wheeled tractors[b]	10
Animal feeds (hog grower mash)[c]	7
(cattle feeds)	17
(layer mash)	20
(broiler mash)	23
Agricultural chemicals[d]	23
Fertilizer[e]	10

Source: David, C., *Economic Policies and Philippine Agriculture* (Makati: Philippine Institute for Development Studies, 1983).

[a]Includes subsidy due to low irrigation fee and low repayment rate.
[b]Based on tariff rate.
[c]Based on weighted average implicit tariff on feed ingredients.
[d]Based on tariff rate and advanced sales tax.
[e]Based on price comparison of urea, ammonium, sulphate, mixed fertilizer, and phosphates from 1973–1981.

Animal feeds likewise had tariffs between 7 and 23 percent. The tariff rates on agricultural chemicals and fertilizers were 23 and 10 percent respectively. The government also has subsidized 60 to 90 percent of the cost of irrigation.[22]

There may be different explanations for the tendency of input prices to be above world prices. The most obvious explanation is that the government promoted local production of most inputs by imposing import tariffs. In the case of inorganic fertilizers, however, domestic prices were higher than world prices in order to subsidize the Fertilizer and Pesticide Authority, a government agency monopolizing and regulating the fertilizer and pesticide trade. In 1974, the agency taxed fertilizer users to recoup some of the losses it incurred while speculating about world fertilizer prices; in that year, the agency doubled fertilizer imports, incorrectly anticipating that fertilizer prices would rise in the next few years.[23]

Whatever the underlying motivation for high input prices, Philippine agricultural policies seem to reveal a pattern of reverse "tariff escalation." Inputs have positive protection rates while outputs have lower or negative protection rates. Typically, in manufacturing, outputs have higher positive rates of protection than inputs, which increases the effective protection rate. In the case of agriculture, effective penalty on agricultural production is reinforced by the deescalating pattern of agricultural trade policies.

A History of Development Policy in the Philippines

It is useful to present a brief history of development policy in the Philippines since the 1950s. The first phase of development policy was the promotion of local import-substituting industries. Trade policies were mainly used to carry out this industrial plan. Emerging from postwar recovery as a newly independent nation in the early 1950s, the Philippines remained economically dependent on the United States. Imports greatly exceeded exports and caused a balance-of-payments crisis. The government responded by imposing restrictive import and exchange rate controls, which conferred a high rate of effective protection to import substitutes.

These protectionist policies did not succeed totally in correcting the balance-of-payments deficit, however; in the early 1960s the peso was devalued to approximately P 4 to $1, and nontariff import barriers were dismantled and replaced by import tariffs. This succeeded in generating some government revenue, but the protectionist bias remained.

Import-substituting manufacturing grew rapidly in the 1950s, but by the late 1950s industrial growth had started to slow down. Although tariffs subsidized import substitution, they simultaneously penalized other sectors, especially exports. Moreover, the structure of protection especially favored the finishing stage of import substitution and discouraged backward integration.

The Technocratic Reformation

In the late 1960s and early 1970s, a number of selective incentives associated with a cadre of well-trained technocrats who occupied high level positions in the Marcos government were put into place to broaden the growth of manufacturing. These included investment incentives (1967), the devaluation of the currency, a floating exchange rate policy, and export incentives (1970).

The Marcos administration also invested substantially in a program to attain self-sufficiency in rice production through irrigation, fertilizer, subsidies, and diffusion of high-yield rice varieties. In addition, land reform, which was already in effect in the late 1960s, was accelerated after martial law was declared in September 1972.

Agricultural exports, however, continued to face the discrimination imposed by the protection of import-substituting industries and the incentives given to selected manufacturing and nontraditional exports. In addition, direct export taxes were imposed under the Stabilization Tax Law of 1970. This law was originally enacted to capture some of the windfall gain to agricultural exporters as a result of devaluation and to finance the partial absorption of windfall losses to consumers. Once in place, however, the export taxes proved difficult to roll back.

Crony Capitalism: The Last Decade

The last decade of the Marcos regime was marked by the growth of rent-seeking activities whereby real resources (labor, entrepreneurship, etc.) were allocated unproductively to set up and appropriate rents. The highest amount of resources wasted in such activities tends to equal the rents that are sought. The mechanisms of rent seeking in general have not been well documented, but several categories of rent seeking have been widely discussed. These are associated with the rents from subsidized credit, tariff and nontariff barriers, public enterprises, and noncompetitive public expenditures. Generalized rent seeking (also known as directly unproductive profit seeking, or DUP, activities) in the case of tariff and nontariff barriers is the subject of an extensive literature in the field of international trade.[24] It is worthwhile mentioning a few patterns of rent seeking in the Philippines.

The coconut industry illustrates the use of both price distortions and government spending to extract rents. Not only did the government impose a large production levy (and at times an export tax), but severe external and internal trade controls allowed the government to set producer prices below their (already distorted) competitive levels.

The activities of the UCPB and the UNICOM illustrate a process of vertical integration of rent-seeking activities, with price distortions and government spending playing complementary roles in the "efficient" production of rents.[25] UCPB was financed by a portion of the revenue from the production levy. The bank in turn helped to finance UNICOM and thereby facilitated control of the processing industry (forward integration). UCPB funds also controlled the seedling industry (backward integration) by mandating that farmers obtain seedlings from only one source. The monopoly producer of seedlings in turn was subsidized through funds from the coconut levy.

The rice sector illustrates a somewhat different pattern of rent seeking. In this case, the government (through the National Food Authority) simply declared itself a monopoly in the international trade in rice and set prices for both outputs and inputs. Despite large government expenditures on fertilizer and credit subsidies, marketing and storage, and price support schemes, rice farmers ended up with a slightly negative effective rate of protection. In other words, rice farmers would have been better off under free-market conditions. In the Philippine case, government expenditures (including subsidized loans from international donors) provide a rough measure of economic waste, both from production inefficiencies and rent seeking. One can only guess at the amount of money earmarked for the construction of warehouses and other marketing facilities that went to the construction of the wrong facilities in the wrong place just as one can only imagine the amounts that have been illegally channelled into private hands. What we do know is that expenditures explicitly designed to improve the terms of trade to rice farmers did not have that effect.

Irrigation has been subsidized heavily and the coverage of irrigation substantially expanded. The government bears roughly 60 percent of irrigation costs at nominal rates and roughly 90 percent based on actual collection rates.[26] Irrigation coverage was increased about 80 percent between 1958/59 and 1967/68 but only by 13 percent between 1967/68 and 1976/77. Nonetheless, irrigation expenditures during the latter period were larger, even after inflation.[27] Although some of these expenditures are justified by higher construction costs and increased spending on rehabilitation, the striking fall in the crude performance indicator is at least suggestive of an increase in rent seeking.[28] Engineering designs sometimes appeared motivated by a desire to increase spending, and construction itself was sometimes substantially divergent from specifications. As a result, the irrigated areas are far less than those originally targeted, operating efficiency is low, and depreciation is rapid—this despite the reputation of the National Irrigation Administration as one of the more efficient government agencies.

These examples suggest extremely poor management of public expenditures in which costs were large and benefits were often negligible. The mismanagement was not confined to agriculture but representative of government spending generally. Perhaps the most dramatic example was the expenditure of more than $2 billion since 1976 on a nuclear electric generating facility in Bataan, slightly north of Manila, which has yet to produce a single kilowatt and perhaps never will.

Negative Agricultural Protection: Some Distinctive Features

Agricultural development in the Philippines has been impeded by trade and industrial policies that promoted nonagricultural, import-substituting industries. Accordingly, key agricultural industries stagnated. Resources were pulled out of agriculture and put into manufacturing. At the same time, export-oriented agriculture suffered from the overvaluation of the currency resulting from import substitution. Based on the 1974 input-output data, negative effective protection rates were computed for copra (− 6 percent), coconut oil (− 5 percent), dessicated coconut (− 12 percent), and lumber (− 10 percent).[29]

This negative protection was compounded by distortionary agricultural policies. Table 5.10 summarizes the worsening discrimination against agriculture by price distortions and policies that limit competition. For example, copra had a − 24 percent effective protection rate, reflecting export taxes and production levies. With UNICOM, the rate became − 29 percent. In addition, the negative effective penalty against agriculture is made even worse by the deescalation of tariffs. Inputs have higher tariffs than outputs, and in many cases, outputs have negative nominal rates of protection, thereby compounding the effective agricultural penalty. This is the reverse

Table 5.10   Effective Protection Rates of Selected Agricultural Products (in percentage)

Products	Reference Year	Rate
Rice	1979	–0.4
Rainfed	1979	–4.7
Irrigated	1979	3.6
Copra	1973–1979	–24.0
	1980–1981	–29.0
Coconut oil	1973–1979	–2.0
	1980–1981	42.0
Dessicated coconut	1973–1979	–4.3
	1980–1981	18.4
Sugar	1974–1980	–23.0 [a]
Cotton	1975–1981	–12.0
Logs	1979–1980	–46.0 [a]
Lumber	1974	16.0
Plywood and veneer	1974	5.0

Source: David, C., *Economic Policies and Philippine Agriculture* (Makati: Philippine Institute for Development Studies, 1983).

[a]Nominal protection rate.

of what happens in manufacturing industries, where inputs tend to have lower tariffs than outputs and thus reinforce effective protection.

There is one additional feature of Philippine agricultural policies that may help explain why the country has done so poorly. Studies show that most of these policies are not unique to the Philippines. Similar tariff and nontariff protectionist structures have been documented in other developing countries in Asia.[30] Negative agricultural protection is also a phenomenon in the other large ASEAN countries.[31] One important difference about Philippine agricultural policies is that the monopolization of major agricultural industries by only a few corrupt individuals facilitated the extraction of agricultural surplus that ultimately found its way out of the country or was wasted in unproductive rent-seeking activities. In any case, such rents can be treated as deadweight losses. Perhaps more importantly, Philippine policies inhibited the private investment that was needed to continue improvements in agricultural productivity. Although in the 1970s Philippine agriculture proved to be one important sector where the country has a comparative advantage, the sector's performance finally faltered in the 1980s, thereby contributing to recession and stagnation.

Recent Reforms

In 1981, the Philippine government decided to unilaterally liberalize its trade policies during a five-year period by lowering tariff rates in four phases and gradually dismantling the restrictive import licensing system. However, the implementation of these reforms was interrupted by the severe balance-of-payments crisis in 1983 and 1984. The government was unable to meet maturing external debt obligations and at the same time finance the country's average imports, and it moved to ration the limited supply of foreign exchange. Direct controls on the foreign exchange market then frustrated the import liberalization program.

The tariff reform program was undertaken in four phases. The first phase covered all commodities with tariff rates of at least 50 percent. The plan was to lower the rates to 50 percent by 1985. The second phase included the food processing, textile and garment, leather and footwear, and pulp and paper sectors. Ten sectors were affected by the third phase: cement, iron and steel, automotive, wood and wood products, bicycles, glass and ceramics, furniture, domestic appliances, machineries and capital equipment, and electrical goods. All three phases were initiated on January 1, 1981. For the second and third phases, the majority of these commodities received a cut of their respective tariff rates. Some of those commodities that previously had low tariff rates were given high rates as long as the 50-percent peak rate was maintained. This was meant to raise revenue and lower the dispersion of tariff rates. Finally, the fourth phase of tariff reform was launched in August 1981 for all the other imports.

The major accomplishments of the tariff reform program were the lowering of the average tariff rate from 43 percent to 28 percent by 1985, the reduction of the dispersal of tariff rate levels from a standard deviation of 32 to 15 during the postreform period, and the limitation of the bias against agriculture and agriculturally based exportables. Before the reform, the relative effective protection rate between manufacturing and agriculture was 30 against agriculture; after the reform, the ratio fell to 26. In terms of traded goods, the relative effective protection rate was 55 against exportables, most of which come from the agricultural sector. The ratio declined to 40 with the new tariff rates. These numbers indicate that where tariffs were binding, the reform program succeeded in reducing the bias against the agricultural sector induced by tariff policies.[32]

The import liberalization program also was undertaken in gradual phases in order to facilitate the structural adjustment process. In 1981, about 262 nonessential or unclassified consumer items were liberalized; 610 items were liberalized in 1982 and 48 items in 1983. According to plan, another 36 items would have been liberalized by 1984 and 201 in 1985. However, the foreign exchange crisis in 1983 prevented the implementation of this plan. The new Philippine government is now debating whether to complete the dismantling of import controls.

It is difficult to assess the impact of the trade policy reforms on agriculture. The system of foreign exchange controls was tightened, thereby blunting the positive effects of import liberalization. Given the severity of the crisis, it is possible that the current tariff policies might have become redundant due to foreign exchange rationing. In agriculture, reforms were initiated in 1985 to privatize trading in key agricultural industries. Pressed by multilateral donor agencies, the Marcos government agreed to dismantle the agricultural monopolies and to restore competition and freedom of entry in the coconut, sugar, and grain industries. The tendency to concentrate continues to linger in the coconut industry, but the new government seems committed to preventing such a concentration.

Conclusion

Agricultural development strategies in the Philippines can be portrayed as comprising a number of elements. Indirect discrimination against agriculture was caused by tariff and nontariff barriers (import licensing, foreign exchange controls, and discretionary regulations) that favored industrial sectors. Programs alleged to offset the adverse terms-of-trade effects of import substitution, such as agricultural price supports, marketing facilities, and input subsidies, created additional layers of distortion and opportunities for rent seeking. Agriculture received negative effective protection. Government control of marketing increased the degree of negative protection. Supply shifters such as irrigation helped keep consumer prices low but did little to enhance the rents received by more than a few privileged farmers.

Economic policy in the Philippines always has been protectionist and rent seeking, and agricultural policy is a cohesive part of that strategy. There can be little doubt that the country's inward-looking policy has played a major role in its poor economic performance. The Philippines did face severe terms-of-trade shocks, but other countries, notably Thailand and Korea, have faced an even worse erosion of their terms of trade and have continued to grow at rapid rates. We agree, therefore, that "while international factors have indeed contributed to the present position, primary responsibility must be assigned to domestic factors."[33]

By comparison, the per capita GDP in Thailand has risen from roughly one-half that in the Philippines in 1960 to slightly more than the Philippine level today. Specific patterns in the sectoral growth of income also stand out. In particular, both manufacturing and agricultural exports were leading sectors in Thailand while these same sectors were stagnating in the Philippines. Although Thailand also had high tariff rates, nontariff barrier protection was much lower.[34] Thailand also had a relatively conservative monetary and fiscal policy, and its policy projects were certainly less glamorous and managed less corruptly than in the Philippines.[35]

One could argue that it was precisely the appearance of relative political stability in the Philippines that allowed the Marcos regime to extract such fantastic rents. Marcos dominated the Philippines for twenty years with very little political opposition. As Olson explains in his theory of the state and economic growth, rent-seeking machinery is only dismantled under dramatic political change. Under the Marcos regime, rent-seeking mechanisms acquired a life and power of their own and could not be undermined by the structural adjustment programs of the World Bank or other agencies. Indeed, it took nothing short of a political revolution to undermine them. The new government in the Philippines thus brings with it new promise of hope.

Postscript on Reciprocal Liberalization

Given the theme of this volume, it is tempting to make speculative recommendations for mutually beneficial reforms of agricultural policy in the United States and in the ASEAN countries, including the Philippines. As a matter of strategy, the most self-defeating approach to cooperation is to demand cooperation by the other party. If the United States were to announce instead its intention to decrease the subsidies to rice and sugar producers, both as part of its domestic policy for reducing the federal budget deficit and as an instrument of stimulating agricultural development, it might help to change the psychology of protectionism and increase the probability that ASEAN and other countries would liberalize their agricultural import policies. The income effects of agricultural development would stimulate the importation of U.S. products, especially wheat, livestock, and feedgrains. Lowering import controls in these latter industries would further increase U.S. exports.

The best way to break the negative psychology of protectionism is not to demand reciprocal liberalization but to stress the rationality of U.S. liberalization for U.S. interests, and let other countries learn by example. The bottom line is that the United States cannot afford to continue running huge deficits. Budget deficits cause balance-of-trade deficits and offset capital account surpluses. Deficit spending, whether internally or externally financed, thus results in huge transfers of financial and real assets to foreigners. A country that sells its own capital stock can hardly promise sustainable growth in levels of living to its citizens. U.S. farm policy continues to be one of the most wasteful and least equitable aspects of the U.S. budget. If the United States is considered to be liberalizing its agricultural policy not to exact reciprocal concessions by other countries but for its own good, this may stimulate other countries to reconsider the high costs of their own distortionary policies.

Notes

1. Unless stated otherwise, the statistical information mentioned in this section is taken from James, W., Naya, S., and Myers, G., *Comparative Studies of Asian*

Economic Development (Honolulu: East-West Center, Resource Systems Institute, 1986, mimeo).

2. Mark, S., and Morrison, C., *Macroeconomic Performance of Developing Countries in the Asia-Pacific Region* (Honolulu: East-West Center, Resource Systems Institute, 1985).

3. James, W., Naya, S., and Myers, G., *Comparative Studies of Asian Economic Development* (Honolulu: East-West Center, Resource Systems Institute, 1985, mimeo).

4. David, C., *Economic Policies and Philippine Agriculture* (Makati: Philippine Institute for Development Studies, 1983).

5. Mark, *Macroeconomic Performance.*

6. Tidalgo, R., and Esguerra, E., *Philippine Employment in the Seventies* (Makati: Philippine Institute for Development Studies, 1984).

7. Bautista, L., and Duremdes, E., "An Overview of Structural Change in the Philippines, 1950–1982," in NEDA, *Towards a Balanced Agro-Industrial Development: A NEDA Workshop on Development Planning* (Manila: NEDA, 1984).

8. De Leon, M., "Intersectoral Capital Flows and Price Intervention Policies in Philippine Agriculture" (Ph.D. diss., University of the Philippines at Los Banos, 1982).

9. In the 1960s, imports and foreign exchange were directly controlled by the government in response to the balance-of-payment crisis in 1949. Such measures were retained after the crisis to protect import-substituting industries.

10. Valdepenas, V., *The Protection and Development of Philippine Manufacturing* (Manila: Ateneo de Manila University, 1980).

11. Power, J., "The Structure of Protection in the Philippines," in B. Balassa et al., eds., *The Structure of Protection in the Developing Countries* (Baltimore, Md.: Johns Hopkins University Press, 1971).

12. This deficit accumulated during the first Marcos administration in the second half of the 1960s.

13. Unnevehr, L., and Balisacan, A., *Changing Comparative Advantage in Philippine Rice Production* (Makati: Philippine Institute for Development Studies, 1983).

14. David, C., and Balisacan, A., *An Analysis of Fertilizer Policies in the Philippines* (Makati: Philippine Institute for Development Studies, 1983).

15. Undoubtedly an aid to rice farmers who receive the loans, the program's goal was unclear in light of the country's exemplary performance in rice production. See Herdt, R., and Gonzales, L., "A Reaction to the Study on the Benefits and Costs of the Masagana 99 Program" (Paper presented at the Fifth National Agricultural Credit Workshop, Zamboanga City, Philippines, March 1981).

16. Unnevehr, *Changing Comparative Advantage.*

17. Nelson, G., and Agcaoili, M., *Impact of Government Policies on Philippine Sugar* (Makati: Philippine Institute for Development Studies, 1983).

18. Ibid.

19. Clarete, R., and Roumasset, J., *An Analysis of the Economic Policies Affecting the Philippine Coconut Industry* (Makati: Philippine Institute for Development Studies, 1983).

20. Cabanilla, L. S., *Economic Incentives and Comparative Advantage in the Livestock Industry* (Makati: Philippine Institute for Development Studies, 1983).

21. Rodriguez, G., and Rodriguez, A., *Corn Policies and Comparative Advantage in the Philippines* (Makati: Philippine Institute for Development Studies, 1983).

22. David, *Analysis of Fertilizer Policies.*

23. Ibid.

24. Bhagwati, J., "Directly Unproductive, Profit-Seeking (DUP) Activities," *Journal of Political Economy* 88, no. 6 (1982):988–1002.

25. The efficient transfer of wealth is sometimes referred to as "third-best efficiency." See Roumasset, J., "The New Institutional Economics and Agricultural Organization," *Philosophy Economics Journal* (1978).

26. David, *Analysis of Fertilizer Policies.*

27. Ongkingco, P. S., Galvez, J. A., and Rosegrant, M. W., *Irrigation and Rice Production in the Philippines: Status and Projection,* Working Paper no. 8 (Los Banos, Philippines: Rice Policies in Southeast Asia Project, IFPRI-IFDC-IRRI, 1982).

28. Wade and Chambers, "Managing the Main System: Canal Irrigation's Blind Spot," *Economic and Political Weekly* 5, no. 39 (1980).

29. Bautista, R. M. et al., *Industrial Promotion Policies in the Philippines* (Makati: Philippine Institute for Development Studies, 1979).

30. DeRosa, D., "Trade and Protection in the Asian Developing Region," *Asian Developing Review* 4, no. 1 (1986):27–62.

31. David, C., *ASEAN Structure and Changes in Agricultural Protection* (Los Banos, Philippines: Agricultural Economics Department, International Rice Research Institute, 1985).

32. Tariff Commission, The Tariff Reform Program (Quezon City, Philippines: Tariff Commission, 1985).

33. Hill, H., and Jayasuriya, S., *The Philippine Economy: Performance, Problems, Prospects* (Canberra: Department of Economics, Research School of Pacific Studies, Australian National University, 1984).

34. See Akrasanee, N., "Industrialization and Trade Policies and Policies and Employment Effects in Thailand," in *Trade and Employment in Asia and the Pacific* (Manila: The Council for Asian Manpower Studies, and Bangkok: United Nations Asian Development Institute, 1977).

35. Hill, *The Philippine Economy.*

part three

Issues for U.S. Policy

chapter six

Agricultural Development and Trade: Broadening the Policy Horizon

George E. Rossmiller
M. Ann Tutwiler

It has become a cliché to say that trade and development are mutually reinforcing and that U.S. agricultural trade policies can support or undermine Third World economic development efforts. Yet, although there has been an increasing awareness of this growing interdependence, it has not improved the ability of U.S. policymakers to design an agricultural trade policy that enhances both U.S. exports and Third World development.

To a large extent, the complexity of the linkages between U.S. agricultural trade policy and the less-developed countries (LDCs) frustrates efforts to craft an effective agricultural trade policy. But more importantly, agricultural trade policy is buffeted by other, larger forces that move the modern economy. Exchange rates, interest rates, and debt payments have more to do with the volume and value of U.S. agricultural trade than does domestic agricultural or agricultural trade policy. The sheer size of international capital flows in relation to agricultural trade flows indicates the relative importance of macroeconomic policies to agricultural trade. To illustrate: In 1982 the value of the worldwide agricultural trade was $189 billion, the value of total trade about $2 trillion, and the value of world capital flows approached $40 trillion.

Thus, any effort to formulate an agricultural trade policy that enhances development must take into account the relationships among the international financial system, the international trading system, and the macro- and microeconomic policies of the United States and the LDCs. It is also important to understand how domestic policies that more directly affect agricul-

Support for preparation of this paper was in part provided by the Economic Research Service of the U.S. Department of Agriculture. The authors would like to thank Rachel Sarko for her advice and comments.

ture in the United States as well as in the developing countries inhibit development.

In this chapter, we explore these relationships and illustrate how the financial, trade, and agricultural sectors have acted on each other since the mid-1960s, often to the detriment of development and trade. In particular, we examine several policies in the developed and developing countries that have wreaked havoc with trade and development efforts in an interdependent economy. In our view, agricultural policymakers and, more importantly, farmers and farm-state politicians must take a broader view of the international economy if agricultural trade is to grow and development efforts in the LDCs are to succeed.

A Model of Macroeconomic and International Linkages to Agricultural Trade

From World War II through 1972, U.S. agricultural exports increased steadily and slowly at an annual rate of $400 million (in 1985 dollars). This relatively dependable increase was fueled by population growth and per capita income gains in importing countries that pushed their demand for agricultural commodities above their ability to produce. During that period, less than 10 percent of the world's agricultural commodities entered international trade channels, with a large portion of that trade flowing between the United States and Western Europe.

In 1973, things changed. In that year alone U.S. agricultural exports jumped by $5.7 billion (1985 dollars) and continued to increase by $2.1 billion each year through 1981—five times the historical rate. Then, suddenly, in 1982, agricultural exports dropped $4.7 billion and have been falling by $1.6 billion a year since then. What made U.S. exports climb to such historic heights and then plummet so sharply?

In 1973, policy changes in other countries sent shock waves through U.S. agricultural export markets. The Soviet Union decided to buy grain on international markets, thereby increasing U.S. exports by more than 8 million tons in one year. The Organization of Petroleum Exporting Countries (OPEC) quadrupled the price of oil, which led to a tremendous increase in international liquidity and an equally large transfer of income from one group of countries to another. Also in that year the United States decided that it would no longer be the world's macroeconomic thermostat and suspended convertibility of the dollar, with important repercussions for U.S. agricultural exports. When the world moved from a fixed to a floating exchange rate system, import prices began to fluctuate with the changing relative prices of national monies. In 1982, the nature and strength of these and other forces underwent a change that affected U.S. agriculture very differently. How did all these forces interact to drive U.S. agricultural exports?

More importantly, what structural links were created between U.S. agricultural exports and Third World development in the post-1973 period, and how have these forces affected U.S. agricultural exports?

It is preferable, in any such discussion, to begin at the beginning. However, in this case, trying to pinpoint the beginning is like unraveling the Möbius infinity strip. But as we are primarily concerned with how U.S. policy might be improved and as U.S. policy to a large extent defines the economic rules of the game for the rest of the world, we will begin by examining U.S. policy.

Macroeconomic Policies and International Finance in the 1970s

United States.   In the early 1970s, U.S. policy accommodated the oil price increase with an expansionary monetary policy and a relatively elastic fiscal policy to lessen the potential recessionary impact of increased oil prices on the domestic economy. The expansionary monetary policy increased the number of U.S. dollars in circulation, which led to low, often negative real interest rates during the 1970s and double digit inflation by the end of the decade.

These low real interest rates, coupled with a dwindling confidence in the U.S. economy, discouraged investors from holding U.S. dollars. The excess supply and the slow demand for dollars kept the value of the dollar down relative to other international currencies. This meant that relative to the products of other countries, U.S. products were cheap.

Nowhere was this more true than with money itself. During the 1970s, the real interest rate on loans made to foreign countries was often negative—meaning foreigners in effect were being paid to borrow money denominated in U.S. dollars. Thus, an expansionary monetary policy coupled with a relatively loose fiscal policy increased the supply of dollars without increasing the demand for those dollars, and the policy mix moved to push the value of the dollar down.

Not surprisingly, investors moved out of the dollar, and the United States experienced a huge net capital outflow during the 1970s. In 1970, net capital outflow from the United States was a little more than $9 billion; by 1980, that figure totaled $86 billion. Much of that money found its way to developing countries that borrowed huge sums from U.S. banks.

Other Developed Countries.   The other developed countries followed strategies similar to the United States in response to the first oil shock. Like the United States, they ran loose monetary policies and comfortable fiscal policies. Like the United States, they experienced relatively high rates of growth and high rates of inflation. From 1971 to 1975, Europe's economies grew at an average rate of 3.1 percent; from 1976 to 1980, they grew 3.4 percent annually. Japan's economy grew somewhat faster at 4.6 percent annually during the first half of the decade and 5 percent annually during the second half. The policies pursued by other developed countries reinforced U.S. policies and contributed to international liquidity, high levels of inflation, and low real interest rates.

Developing Countries. Macroeconomic policies in the developing countries also reinforced U.S. policies. Developing countries, particularly in Latin America, often overvalued their currencies and at the same time pursued expansionary monetary policy, thus making it cheaper to borrow money on the world markets than at home.

In Chile, for example, the exchange rate was overvalued in order to maintain stable purchasing power in international markets. With Chilean inflation substantially higher than international inflation, by the end of 1979 the interest rate on dollar-denominated borrowings in Chile fell to a negative 27 percent, while the interest rate on peso-denominated loans was a positive 22 percent. Such policies encouraged a net capital inflow into Chile of mostly dollar-denominated loans of $3 billion in 1980 and almost $5 billion in 1981.

These capital inflows tended to finance consumption and imports rather than investment. In middle-income countries, which received most of the petrodollar loans, public and private consumption rose 12.1 percent annually from 1970 through 1981; imports rose by 9.2 percent, and gross domestic investment rose by 7.5 percent.

Another group of developing countries in Asia followed different macroeconomic policies that also encouraged international borrowing. For example, the so-called "Gang of Four" (Hong Kong, South Korea, Taiwan, and Singapore) followed an export promotion strategy that combined an undervalued exchange rate and substantial foreign borrowing which financed industrial sector expansion. Long-term capital flows into South Korea increased from $430 million in 1970 to $3.6 billion in 1981, and short-term capital flows increased from $191 million to $1.1 billion in the same period. In Singapore, direct investment rose from $93 million to $1.8 billion between 1970 and 1981; long-term capital flows increased from $47 million to $113 million; and short-term capital flows increased from $33 million to $615 million in the same period.

From 1970 to 1981, Hong Kong, South Korea, and Singapore devoted a larger percentage of their Gross Domestic Product (GDP) to investment than did other developing or industrial market countries. These three countries also imported far more (as a percentage of their GDP) than did other developing or developed countries. With these investments and imports the Gang of Four developed export-oriented industries. In Singapore, exports rose from $1.5 billion in 1970 to $20.5 billion in 1981. In Korea, exports rose from $880 million to $20.9 billion in the same period. Similarly, Hong Kong's exports grew from $1.1 billion to $23.4 billion.

A third group of developing countries discovered the power of cooperation in the early 1970s and banded together in a cartel to increase the price of oil from $3 a barrel to $12 a barrel almost overnight. The OPEC economies grew at an astounding 9 percent annual rate from 1971 to 1975 and 5 percent annually from 1976 to 1980.

Unlike other developing countries, OPEC nations had small populations and could not absorb all their new wealth without risking substantial domestic inflation, so they invested it with U.S. and European banks. Much of that money eventually wound up in those bargain-basement loans to the non-oil-producing developing countries.

During much of the 1970s, commercial bank lending to LDCs increased at a rate of about 20 percent annually. In 1970, middle-income countries had long-term capital inflows of $5.8 billion and short-term inflows totaling $1.9 billion. By 1981, long-term flows reached $61.2 billion, and short-term flows amounted to $8.6 billion. The external debt of the twenty-one major LDC borrowers totaled $500 billion.

The macroeconomic policies of developed and developing countries in the 1970s impinged on the international financial system in a way never before known in history. The expansionary policies followed by the United States and other developed countries in response to the first oil shock led to high inflation domestically, low, often negative real interest rates, and a weak dollar internationally. At the same time, many developing countries followed exchange rate policies that made dollars even cheaper and that encouraged consumers to buy foreign goods. Simultaneously, OPEC came along to supply the world with additional liquidity in the form of petrodollar deposits in international banks.

This confluence of economic events made the world smaller than any development in transportation or communications could have. The abandonment of the Bretton Woods system of fixed exchange rates coupled with a massive increase in international liquidity meant that the health of the U.S. economy and the strength of international demand for U.S. agricultural products depended on macroeconomic policies in Europe, policy decisions in Moscow, the price of oil, and exchange rate policies in Latin America.

If any link were to give way, the stage already would be set for collapse of the international financial system. With developed and developing countries alike expanding their economies rapidly, some with the aid of misaligned international exchange rates and many with the sea of liquidity provided by petrodollars and easy monetary policies, runaway inflation and rising real interest rates in industrial countries began to cause concern. In developing countries, massive capital inflows encouraged by negative or low real interest rates often financed consumption rather than capital formation, and

developing country governments began making promises to poor populations that they knew they could not keep. Under the weight of double digit
inflation in the developed countries and rapid economic growth financed
by unsustainable capital flows in the developing countries, the three-legged
stool of domestic, financial, and trade relations began to wobble.

The International Trading System in the 1970s
Macroeconomic policies and performance as well as the international financial system affected the international agricultural and industrial trading system through several channels.

Agricultural Trade.   During the 1970s, strong growth in developed and
developing countries alike led to a ninefold increase in the value of
worldwide agricultural trade. The rise in international liquidity also fueled
import demand. This was particularly true in the developing countries. Although in some çases developing countries did invest in infrastructure and
productive endeavors, in many cases the borrowed funds were used to buy
food.

Much of this trade was captured by the United States, in part because the
dollar exchange rate made U.S. products cheaper to foreign consumers.
(With large stocks and substantial idle land, the United States also could respond quickly to increasing export demand.) U.S. agricultural exports as a
percentage of world agricultural trade rose from 37 percent in 1970 to 54
percent in 1980. In dollar terms, U.S. agricultural exports increased from less
than $20 billion in 1972 to $44 billion in 1981. In 1972, exports to Latin
America, Asia (excluding Japan), and Africa accounted for more than 10 percent of all U.S. exports. By 1981, exports to those countries accounted for 43
percent of all U.S. exports. The dollar values increased from $2.7 billion in
1972 to $18.9 billion in 1981.

Income growth in developing countries coupled with favorable exchange rates vis-à-vis the dollar increased the demand for imported food as
well as other items. Total developing country agricultural imports increased
from $45 billion in 1972 to $165 billion in 1980.

Industrial Trade.   But trade in agricultural products is only half the
story. During the 1970s, the developing countries found good markets for
their products in the developed countries. Total exports from developing
countries increased from $65 billion in 1970 to $615 billion a decade later.
Strong growth and low unemployment in Europe, Japan, and the United
States meant that few industries tried to restrict LDC imports. Furthermore,
the level of exports from LDCs was low enough in this decade that they did
not come up against trade restrictions and did not attract much attention
from competing industries in the developed countries.

During this period, despite increasing exchange rate instability, world trade flows grew substantially. Aided by healthy growth and the absence of protectionist sentiment in the developed world, a number of trade agreements were consummated, including the important Tokyo round of tariff reductions. Concurrently, after having failed to persuade the developed world to grant them concessions for joining the General Agreements on Trade and Tariffs (GATT) process, developing countries pursued bilateral and regional trade agreements and began shifting away from import substitution and toward export-promotion strategies.

Microeconomic Policies in the 1970s

Supporting these trade flows were microeconomic policies in the United States and other developed countries that increased the supply of agricultural products and microeconomic policies in developing countries that increased the demand for imported agricultural commodities.

U.S. and EEC Agricultural Policies.   U.S. agricultural policy in the 1970s made the United States extremely competitive in the world economy with reasonable prices, large stocks of agricultural commodities available for export, and vast areas of idle land that could be brought quickly into production to meet increasing world demand. This allowed the United States to increase its market share dramatically in an increasing world market.

The European Economic Community (EEC) also pursued agricultural policies that increased exportable surpluses. High internal support prices encouraged production while high internal food prices kept a lid on consumption. To dispose of some of the resulting excess supply, the EEC offered export subsidies equal to the difference between the high producer prices and the lower world prices. During the 1970s, the EEC switched from being a net importer to a net exporter of cereals, beef, and sugar, thereby increasing the supply and depressing the price of agricultural commodities on the world market.

Developing Country Policies.   On the demand side, a number of developing countries used their borrowed funds to purchase groceries, but increased food purchases were not the result only of a cheaper dollar and additional funds. Quite a few developing countries followed agricultural policies that kept food prices low to urban consumers. Low food prices dampened incentives for subsistence farmers to increase their production to sell to urban markets. With domestically produced food supplies inadequate and foreign food inexpensive, urban consumers in developing countries ate U.S. wheat.

Strong demand for U.S. exports, which was fueled more by a cheap dollar, stimulative macroeconomic policies, and international liquidity than by increases in population growth and income-producing investment, encouraged U.S. farmers to bring idle resources into production. The value of farm marketings increased from $50.5 billion to $143 billion during the 1970s. Investment in agriculture, encouraged by negative real interest rates, increased from $6.7 billion in 1970 to $17.9 billion in 1980. Land values soared, and on the basis of that collateral, U.S. banks lent $128 billion to U.S. farmers between 1970 and 1980. Net farm income doubled in the 1970s, rising from $14.4 billion in 1970 to $32.3 billion in 1979.

Macroeconomic Policies and International Finance in the 1980s

United States. In 1979, OPEC served the world a second oil price increase. By this time, the United States was faced with double digit inflation. It responded to the oil shock with a contractionary monetary policy designed to wring inflation out of the economy; this policy was accompanied by an expansionary fiscal policy that saw the federal budget deficit move from $34.5 billion in 1980 to $139 billion in 1985. Europe followed suit with a tight monetary policy but also a tight fiscal policy.

As the supply of dollars printed by the U.S. government declined and as the demand for dollars by the government increased, interest rates rose. High rates and the underlying strength of the U.S. economy attracted foreign capital and thus increased the value of the dollar exchange rate vis-à-vis international currencies. In 1975, for example, the French franc was worth 23 cents. By 1984, its value had fallen to 11 cents, making U.S. products twice as expensive for the French. On a trade-weighted basis, the value of the dollar increased 44 percent between 1973 and its peak in the first quarter of 1985.

Other Developed Countries. Other developed countries were forced to follow the U.S. lead and maintain high interest rates to attract investors. Tight monetary policies led to money market rates of 16 percent in England in 1980, 15 percent in France in 1980, and 12 percent in Germany in the same year. These figures were several points higher than normal levels and were historically high in real terms; still, the developed countries experienced capital outflows. In 1981, capital outflows approached $6 billion from France and $10 billion from the United Kingdom.

The increase in interest rates and restrictive monetary policies hurt the developed economies and sent them into the deepest recession since the 1930s. In 1982, industrial production in the United States and West Germany was 5 percent less than 1980. In Canada it was 11 percent less than the 1980 level. Also in that year, unemployment reached 9 percent in the United States, 11 percent in Canada, 8 percent in France, and almost 12 percent in the United Kingdom.

Developing Countries.   The increase in worldwide interest rates and dollar exchange rates in the early 1980s had severe repercussions for those developing countries that had borrowed heavily in the 1970s. Because the bulk of their debt payments were denominated in dollars, with the interest rates pegged to the U.S. prime rate or the London interbank borrowing rates (LIBOR), many saw their debt service payments skyrocket. Suddenly, a number of countries were unable to repay the interest on their debts, much less the principal.

To avoid default, these countries—Mexico, Brazil, Poland, Argentina, to name a few—sat down with their international bankers to renegotiate their debt payments. As part of the rescheduling process, the banks required the debtor countries to adhere to austerity plans drawn up by the International Monetary Fund (IMF). These often called for a set of restrictive macroeconomic policies that forced debtors to devalue their exchange rates, cut their imports, and contract their fiscal and monetary policies. With bank lending slowing to a trickle, beginning in 1982, the debtor LDCs experienced a net outflow of capital. Yet, even with these repayment schedules, LDC debt by the end of 1986 is expected to stand at $1 trillion.

The international finance leg of the three-legged stool was bending under the pressure of higher real interest rates and a soaring dollar. Debt that was denominated in dollars suddenly became very expensive, and the developing countries were forced to increase dramatically their exports and drastically decrease their imports, moves that affected the other two legs of the stool: domestic economies at home and abroad and trade flows.

The International Trading System in the 1980s

U.S. Agricultural and Industrial Trade.   The international trading system felt the impact of these policy changes after a lag. Although U.S. agricultural exports peaked in 1981, the rate of increase already was slowing. By 1985, U.S. agricultural exports were down $10 billion.

In part, demand for U.S. commodities fell because of the high dollar, but the decline also was caused by falling per capita incomes in the developing countries. Although LDC incomes (in terms of Gross National Product—GNP) had risen 6 percent annually during the 1970s, they increased by only 1.4 percent in 1981, 0.9 percent in 1982, and 0.4 percent in 1983. IMF austerity programs, which required sharp cuts in imports, also hurt demand for U.S. food and industrial products.

At the same time as demand for U.S. products was declining, U.S. demand for foreign products was increasing. The overall balance of trade on goods and services fell from a positive $8.9 billion in 1980 to a negative $95 billion at the end of 1984. By the end of 1985, the trade deficit topped $150 billion. The trade deficit was financed by a tremendous inflow of capital from overseas; in 1984 capital inflows from abroad exceeded U.S. investment overseas by $95 billion. In early 1985, the United States became a net debtor.

Developing Country Foreign Exchange Earnings. An equally important factor hampering U.S. exports was the decline in developing countries' foreign exchange earnings. Hardest hit were countries exporting basic commodities and raw materials, whose export earnings fell in the face of low commodity prices caused by weak demand. Africa's export earnings rose from $12.9 billion to $94 billion between 1970 and 1980. Since 1980, export earnings have fallen to $62 billion. In Latin America, export earnings rose from $15.9 billion in 1970 to $108.2 billion in 1981; after falling to $97.5 billion in 1982 and 1983, export earnings in 1984 have recovered to their 1981 levels.

Two individual countries are illustrative of these trends. In 1980, exports of goods and services from Argentina increased at an annual rate of 26 percent. Argentine exports fell 7.5 percent in 1981 and another 7.5 percent in 1982. Chile's exports rose an average of 28 percent annually from 1976 to 1980, then fell 4.5 percent in 1981 and 1982. In Chile's case, the decline in export earnings—induced by falling copper prices—was exacerbated by the country's exchange rate policy. The Chilean peso is pegged to the U.S. dollar, and as the dollar appreciated so did the peso. This reduced Chile's competitiveness and Chile's ability to export copper to industrial countries. What foreign exchange remained after these declines usually went to pay interest on international debt, not to purchase U.S. wheat and corn.

There is evidence to suggest that without the U.S. trade deficit the developing countries would be under more stress than they already are. According to the Annual Report of the President, the U.S. balance of trade with six high debt Latin American countries has fallen from a positive $4.4 billion in 1981 to a negative $20.6 billion today. Our purchases from these countries are helping to repay some of their debt to U.S. and European banks.

Microeconomic Policies in the 1980s

U.S. Agricultural Policies. The U.S. farm sector, like the LDCs, had taken on debt in anticipation of a strong future. Total agricultural debt in the United States reached about $220 billion by 1985. With the fall in exports and simultaneous rise in U.S. interest rates, the farm sector came under severe economic stress trying to repay those loans.

U.S. farm policy did not help matters. The policies that helped farmers in the booming market of the 1970s hurt them in the sagging market of the 1980s. Based on expectations of double digit inflation that did not materialize, loan rates supported prices at a level far greater than the depressed world market was willing or able to pay. Farmers sold their crops to the U.S. government. High loan rates, coupled with an expensive dollar, supported world prices and encouraged foreign competitors to increase production.

As U.S. farmers saw the agricultural trade surplus fall from $26.6 billion in 1981 to approximately $10 billion in 1985, they began demanding protection from imports and from competition in third world markets. At the same time, a budget-cautious government increasingly resorted to import quotas to keep costs down and protect domestic policies. U.S. policymakers shifted the burden of adjustment away from the domestic market and into the international market.

Despite the rhetoric, the 1985 farm bill does not represent a fundamental departure from this strategy, although it does retool some policies in an effort to make U.S. products more competitive on world markets. The 1985 farm bill makes U.S. commodities, not U.S. farmers, more competitive. The burden of adjustment still falls on the international market, as falling U.S. loan rates bring down world prices. It also falls on the U.S. budget, as stable target prices and falling loan rates increase deficiency payments to farmers.

Since the Great Depression, U.S. farm policies have been determined by domestic political and economic considerations, and the financial health of farmers was dependent on these policies. But after 1973, U.S. farmers became irrevocably dependent on the level of U.S. exports as well. As soon as farmers in the United States expanded their acreage based on expectations of increased exports, their financial health became tied up with the health of the rest of the world economy, with exchange rates, interest rates, international liquidity, and the level of GDP in Argentina, Chile, and South Korea.

When world demand was strong, loan rates had no effect on world prices, and agricultural price policy was irrelevant to the well-being of the U.S. farmer. But when demand fell in the 1980s, the 1930s farm policies did not perform well for U.S. agriculture because they supported U.S. commodity prices greater than the world market prices. These policies developed with a domestic, or "closed economy," perspective and in many cases have been counterproductive in the international environment.

EEC Agricultural Policies.   Like the United States, the EEC did not alter its policy path when conditions changed in the 1980s. Higher world prices, coupled with an expensive dollar, raised world price levels and lowered the cost of EEC export restitutions, and the EEC was able to increase its exports without substantially increasing its costs. U.S. wheat exports declined 6.7 million metric tons between 1981 and 1985, while EEC exports of wheat increased by almost one-half that.

Developing Countries.   The debt crisis forced many LDCs to follow austerity plans that affected their ability to support microeconomic policies. In some cases, these cutbacks are having severe repercussions. Subsidies for many necessities like gasoline, fertilizer, and electricity had to be reduced. Foreign exchange shortages have cut into imports of spare parts and replacements, thereby severely hurting productivity. In other cases, austerity has forced many LDCs to become more export oriented and to exploit their comparative advantage.

Although in the longer term these policies should put LDCs on a growth track, the short-term costs can be quite high. In the long term these policies also should increase LDC imports of food from the United States and other countries, but in the short term LDC food imports will likely stagnate.

It should be clear from the preceding discussion that national economic policy decisions have fundamental impacts on the international economy, on other national actors, and on the agricultural sector. Yet because these policies are determined according to the dictates of national economic and political necessity, their international ramifications are seldom, if ever, considered. National policies are made in a vacuum, even though their effects may boomerang through the international economy and end up hurting the very country that initiated them. Conversely, agricultural policy is determined with little appreciation for exchange rates, capital flows, or debt reschedulings.

In the second half of this chapter, we look at a number of policies—industrial, developmental, and agricultural—that are pursued by developed and less-developed countries alike and that impair agricultural trade and development.

Counterproductive Policies

There exists a whole range of industrial country trade restrictions that impede economic development in the LDCs and eventually impede U.S. agricultural exports.

Import Restrictions

Textiles. One such restriction is the Multi-Fiber Arrangement (MFA), which effectively restricts the quantity of textiles from LDCs that may be imported into developed countries. The MFA is a series of bilateral agreements between industrialized countries and textile-producing developing countries that allows developed countries to limit imports of specific textile products when those imports threaten domestic production.

The MFA creates economic distortions in both importing and exporting countries. Textile quotas permit the textile-importing country to commit more resources, both labor and capital, to its textile industry than might otherwise be warranted under a more liberalized trading regime. Textile quotas also raise the price of clothing to consumers in importing countries by restricting the supply of apparel available on the domestic market.

In exporting countries, textile quotas limit the size of the textile market and force textile industries to operate at less than full capacity. They also encourage countries such as China to invest in noneconomic raw materials such as ramie in order to circumvent quota restrictions. Textile quotas also decrease demand for U.S. cotton exports—about one-quarter pound for every pound of imported cotton fabric the United States prohibits. More importantly, quotas limit the capacity of textile-producing LDCs to earn foreign exchange with which to buy U.S. agricultural commodities.

It should be noted that textile-producing countries are, by LDC standards, relatively high-income countries that are just at the stage of development where they are rapidly increasing food (and especially protein) consumption and are trading actively with the United States. Recent legislative efforts in the United States to tighten (in effect, kill) the Multi-Fiber Agreement will serve to constrain further the textile-producing nations' ability to sell to and thus buy from the United States.

Steel.   Another product that illustrates the relationship between trade and development is steel, and here an anecdote is useful. In 1980, Brazil began to modernize its steel industry, with encouragement and money from developed countries. By 1984, Brazil had developed what is probably the world's most modern, technologically advanced, efficient steel industry and was ready to produce large quantities of steel for export. However, with overcapacity in their own steel industries, the developed countries all balked. In fact, the United States (among others) steadfastly refused any additional imports of Brazilian steel and threatened to impose quotas unless Brazil agreed to voluntary restraint agreements.

Once again, the developed countries cut off their noses to spite their faces. Brazil is one of the largest Third World debtors. It is also an important customer of the United States—in fact, its third largest wheat customer. In 1984, Brazil bought $26 billion worth of U.S. agricultural products. If Brazil is to continue to be a good customer, Brazil must have markets in which to sell steel and other products for which it is a low-cost producer.

U.S. and EEC Agricultural Policies

Sugar Policies.   A number of U.S. and EEC agricultural policies inhibit LDC development, but the most prominent examples are those policies for sugar. The story starts with the European Community's Common Agricultural Policy (CAP). The CAP established a producer price for sugar that provided incentives for rapid expansion of sugar production within the European Economic Community. By 1981, domestic sugar production, plus imports from the African, Caribbean, and Pacific countries (which are guaranteed preference under the Lome Conventions) created a huge surplus of sugar within the EEC. In 1981, the EEC dumped 4 million metric tons of sugar on the world market, thereby severely depressing the world market price.

In the meantime, the powerful sugar lobby in the United States was pushing for a "sweet" sugar program. It obtained a guaranteed producer price of 18 cents per pound, three to six times the world market prices. By April 1982, the duty and fee system used to sustain the U.S. support price was not sufficient to keep out cheap imported sugar without massive purchases of domestic sugar by the Community Credit Corporation. The secretary of agriculture, not wanting to make such purchases, asked the president to impose quotas on sugar imports.

In the first year of sugar import quotas, allowable imports were only slightly less than those of a year earlier. Because the import fees were reduced, countries with a right to export to the United States benefited from high U.S. prices. However, the high U.S. domestic price of sugar created incentives for rapid increases in the production of sugar substitutes, especially corn sweeteners, thereby threatening to increase the excess supply of sugar on the domestic market. In 1985, the sugar quota fell to 1.85 million tons, and some observers believe that in the next two to three years the United States will have to prohibit all sugar imports in order to maintain domestic prices.

The effect of these quotas on world sugar prices is obvious. The U.S. import price of sugar was 21.74 cents per pound in 1984; the EEC support price was 16.04 cents per pound. The price of sugar in the Caribbean stood at 5.2 cents per pound in 1984.

U.S. and EEC sugar policies also have exacerbated trade tensions regarding corn gluten feed, with important repercussions for developing countries. Corn gluten feed is a by-product in the production of corn sweeteners and presently commands a relatively high price in the EEC as a substitute for corn and soybeans in the feed ration for livestock. Corn gluten feed is imported into the Community at "zero tariff binding," meaning the Community does not collect a tax on imports, creating an irritating situation for the EEC.

The EEC argues that much of the corn gluten feed winds up as dairy feed rations, thus exacerbating the dairy surplus problem in the EEC. The United States, on the other hand, argues that imposing quotas or tariffs on corn gluten feed would set a precedent for eventually setting restrictions on soybeans. Although in some ways the corn gluten feed issue is a "tempest in a teacup," it easily could add fuel to the ongoing trade fire and result in increased trade restrictions and/or increased export subsidies.

The combined effect of the European and U.S. policies has been to depress the price of sugar on the world market, to destabilize prices, and to restrict export markets for LDC sugar. This has had a devastating impact on sugar-producing developing countries and has limited both their foreign exchange earnings and their ability to import. Caribbean sugar prices have fallen from 28.67 cents per pound in 1980 to 5.2 cents per pound in 1984. Overall export earnings (which include other products as well as sugar) for Caribbean sugar-producing nations have fallen by approximately 10 to 15 percent in the same period.

The United States and European sugar policies also distort comparative advantage and force U.S. consumers to spend approximately $2.5 to $2.9 billion more each year on sugar than they otherwise might spend. Of that, $1.6 to $1.8 billion is transferred to domestic sugar producers and $0.5 to $0.66 billion is transferred to countries holding import quotas. The rest, approximately $500 million, is simply lost to the economic winds.

Agricultural Export Subsidies. Subsidies also affect development. The impact of the subsidy depends on the nature of the subsidy and on who is doing the subsidizing. All countries subsidize agriculture to one degree or another. In the broad sense of the term, a subsidy may be defined as any government program that directly or indirectly lowers the market price of an input or of a final product.

When wheat is subsidized, the price of bread to consumers does not reflect the full cost of producing wheat and is lower than it would otherwise be. So, the quantity of bread demanded by consumers is greater than it would otherwise be. The farmers, viewing the subsidy plus the price received as their return, commit more resources to wheat growing than they would if there were no subsidy.

As wheat production increases under a subsidy, the price of bread falls, thus making it difficult for other nonsubsidizing bakers to stay in the market. That may seem all well and good for the subsidized wheat farmer until he realizes that that out-of-business baker was an important customer.

Subsidies most often are justified on political and social grounds, such as food security, economic development, income redistribution, rural settlement, or international market share gain. Aside from the infant industry argument (which is valid for some developing countries), there is little economic justification for subsidies because they introduce so many economic distortions, the most important of which is the misallocation of resources to production and the misguided incentives to overconsumption.

Of all forms of subsidy, export subsidies are probably the most directly linked to economic development. Export restitutions by the European Economic Community and export credit programs, export payment-in-kind programs, and other direct export enhancement schemes directly or indirectly depress the price of agricultural goods on international markets. To the extent that these artificially depressed prices are reflected in the domestic economies of LDCs, they signal LDC producers to allocate fewer resources to agriculture than would be appropriate, and they signal consumers to buy their food on world markets instead of from possibly more efficient domestic producers.

Sometimes the specific way in which an export subsidy is administered can adversely affect development. For example, the U.S. GSM-102 export credit guarantee program encourages countries to take on debt in order to buy food and has probably contributed to the debt burden of many LDCs. Mexico could save foreign exchange by purchasing grains from other, less-expensive suppliers. However, Mexico's foreign exchange shortages and large debt service requirements have made grain imports under U.S. credit guarantees attractive despite higher prices. Thus, GSM-102 funds have provided Mexico with short-term balance-of-payments support but in the longer term have increased Mexico's overall debt burden.

The GSM-102 and other credit programs also rob developing countries of their export markets. For example, Argentina lost a wheat sale to Brazil, a long-time customer, when the United States offered Brazil wheat on credit. A recent evaluation of the GSM-102 program completed by the Foreign Agricultural Service (FAS) suggests that should the United States discontinue the program in Chile, Argentina would be able to enhance its market share. Credit programs have forced countries like Argentina, who can only sell for cash, to seek export markets where the United States does not offer such credit packages. The FAS study concludes that the GSM-102 program has not expanded the U.S. market but has helped the United States retain or expand its market position in targeted countries.

The cost of these programs to developing countries has been to disrupt traditional and efficient trade ties and force these countries to seek other markets where they can sell for cash, at a discounted price, in order to compete with subsidized U.S. credit or credit guarantees. Thus, it appears that these credit programs have not increased U.S. market share significantly; rather, they have shifted trade flows around and moved prices lower, to the detriment of developing countries.

The PL-480 program donations, although not a direct subsidy, can lower food prices enough to depress producer incentives. The program has humanitarian, foreign policy, and market development objectives, although the primary and original objective was surplus disposal. Under PL-480 Title I, the long-term concessional sales title, usual marketing requirements must be certified (an assurance the recipient country will not be substituting PL-480 commodities for commodities that they would otherwise purchase commercially). Charges often are made that since it is difficult, if not impossible, to target and isolate recipients of the program—the needy who cannot translate that need into effective demand in the marketplace—it increases market supplies and thus depresses prices in the recipient country. To the extent that this is true, it will provide disincentives to domestic producers in recipient countries and lead to underallocation of resources in agriculture.

Under Title III, Title I loans are forgiven when the local currencies generated are used for development purposes, and under the new Food for Progress program commodities are donated when the recipient country agrees to move to more market-oriented policies. If not carefully administered, these programs may distort the market in the short term, but if the development projects or market-oriented policies are carefully designed and implemented, the longer-term effects should be positive for agricultural development.

Finally, targeted export enhancement programs have heightened political tensions between the United States and the EEC and could lead to an all-out trade war between these two economic elephants, thereby further depressing world prices and further lowering export earnings of many developing countries.

Macroeconomic Policies

As indicated earlier, the recent combination of U.S. macroeconomic policies has been particularly painful for the LDCs and has contributed to the decline in U.S. agricultural exports. The recent fall in the value of the dollar and interest rates should ease debt repayment problems as well as promote development and U.S. exports. The decline in the U.S. dollar might also help the exports of those countries, such as South Korea, whose currencies are pegged to the U.S. currency.

Development Assistance Policies and Support

The type of Third World development policies that should be pursued depends quite fundamentally on how the process of development occurs. Since 1945 and the Marshall Plan, the U.S. understanding of the development process has undergone several evolutions. At first, the United States assumed development meant technology and focused its efforts on bringing the fruits of modern technology to a "primitive" world. We look back sadly on the dinosaurs of development—the dams ready to produce electricity for people who have no lightbulbs, the sophisticated research stations next to fields of subsistence farmers, the international airports for countries with one plane. We waited for development to "trickle down."

The second stage in the evolution of U.S. development philosophy saw development in terms of bottlenecks, and the United States sought to stimulate certain sectors, be it energy, roads, or irrigation. Once again, the United States left behind many useless monuments. In a third change, the United States sought growth with equity and focused on basic human needs, participation, and self-help strategies. Indeed, babies were now born who would have died ten years earlier. The problem was that food production did not keep pace with population growth, and those babies grew up undernourished.

Today there is increasing recognition that an important, indeed necessary, part of economic development is the development of agriculture. In order for countries to progress, they must be able to draw resources out of their agricultural sector and into the industrial sector. This will occur only when farmers begin producing more food than they can eat themselves. Once this happens, labor and resources will be released from agriculture into the industrial sector, and surplus production in either sector can be traded for products that cannot be produced domestically.

The agricultural sector provides an important market for the products of the nonagricultural sectors, such as clothing, household goods, and farm implements. With the money earned by the nonagricultural sector, tailors, merchants, and hardware store owners can buy more, better quality food from farmers. So as resources become more productive, they create more value added, thereby increasing per capita incomes. Eventually the increases in per capita incomes translate into improved diets.

This focus on agricultural development is changing the face of development assistance. There is now a shift away from project lending and toward policy-based lending. Development assistance is beginning to help developing countries bring their economies through the transition from distorted to more market-oriented policies that will provide farmers with appropriate incentives to produce.

A key part of this development strategy is trade. There are two reasons why trade is important. First, developing countries have too few resources to waste on producing goods in which they do not have a comparative advantage. It is preferable for them to specialize, to whatever extent possible, in producing those goods each country can produce efficiently and trade with other countries for those goods that cannot be produced efficiently on the domestic level. For this to work, it is critical that the economies of developing countries be open and follow market price signals and that these economies operate with a liberal trading system. Second, once a population shifts from a predominantly starch diet to a protein diet, few countries have the agricultural capacity to fulfill the demand for the necessary feedgrains, foodgrains, oilseeds, and other products required by a growing population with increasing incomes. Eventually, higher-income LDCs must import food from countries such as the United States.

Domestic commodity groups often charge the United States Agency for International Development (AID) and the World Bank with helping LDCs compete with the United States, and in the short term this is true in some cases. For example, the United States helped Brazil develop its soybean subsector, which competes with U.S. soybean exports. But with the foreign exchange earned from sales of soybeans, Brazil has become a significant trading partner of the United States. In 1981, Brazil bought $843 million in U.S. agricultural products and is its third largest wheat customer. South Korea, which has no comparative advantage in agriculture to exploit but does have a comparative advantage in textiles, electronics, and small automobiles, bought $2.1 billion in groceries from the United States in 1981. Increased incomes in South Korea have translated into increased U.S. exports to that country. Since the advent of the debt crisis and world recession, Brazilian imports have fallen to $437 million and South Korean imports to $1.2 billion in 1984.

It is in the interest of the United States and other industrialized countries to do whatever they can to help LDCs improve their agricultural sectors, including promoting freer trade and increased funding for development efforts. AID recognizes that developing countries must become agriculturally self-reliant. This means that LDCs would develop their agricultural sectors in those areas where they held a comparative advantage and import other agricultural requirements with the foreign exchange generated by more efficient enterprises. But AID's wishes cannot be translated into tangible U.S. policy when U.S. producers demand protection and are unwilling to allocate money to fund development.

Unfortunately, political pressures in the United States make it difficult for commodity groups, and hence members of Congress, to support liberalized trade and increased funding for the IMF, the World Bank, and AID. Unfortunately, the type of development that is needed is going to be much more difficult, painstaking, and labor intensive than building dams in the desert.

Developing Country Policies
The developed countries are not solely responsible for the poor progress of LDCs. The LDCs themselves must share some of the blame. As has been pointed out, instead of investing the monies lent them by international bankers, many LDCs bought food, postponed needed adjustments to higher oil prices, and put off until tomorrow what they were unwilling to face today. It is clear that money is not enough. In the past, many LDCs used borrowed money to pursue policies that undermined development efforts. All the money in the world will not buy prosperity if LDC policies are not supportive of agricultural development.

Food Pricing Policies.   Many developing countries have followed pricing policies that keep food prices low to urban consumers. But by depressing prices for agricultural goods, food pricing policies depress incentives for farmers in rural areas to increase their production, invest in new technology, or invest additional hours in tilling the fields.

In many African countries, food prices to urban consumers are too low to compensate the farmer (or market agent) enough to bring his (or more often her) produce to market. Inadequate compensation not only limits the amount of domestically produced food available in urban centers, but also diminishes the incentive to improve roads and railways or to invest in trucks or railcars.

The short-run effect of these policies usually is to increase a country's food imports. In the longer term, these policies tend to exacerbate income distribution problems by lowering the incomes of farmers relative to their urban cousins. Rapid rural to urban migration occurs and creates socio-economic and political problems for the national government. Usually there are no jobs available for these uprooted farmers; instead of becoming productive farmers or workers, they become a drain on the national budget and a picture of human misery. In the end, these policies can reduce a country's ability to either feed itself or pay for imported food.

What has happened in Zambia is a good example of such deterioration. There, the rural-urban terms of trade (in barter terms) deteriorated from a base of 100 in 1965 to 35 in 1979. The rural producer had to market three times as much in 1979 as in 1965 in order to purchase the same amount of urban goods. Part of this shift is a result of subsidies, especially on maize meal. The government purchases maize from farmers at a fixed, uniform price, and the maize is resold to urban consumers at a subsidized price. Since the early 1970s, the rate of rural-urban migration has increased, thereby exerting pressure on employment in the formal and informal sectors and lowering incomes in the cities. Overall, Zambia's food imports have risen since 1973.

Investment and Credit Policies.   In an effort to spur investment many developing countries subsidize interest rates. Usually these policies are counterproductive. Subsidized interest rates hurt development in a number of ways. Low rates underprice capital and encourage firms and farms to employ capital instead of labor, thereby limiting the benefits of growth to the owners of capital. Subsidized rates also discourage savers, thereby limiting the capital available for investment in new technology, new businesses, and improved infrastructure. Subsidies also encourage investment in opportunities that may not be economically productive—that is, the investor does not need to achieve high returns in order to repay his or her investment, so the economy does not benefit from the most productive use of its resources. Finally, subsidized rates encourage banks to ration their limited capital to less risky (read "larger") farmers and businesses that are more likely to substitute capital for labor. For example, in Ecuador the interest rate on commercial paper in 1976 was 8 percent less than the prevailing rate of inflation. Low legal lending rates have rationed long-term credit and encouraged banks to hold substantial reserves rather than lend out funds for the low returns available in the market.

Exchange Rate Policies.   Exchange rate policies also can be counter-productive to development efforts. In the 1970s, many developing countries, especially those in Latin America, followed import-substitution strategies. Under this development strategy, LDCs set up high levels of protection from imported goods in order to develop their own industries, which would eventually produce goods domestically to substitute for imported goods. The primary result of this strategy was often an overvalued exchange rate.

For example, from 1978 through 1981, Mexico increased public expenditures and encouraged private expenditures to generate employment and improve living standards. Although these policies succeeded in increasing real per capita GNP by 25 percent, the dramatic growth in demand for goods and services placed the economy under extraordinary inflationary pressures. Instead of cutting public expenditures (a politically difficult accomplishment even in wealthy countries), Mexico overvalued the peso, thus making imports cheaper. The overvalued exchange rate calmed inflationary pressures because imports were less expensive and domestic companies that competed with those imports were forced to match the import price. The overvalued exchange rate also allowed the Mexican government to borrow cheaply in international capital markets when oil revenues fell off and the Mexican government could no longer finance its expenses domestically.

The exchange rate policy undermined the import-substitution policy, distorted domestic production, and penalized industries that competed with cheaper imports as well as exporting industries, like oil. Eventually, many firms in these industries were forced out of business, which did permanent damage to the Mexican economy.

Sometimes exchange rates inadvertently can undermine rural-urban terms of trade. For example, when the price of oil rose in the 1970s, Indonesia experienced rapid inflation as oil dollars flowed into the economy. Internally, each rupiah was worth less than it had been a year earlier, but externally, the rupiah's value against the dollar did not change. Thus, the real value of the rupiah vis-à-vis the dollar appreciated by 50 percent due to relative differences in the rates of inflation between the United States and Indonesia. Although policy itself had not set an overvalued exchange rate, the high international exchange value of the rupiah reduced Indonesian agricultural competitiveness in world markets, thus hurting agricultural productivity and incomes.

Summary and Conclusions

For a chapter meant to focus on U.S. agricultural trade policies and Third World development, we have painted a broad canvas. But it is clear from the foregoing discussion that a narrow approach is outdated at best. Since 1973, when capital flows surged and trade became increasingly dependent on the international financial system, the world has become irrevocably intertwined. Decisions made by one actor affect others, and policies implemented in one sector reverberate to other sectors. Consequently, agricultural policymakers who want to improve U.S. agricultural trade can no longer be content with trying to influence target prices and loan rates or to develop a new export enhancement program or revise the PL-480 program. What sorts of policies, then, should the agricultural community and agricultural policymakers promote?

1. The agricultural community should promote economic development efforts through bilateral and multilateral institutions such as the Agency for International Development and the World Bank. It is especially important that aid be devoted to self-sustaining and productive projects that increase the incomes of a broad segment of the population. Instead of opposing increased funding for these institutions, the agricultural community should lead the way for further support.

2. The agricultural community should recognize its stake in finding a solution to the debt problem. Until the debt problem is resolved, some of the wealthier developing countries that buy U.S. agricultural commodities will be spending all their surplus foreign exchange on interest payments, not imported food. Thus, it is in agriculture's interest to support efforts to reduce the debt burden. This includes supporting increased allocations to the International Monetary Fund.

3. The agricultural community should work for a more liberalized trading system, not only in agricultural commodities but also in industrial products, through the next round of the Multilateral Trade Negotiations and through bilateral negotiations. It is clear that if LDCs do not have a market for their products, they cannot buy U.S. farm or industrial products.

4. The agricultural community should support increased technical assistance in all areas of development, especially in developing the capacity of LDCs to perform policy analysis. It is important that the LDCs develop their own institutional capacity to assess and direct their economic destinies.

5. The agricultural community should encourage policymakers to work toward an amicable solution to the trade tensions between the United States and the EEC. A trade war between the world's economic giants will benefit no one. What is needed are quiet, high-level discussions between decisionmakers in the United States and Europe, not inflammatory headlines and rhetoric.

6. Similar quiet diplomatic efforts should be encouraged in the multilateral arena as well. Although publicity and rhetoric are de rigueur in international negotiations, they do not necessarily produce the desired results.

7. The agricultural community should learn patience. The international

environment *has* improved since the early 1980s, but in the short run there is little chance that macroeconomic forces will improve the export picture for U.S. agriculture.

Declining oil prices and falling commodity prices, although benefiting consumers, have severely damaged the economies of several of the larger U.S. trading partners, thus making it unlikely that they will become larger markets for U.S. agricultural products. The austerity programs imposed as a precondition to debt rescheduling also promise to dampen LDC economic growth and hence the demand for U.S. commodities. Although the fall in the dollar may provide some boost to U.S. exports, it probably will not do so as soon and as much as U.S. farmers would want. Increased demand for exports usually lags behind a fall in the exchange rate by eighteen months or more. Given that the currencies of some of the larger U.S. trading partners in the developing world are pegged to the dollar, U.S. products have not become cheaper for them.

Finally, the debt picture has improved, but the international financial system is not out of the woods yet. A number of countries will need to come back to the IMF and their international creditors to reschedule. There are a number of other countries that are not in difficulty but are beginning to pile up considerable international obligations.

The important indicators are moving in the right direction, but they are not moving quickly. U.S. exports will recover but not rapidly and not to the high levels of the 1970s. When 1986 and 1987 exports do not fulfill expectations and when developing countries begin to develop and compete with U.S. exports, some groups will find the present policies wanting and will push for greater subsidies and protection. As tempting as it is to reach for export enhancement programs and subsidies, the U.S. farm community should refrain. Altering domestic farm policies will not change the U.S. agricultural export picture. U.S. agriculture must wait for a healthy international environment and then be able to compete in the world market. Export enhancement programs and subsidies, when coupled with the 1985 farm bill, currently are buying the United States more hostility than customers and in the longer term will only ensure smaller markets and poorer customers.

Commentary

D. Gale Johnson

It is all too rare in discussions on agricultural trade to hear U.S. policymakers give balanced attention to U.S. import as well as export policies. Yet agricultural and trade policies affect both exports and imports. As is well known, although generally ignored in policy discussions, in the long run the value of a nation's exports must be about the same as the value of its imports. Consequently, there should be some recognition that there is a relationship between U.S. imports of agricultural products and U.S. exports of farm products.

Given that developing countries as a group are net exporters of agricultural products, U.S. policies affecting imports of farm products have a particular relevance. If the United States shuts out the exports of developing countries for which they are low-cost producers, then it limits the potential export demand for those products for which the United States is a low-cost producer. It is as simple as that.

Fortunately, Rossmiller and Tutwiler do not neglect U.S. domestic farm programs and their impact on U.S. imports. I found little in their analysis with which I disagree. Consequently, my comments should be considered supplementary to theirs. I amplify their comments concerning the 1985 farm bill and its subsidization of U.S. exports. I also discuss some U.S. import policies that adversely affect Third World countries.

The 1985 Farm Bill and Export Subsidies

Rossmiller and Tutwiler succinctly describe the 1985 farm legislation and its effects upon world trade. Clearly the newfound competitiveness of U.S. farm products in export markets will be due to the U.S. Treasury, not because U.S. farmers are now low-cost producers. Even so, with high target prices for grains and cotton, there is no way of knowing if U.S. farmers are low-cost producers.

The authors only hint at how the 1985 farm legislation will impinge upon international markets for grains and cotton and, thus, upon the markets for farm products from Third World countries. On April 15, 1986, the United States took an action that deliberately reduced the export price of rice by more than 20 percent. On that date farmers could redeem their 1985 rice price support loans at the world market price. They did not have to repay the amount of the original loan of $8.00 per hundred weight, nor did they have to pay interest or carrying charges on the loan. The loans could be redeemed by paying what the secretary of agriculture deemed was the world market price for rice. On April 15, Arkansas number 2 milled rice was priced at 16.5–18.0¢ per pound; by May 1, the price had fallen about 22 percent to 13.0–14.0¢. The forgiveness of a significant part of the price support loan amounted to nothing more than an increase in the deficiency payment on the 1985 rice support loans. Note that this adjustment applied to 1985 rice, rice that had been pledged as security for a nonrecourse loan from the Commodity Credit Corporation (CCC).

For 1986 and each subsequent year through 1990 the loan repayment rate for rice will be the higher of world market price or some fraction of the basic loan rate, such as 50 percent for 1986 and 1987, 60 percent in 1988, and 70 percent in 1989 and 1990. The basic loan rate for 1986 rice will be $7.20 for rough rice. It is of more than passing interest that the forgiveness of part of the price support loan will not be counted toward the maximum annual subsidy payment to any one person of $50,000. Thus, for all intents and purposes, the 1985 bill eliminated the price support loan for rice, greatly increased the deficiency payments, and negated most of the payment limitations.

The 1986 target price for rice is set at $11.90 per hundredweight. If the price for the 1986 rice crop averages approximately what it was in May 1986, the sum of the regular deficiency payment of $4.70 per hundredweight plus the forgiveness of the price support loan may result in a total deficiency payment of about $6.00 per hundredweight. Thus, for the 1986 rice crop the farmer will receive as much in governmental subsidies as from the market. This is what rice producers in the developing countries must compete with—not with low-cost rice produced in the United States.

This magnificent bounty is provided for the benefit of less than eleven thousand rice producers. If rice production is held to the low 1984 level of about 100 million hundredweight—there has been and will be an acreage diversion program—the cost of the two payments will come very close to $600 million. Thus, the average cost per producer would be more than $50,000. The largest four hundred rice producers will receive total deficiency payments plus loan forgiveness that will average in excess of $100,000. As one can see, the $50,000 payment limitation is no longer of any consequence.

U.S. price subsidies for rice have been strongly protested by the government of Thailand as disruptive, predatory, and distinctly unfriendly. Why has the United States hit Thailand so hard? Is there any evidence that Thailand has been subsidizing its exports of rice? Thailand has during the years followed a contrary policy—namely, that of taxing its rice exports—and thus has helped to maintain world rice prices. What does the United States gain by harming one of its strongest allies? It increases rice exports by about 1 million tons.

On August 1, 1986, a provision similar to that used for rice was applied to cotton. The one difference is that the payments applied not to stocks pledged as security for a CCC loan, but to all free stocks of cotton held in the United States on August 1, 1986. The owners of free stocks of cotton, which means all stocks not held by CCC, received a payment per pound of such stocks equal to the difference between the 1985/86 loan rate of 57.3¢ per pound plus carrying charges and the world price as determined by the U.S. Department of Agriculture (USDA). Thus, every individual or corporation that owned any cotton located in the United States on August 1 received a negotiable certificate, payable either in cash or in kind, equal to the quantity of owned cotton multiplied by the subsidy rate. Given that the world price of cotton is little more than one-half the U.S. loan rate plus carrying charges, the aggregate payment was substantial. The reason for this scheme was to induce redemption of the 1985/86 price support loans to create free stocks in order to receive the subsidy. Obviously, the net effect will be a substantial reduction in the market price of cotton.

In the case of cotton, as is true for rice, the competing producers are not found in the EEC but in developing countries. In other words, most foreign producers of cotton are substantially poorer than are U.S. producers. Yet the United States has shown no reluctance in using the power of its treasury to force U.S. products into world markets at low prices. Certainly, the pricing policies for rice and cotton will make it more difficult for a number of countries to import more U.S. agricultural products.

Cotton and rice are not the only farm crops that will have large subsidies as a result of the 1985 farm bill. Although target prices for wheat and feedgrains were kept at the 1985 level for 1986 and 1987, the price supports were reduced substantially when the secretary of agriculture used the discretion given him to reduce the loan rates by 20 percent. Thus, the loan rate for wheat in 1986 will be $2.40, down from $3.30; for corn the rate will be $1.92, down from $2.55. The secretary has the discretionary authority to permit farmers to repay their price support loans at less than the original value. However, assume that the price support loan rates are maintained and that market prices are at the loan rates. How will the deficiency payments compare to farm prices? Given these assumptions, the deficiency payment for wheat will be 82.5 percent of the farm price, and the deficiency payment for corn will be 58 percent of the farm price. Wheat producers will receive 45 percent of their cash receipts from subsidies and corn producers, 37 percent. This is hardly a market-oriented program. Competing grain producers in the Third World will find the market prices they face significantly lower as a result of U.S. policy changes and large subsidies.

There are those who argue that the U.S. target price and deficiency payment systems are not nearly as disruptive of international markets as are the export subsidies of the EEC. Two justifications are given for such a position. One is that the low prices prevail for both domestic and export use, and thus domestic consumption is not discouraged as it is by high consumer prices in the EEC. This is a valid statement, although how important it is in fact depends upon the price elasticity of demand in the domestic market. For wheat the argument has little empirical validity. The price elasticity of demand for food use of wheat is very close to zero—the low domestic price does not encourage increased food use. True, the elasticity of demand for wheat as feed is relatively high, but that only shifts the excess production encouraged by high target and support prices to the feedgrain market, a shift that does the Thai corn producer no favor.

The second argument is that in order to obtain deficiency payments farmers must participate in acreage diversion programs, and thus U.S. farm production is restricted. When the difference between target prices and loan rates or market prices was small, as was the case for corn during the late 1970s, it probably could be argued that the acreage diversion program at least offset the output increasing effects of the target prices and price supports. But when target prices are 50 percent or more than market prices, as was the case for wheat during the period of the 1977 farm act and is now the case, it requires some evidence to make the case that U.S. subsidies have a different effect upon world market prices than do EEC export subsidies. Saying it doesn't make it so. It is time that U.S. policymakers undertook systematic analyses of the output effects of recent farm programs. Until we do so, I do not see how we can seriously prepare for a new round of General Agreements on Trade and Tariffs (GATT) negotiations.

The 1985 Farm Bill and Imports

The authors mention U.S. sugar policy and its severe limits upon U.S. imports of sugar. The 1985 legislation represented no change from the 1981 sugar program. However, this is hardly good news because under the 1981 act U.S. sugar imports declined from 4 million metric tons in 1980 to 1.7 million metric tons in 1985. The U.S. sugar program clearly violates Article XI of GATT, which requires that quantitative limitations on imports of farm products should be used only when domestic production is being restricted or controlled and imports are not reduced proportionately more than domestic production. True, the United States procured a waiver to this article in 1955, but why should this country expect others to abide by GATT rules on such matters as export subsidies if it flouts the rules on import restraints? The U.S. waiver does not make U.S. actions consistent with the liberal trade policies that the United States espouses for the world. The U.S. sugar program is clearly inconsistent with the U.S. effort to increase exports of agricultural products to Third World countries.

The authors do not mention the U.S. peanut program. The 1985 legislation makes only a modest change in the 1981 program by authorizing an increase in the 1985 price support for quota peanuts if there were an increase in production costs between 1981 and 1985. The application of this provision resulted in an increase in the price support for quota peanuts from $559 per short ton in 1985 to $607 in 1986.

The quota applies to peanuts used domestically for direct consumption as nuts or peanut butter. Excess peanuts are processed for oil and oilmeal. In recent years imports of peanuts have been nil even though the price for additional peanuts has been one-third or less than the quota price. The price of greater-than-quota peanuts are an approximation of world market prices. In other words, even though world market prices of peanuts have been less than the support price of quota peanuts, the United States has refused to import peanuts. It should be noted that the United States is the only industrial country that produces any significant amount of peanuts. The competing producers are such countries as the Sudan, Zaire, Senegal, India, and China.

Price Policy and Agricultural Adjustment

There is no inconsistency between the growth of U.S. agricultural exports and Third World development, if U.S. exports are based upon comparative advantage. There is a clear inconsistency, of course, when the United States embarks upon policies that create excess productive capacity and then uses the power of the treasury to find export outlets for the surplus production. This is the course on which the United States now finds itself, and it will continue on that road during the remainder of the life of the 1985 farm bill. Unless the legislation is amended to reduce the target prices from the levels specified, U.S. farmers will not make the few resource adjustments required to make U.S. agriculture competitive in world markets.

During the 1950s, the United States had substantial excess productive capacity in agriculture, just as it does today. The country first tried to adjust to that fact by passing Public Law 480, which subsidized U.S. exports under the guise of assisting developing nations to achieve further economic development. The United States now is subsidizing exports, although without any hidden objective. The country simply means to dispose of excess stocks and the continuing excess flow that it will produce each year for the next few years. The United States attributes the necessity for such actions to the policies that others follow (such as the EEC) or the need to regain markets lost to efficient competitors. But these excuses don't help competing producers in the developing countries.

But starting in the late 1950s, the United States did more than subsidize exports in order to handle excess productive capacity and low farm incomes. During the next fifteen years, the incentives to produce farm products were reduced and drastically so. From the early 1950s to 1968–1972, the price support for wheat was reduced (in real terms) by more than 60 percent, the corn price support by nearly 60 percent, and cotton price support by almost 60 percent. True, farmers received direct payments during the latter period. However, even if the direct payments were added to the loan rates, the reductions in guaranteed returns were 40 to 50 percent.

But what signals has the government given to producers of grains, cotton, and soybeans since that time? In real terms, price supports have increased since 1968–1972 in the face of market prices that have been declining. (The nominal price supports have been deflated by the Gross National Product price deflator.) If we compare the real price support levels for 1982–1985 (the period of the 1981 farm act) with the levels for 1968–1972, we find that wheat price supports were increased by 20 percent, corn price supports by 6 percent, and cotton price supports by 22 percent. Soybean price supports declined by 5 percent.

Milk price supports declined by only 17 percent from the early 1950s to 1968–1972. However, the 1981 act brought real milk price supports back to the level of 1950–1954—$4.80 per hundredweight in 1967 prices. It should not be too much of a surprise that farmers find milk production relatively attractive.

The target price concept was introduced in the 1973 farm bill. How have real target prices that apply to grains and cotton changed from 1974 to date? In 1985, the target prices for wheat, cotton, corn, barley, and sorghum were each higher than in 1974 after adjustment for inflation. In real target prices, each was to increase after 1975, reach a peak in 1977 or 1978 (1979 in the case of cotton), and then decline somewhat. However, in real terms the 1984 target price for cotton was higher than in 1973. Thus, the pattern of target prices hid from farmers that there was a problem of excess productive capacity. In fact, in the face of continued productivity improvement, the signal given by the target prices has been to expand production. That is exactly what has occurred, and no one should consider this outcome an unreasonable one—no one, that is, except U.S. taxpayers, consumers, and competing producers.

Conclusion

Trade can be a powerful instrument for assisting economic development. But trade, if manipulated by governments, may fail to play that role to the degree that is both possible and desirable. Trade in agricultural products now is being manipulated by almost all governments. Most developing countries either tax agricultural exports directly or through overvalued exchange rates. Most developed countries subsidize agricultural exports, either by providing export subsidies or by encouraging excess output through high returns, and severely limit the imports of agricultural products that compete with high-cost domestic production.

The 1985 farm bill has made the United States a very bad actor in international trade in farm products. For the next five years the government will pay enormous subsidies to U.S. farmers. When the legislation expires in 1990/91, there will have been very little change in excess productive capacity in agriculture. The current legislation makes no significant contribution to the adjustment in U.S. agricultural productive capacity that is required if U.S. farmers are to receive adequate compensation for their resources through the market. What the 1985 farm bill assures is that farmers will receive somewhat inadequate returns, a significant part of which come as subsidies from the government. At the same time, the U.S. reliance on subsidies will continue to cause disorganization and depression in world markets.

chapter seven

Food Assistance: Implications for Development and Trade

Edward J. Clay

Food aid policy, from the inception of PL-480 in 1954, has been a Janus-faced creature. One face reflects the complex humanitarian, developmental, and political concerns that characterize all bilateral and internationally mediated aid flows. The other face reflects agricultural trade policy. Food aid has always been used to manage exportable agricultural surpluses and to promote long-term agricultural trade development. There are internationally negotiated rules on surplus disposal to ensure that food aid is managed as an orderly part of agricultural trade. The Food Aid Convention (FAC), part of the International Grains Agreement, establishes minimum annual commitments. A representative of USDA, not of the United States Agency for International Development (AID) or the State Department, heads the U.S. delegation in meetings to supervise the operation of these international arrangements. Other food aid donors have administrative practices that accord a less-visible role to their agencies responsible for agriculture trade. But the management of exportable surpluses in relation to domestic agricultural policy, particularly as that management expresses itself in political administrative practices, separates food aid from other forms of developmental and humanitarian assistance.[1]

Given that complex interests and policy concerns influence all aid policy practices, it must be asked to what extent food aid has been and can be both a significant resource for development (and humanitarian assistance) and an important instrument of agricultural trade policy. The economic policy model associated with Tinbergen suggests the need for a multiplicity of instruments to manage multiple policy objectives. Can food aid be simultaneously an active instrument of these different sets of policy concerns? An alternative approach regards agricultural trade concerns as constraints within which food aid policy could be formulated for developmental and humanitarian goals in a frankly political context.

The difference in approach can be illustrated by examples. In a review of Swedish and some other donor policies it was suggested that agricultural concerns act as constraints on the food aid program. Domestically available commodities for export are expected to be programmed, and commodity levels are determined in a classic bureaucratic policy process. However, the formulation of policy, including country programming and choice of commodities, is the concern of the Swedish International Development Agency (SIDA) and the Foreign Ministry.[2] A contrasting model is provided by agricultural export agency practice, which regards food aid as one of a range of possible export options that can be combined in a bilateral agricultural export agreement. This implies that at the level of the individual food aid agreement trade policy objectives could override other concerns. Sri Lanka's food aid relationship with donors, examined by this author in the early 1980s, appeared to have some such elements.[3] Likewise, a number of donor food aid agreements with Egypt often are considered to have such a complexion.

This chapter is concerned primarily with the developmental and humanitarian objectives of food aid. The trade promotion objectives of food aid are considered important insofar as they indicate potential areas of tension in policy practice. As much of the support for food aid (and probably substantial, additional resource flows) results from support by agricultural interests, it is appropriate to ask to what extent the record suggests food aid has contributed simultaneously to trade policy goals.

Food Aid and the Recipient Economy

Trade Case Studies

There are few areas in the development literature more controversial than the impact of food aid on the general, and in particular the agricultural, economy of recipient countries. Food aid has had both proponents and detractors who have identified a range of potentially positive (incentive) and negative (disincentive) effects on recipient economies. A taxonomy of the potential effects most commonly identified in the literature provides some indication of the complexity of the issues and the opportunity for confusion.[4] For every positive effect identified as an illustrative case, it is possible to provide a contrasting negative case and vice versa.

The direct disincentive effects that occur when food aid imports lower prices for domestic food producers have received the most attention.[5] But some observers, in turn, point to circumstances in which such effects are absent, noting that, in any case, a counteracting effect encourages growth in consumption of basic foodstuffs from lower prices.[6] Potentially positive or negative effects of food aid on income distribution and poverty also often are identified.[7]

Food aid may bring about long-term changes in consumer tastes, either by creating a dependence on imports or, alternatively, by providing a market that makes possible the expansion of domestic production of previously little-consumed commodities.[8] The technological basis of import dependence is also important.[9] Capital- or labor-intensive technologies, with their positive or negative employment effects, can be promoted.[10] These potentially contradictory effects all concern prices and interventions in agricultural markets by governments.

There are also budgetary, public expenditure implications of food aid, which include the dangers of becoming fiscally dependent on the sale of aid commodities, although such sales also can relieve otherwise unsustainable budgetary pressures on a government that has little scope for increasing domestic taxation in the short run.[11] Reliance on concessionary food imports may have disincentive complacency effects by reducing the priority accorded to agricultural policy. Alternatively, the direct use of food as wage goods and of revenue from the sale of food imports can provide resources for investment in agriculture.[12] Many observers have stressed the macroeconomic growth and anti-inflationary possibilities of food transfers.[13] Others see in such transfers the dangers of enabling governments to avoid adjustment to overvalued exchange rates. They also see distortions in the internal structure of prices that in the long run inhibit growth.[14]

When confronted with such a range of possibilities and in reviewing frequently contradictory interpretations of evidence from the same experiences,[15] some observers, myself included, conclude that the debate is intrinsically indeterminate. Judgments rest on the interpretation of unavoidably selective, and often different evidence. Food aid does offer positive opportunities for development, but realization of these depends on the adoption of constructive policies by recipients and donors and on effective implementation.[16]

Surveys covering the period up to the late 1970s reflected both the sense of the opportunity provided by food aid and the concomitant need for appropriate policies.[17] Subsequently, there has been a growing interest on the part of researchers and policy analysts in the economic and, in particular, the agricultural impact of food aid. There also have been two other important developments. First, since the early 1970s most recipients have received aid from a number of sources, whereas in the earlier period, the bulk of food aid was provided by the United States. Most members of the Western or Organization for Economic Cooperation and Development (OECD) donor community now have some interest in food aid. Second, there has been a dramatic shift of flows from the newly industrialized countries (NICs) in South America and Asia to a large number of smaller economies in sub-Saharan Africa.

Two important analytic implications proceed from these developments. First, it is difficult to isolate the role of PL-480 flows, and it is necessary from a developmental perspective to assess the impact of all food aid. As there is at least informal partial coordination of PL-480 and other aid to individual countries, this is simplified by actual policy practice. Second, the evaluation record tells us little about many of the currently important countries. Faced with the need for selectivity, I have chosen here only to examine recent writings that have minimized confusion and clarified conflicting findings and to search for any shift in the evidence on the actual effect of food aid emerging from recent impact assessments.

Additionality or Balance-of-payments Support?

The apparent confusion regarding the economic impact of food aid indicates that any discussion of these issues should begin with a careful restatement of the macroeconomics of food aid.[18] An intentionally simplified, analytic exposition helps to identify the important relationships and interactions that must be taken into account both in impact assessment and in prescriptive policy analysis. This analytic exposition also provides the basis for a review of the donor/export trade implications of food aid transactions.

Additional Food Imports.   The potentially negative effect on domestic production and the counteracting positive consumption effects of food aid are illustrated most clearly in the introduction of food aid imports that are wholly additional and without direct substitution effects on commercial imports or exports. The shift to the right in the supply curve (more food available at any given price) has a depressive effect on domestic prices and production. However, such a reduction in prices also would have a partially or wholly compensating positive effect on demand. This consumption or demand effect will be maximized where government intervenes to segment the market and target food subsidies (or in the extreme case, provide food free) to low-income households with the highest income elasticity of demand for basic foods.[19] The direct disincentive effect will be greatest where government engages in open-market, unsubsidized sales.

Some of the potential, indirect effects of food aid in the pure additionality case also should be noted. In general, the highest real income effect of the transfer to final recipients, assuming decreasing marginal utility, will be achieved by perfectly targeting freely distributed food to the poorest households.[20] Where the structure of asset holding and production results in undernutrition of children in poor households, the positive impact on human capital formation through improved nutritional status will be maximized in this special case.[21] If there is underemployment of labor for technological or structural reasons (such as the seasonality of agricultural operations or the way control of land is distributed between small and large farms and estates), then the use of food aid commodities to create additional employment would have multiplier effects on aggregate demand, including food consumption, and would allow investments that reduce the costs of production.[22]

Local currency proceeds from sales of food aid by governments (counterpart funds) generate revenue.[23] This budgetary support is maximized at market clearing prices, indicating a tradeoff between the potential, direct consumption income transfer to beneficiary households and financial support to the government.[24] This support is fungible and available for any purpose, developmental or otherwise.[25] It is possible simultaneously to lower food prices to consumers, pay higher prices to producers, or reduce their costs through input subsidies, agricultural investments, or intensified extension services. The developmental impact depends on government policy. Donor desire to obtain commitments and to monitor actual uses of revenues has led to the establishment of special accounts for sales proceeds.[26]

Balance-of-payments Support.   In the other boundary case of an open economy, where domestic prices are set by the world market, food aid would substitute for commercial imports by providing balance-of-payments support.[27] The impact would depend on the use of the freed foreign exchange, which in practice is a function of general development policy including the strategy for the agricultural sector. *There can be no direct disincentive effects through prices.* Balance-of-payments support, on the one hand, can have a potentially important, positive impact on a country's overall development effort, and, on the other hand, can have complacency effects on policy, particularly in avoiding adjustments in exchange rates and reducing the financial and political pressures to invest in domestic food production capability.

The mythology of good neighborly agricultural trade policy, as enshrined in the Food and Agriculture Organization's (FAO) Rules on Surplus Disposal, is that food aid is not supposed to substitute for usual commercial imports. Historically, much of the opposition to food aid being used explicitly as balance-of-payments support and thereby militating against the proper planning of such aid has come from agricultural interests. The recent U.S. Food Security Act contains only a minor concession on the formal operation of the rules of surplus disposal, which require countries to maintain the usual marketing requirement (UMR) provision of commercial imports as a condition of food aid. The UMR is the responsibility of USDA, and in the European Economic Community (EEC), of the Directorate General for Agriculture, rather than of food aid administrators. The EEC Council of Ministers also explicitly rejected the objective of balance-of-payments support put forward in the EEC Commission discussion paper on food aid in 1983. Yet the practical reality is that a large proportion of food aid imports is being channelled into urban and formal sectors of national food systems in Africa, and the underlying rationale is that this aid is intended to reduce the burden of imports, thereby providing balance-of-payments support. Whether that is the real intent of food aid imports is a sensitive question in donor/exporter agricultural circles. Such sensitivity inhibits research and explicit policy analysis of the balance-of-payments issue.

A Widespread Donor Aspiration: To Have Your Cake and Eat It Too
An important implication of the one-to-one substitution case for policy analysis is that there is no net budgetary gain to the recipient government, whether foreign exchange savings are used to finance other, possibly non-food imports (an expansionary policy) or to reduce other foreign borrowing (a disinflationary alternative). Relatively simple analysis of the substitution case therefore provides another criterion for discriminating between logically consistent and inconsistent writing on the impact of food aid.

Even though the provision of balance-of-payments support and additional budgetary resources are logically alternative, mutually exclusive consequences of food aid, in both impact assessment and policy prescription the practice of considering these effects sequentially and independently remains widespread.[28] The criterion given for assessing the impact of food aid for balance-of-payments support is the performance of the whole economy.[29] There is a further policy implication. Where food aid provides even partial balance-of-payments supports, a donor who enters into a policy dialogue about the uses of revenue from all local sales is seeking to influence the allocation of the government's existing revenue.

Neither boundary case is typical.[30] The opportunities for trade, legal or otherwise, open up the possibilities for alternative outlets that dampen the direct effects. First, entirely additional cereal imports may promote smuggling of domestically produced food into neighboring economies, thus leaving foreign exchange in private hands. This issue is probably most significant in sub-Saharan Africa where traditional trade patterns do not conform at all to postindependence political boundaries. Second, government interventions in domestic agricultural markets are pervasive with or without food aid.[31] These can increase the aggregate demand for food, dampen the disincentive impact of additional imports, or, alternatively, intensify balance-of-payments pressures where imports are the marginal source of supply. Third, food aid can free foreign exchange or act as an additional means to relax constraints on economic growth, which, in turn, increases demand for food staples and other agricultural commodities. Alternatively, these resources may provide a cushion for "bad," nondevelopmental policies. Fourth, the uncertainties of programming food aid have resulted in correlated movements in both commercial and concessional imports where risk-averse governments have sought to manage the food system with imports (examples are Bangladesh and Kenya).

There are two distinct responses to the problems of assessing the food aid record when confronted with these potential effects. Many analysts consider it necessary to model the food sector and intersectoral interactions formally with econometric techniques or at least consider effects within a conceptual framework that recognizes intersectoral interactions.[32] However, the greater part of the assessment literature, even for the recent past, consists of studies in which there is partial analysis of each separately identified aspect of the food aid transaction. The advantage of this approach is that it includes the effects of policy, commodities, and technology that rarely are considered explicitly in sectoral modeling research.[33]

The Disincentive Question: Agricultural Sector Models
The overall impact of food aid is a priori indeterminate, but theory provides a number of alternative hypotheses. This complex but real set of possibilities implies that meaningful quantitative estimates of the impact of food aid can be obtained only through multiequation models that can handle simultaneously the direct and indirect supply and demand side effects on production of the imported goods (wheat in wheat-growing economies for example), close substitutes (maize or rice where food aid is received as wheat), and alternative land use (including export crops). This consideration also provides criteria for assessing attempts to estimate the overall macroeconomic and narrower agricultural (disincentive) effects of food aid on recipient economies. There are no formal procedures for testing models that are equivalent to those provided by statistical theory for scientific experimentation. Rather, a model reflects judgments by the analysts based on a priori reasoning drawing upon statistical exploration of the characteristics of the particular economy and the particular forms of public intervention. The results of modeling exercises may be interpreted as plausible quantitative values where analysis otherwise provides only qualitative assessment. Some of the desirable features of satisfactory models have been identified by writers making a critical analysis of the earlier literature on the economic effects of food aid, particularly for India and some previously important recipients of cereals aid, in per capita and total terms.[34] These cases provide evidence on the impact of PL-480 until the early 1970s.

India, 1954–1970.   Much of the earlier modeling literature on the economic effects of food aid was formulated within a partial equilibrium of the framework focusing on national supply and demand relationships for cereals only. Within the restricted assumptions of these models the implied cumulative effect on cereal production ranged from a 15 to 31 ton reduction in domestic production, and the additional food grain consumption ranged from 59 to 93 tons, for every 100 tons of food aid shipments within the reference period of the models. This variation in results contributed to wider confusion on the impact issues.[35] Blandford and Plocki show the importance of clear specification of the way in which government intervention through dual-price operations affects price determination and output. They also demonstrate the sensitivity of results to analysts' choices, such as the sample periods and specification, underlining the lack of robustness of such models. The issue cannot be determined on a head count of modeling exercises, therefore, but has to be decided in terms of the realism with which models characterize the strategic interrelationships within the agricultural sector and linkages to the general economy.[36] More recent studies for India and other countries that were formerly or are currently large-scale recipients of food aid indicate the ways in which earlier work has been superseded.

Colombia, Brazil, and Tunisia.   These three countries are graduates from large-scale food aid where controversy surrounds the impact of U.S. PL-480 shipments. For Colombia, Goering originally argued that wheat food aid in effect provided balance-of-payments support while counterpart funds (budgetary support) contributed to investment.[37] Dudley and Sandilands subsequently challenged these conclusions, finding a dramatic impact of imports and low prices on domestic wheat production.[38] Analyzing within a restrictive partial equilibrium framework and focusing only on wheat, they concluded there was a severe tradeoff between food imports, aid-supported policies and low prices in terms of the negative effects on wheat production. A subsequent reanalysis by Hall, still modeling only the agricultural sector but disaggregating to consider other commodities, reached a contradictory conclusion. The negative impact of wheat pricing policies was outweighed by higher relative prices of rice. Hall also noted a finding generalized in many more recent impact assessments—that the role of food aid was relatively restricted and was only a small proportion of total wheat imports.[39] A parallel study for Brazil by Hall showed how food aid resources were used to help finance a dual-price system, which supported producers, subsidized consumers, and resulted in both higher production and consumption.[40] Tunisia also successfully operated a dual-price system involving imported and domestically grown cereals as well as imported soybean oil and domestically produced olive oil. These policies were favored by the high-income elasticity of demand for imported products.[41] A pattern begins to emerge from these country experiences of food aid imports used as part of a relatively complex food pricing policy that involved, depending on local circumstances, discrimination between commodities and two-tier pricing for consumers and producers. In the long run, these countries ceased to be dependent on large-scale food aid, relative to the size of their food system.

Such agricultural sector models can be criticized as too restrictive in treating government expenditure, nonagricultural production, and foreign exchange as, in effect, exogenous, when these variables are likely to be influenced heavily by food aid resources and also to have significant effect on agricultural sector productivity.[42] The earlier Indian models, for example, ignored substitution possibilities in both production and consumption, as did the earlier Dudley and Sandilands model for Colombia.[43] Changes in the composition of agricultural output can have important implications for farm incomes, trade (and therefore foreign exchange), and the price structure of agricultural and nonagricultural commodities.

Intersectoral Linkages: Agricultural-nonagricultural Interactions
Recent studies for Bangladesh, Egypt, and India illustrate the two ways in which analysts have sought to transcend the restrictions of working within a partial equilibrium framework when measuring impact on the agricultural sector and on food consumption. The first approach, exemplified by Mellor[44] on India and Nelson[45] on Bangladesh, may be characterized as partial analysis within a general equilibrium framework. Mellor explored the differential effects of food price changes in India on consumer incomes, producer incomes, the level of agricultural production, and employment up to 1970/71. He found that both real consumer and producer incomes in the lowest two deciles diminished significantly with a rise in food prices. In a parallel study, he also concluded that the accelerated rate of increase in employment in the early 1960s was sustained by food imports. Contrary to the assumptions of earlier studies, food aid probably provided significant balance-of-payments support and sustained growth by forestalling massive diversion of foreign exchange from capital goods to food imports in poor crop years.

Nelson, adopting a broadly similar approach, undertook a reassessment for Bangladesh that questioned the widespread view that food aid had had adverse effects on domestic agriculture. The advantages of this informal approach is that it permits analysis where the time period under study is too short for satisfactory econometric modeling (in this case Bangladesh for a period of less than a decade since independence and the end of large-scale emergency relief). It also allows the analyst to consider structural and technological constraints as well as difficult-to-quantify tensions in macroeconomic and agricultural sector policy. Nelson's cautious conclusion, which might be generalizable to a number of other low-income countries during periods of severe economic and food system disruption, is that it is difficult to envisage a sustainable counterfactual scenario in which significantly lower levels of food aid would have resulted in more rapid, equitable agricultural development.

Bangladesh and Egypt, the largest recipients of food aid through the 1970s, have displaced India as the most discussed cases. The divergence of opinion on the overall economic impact of food aid on the economy, particularly agriculture, indicates the limitations of the informal factor by factor approach.[46] First, the data, particularly regarding policy and implied counterfactual scenarios to historical levels of food aid, are susceptible to differences of interpretation. Second, in a qualitative analysis, unless all the indicators are consistently positive or negative, the overall assessment becomes a matter of judgment and disagreement.[47]

The alternative formal approach is to explore output and price behavior in a general equilibrium model in which behavior in the agricultural and other sectors of the economy is linked. The potential power of such an approach is illustrated by Ahluwalia's relatively simple model of the Indian economy, which explores output and price behavior in two sectors (agricultural and nonagricultural), thereby quantifying the broader economic implications of food imports that only can be handled qualitatively in an informal approach.[48] Simulations suggest that a relative decline in the price of food grains (prima facie evidence of a disincentive effect) is compatible with an overall marginally positive impact on agricultural output through the effects of lower wage rates in the manufacturing sector and a shift away from food grains to other crops. The simulation approach inevitably precludes empirical verification but obliges the analyst to quantify relationships. A whole generation of models comparable to that of Ahluwalia is now being developed.[49] These models offer the opportunity to explore the role of food imports (supported by food aid) in a wider macro context. This would be an advance because the lesson from the literature on former recipients and countries, such as Bangladesh, Egypt, and Sri Lanka,[50] which continue to be significant recipients, is that partial and sectoral analyses seem likely to sustain an inconclusive debate. But, as Blandford and Plocki show in their careful review of Indian sectoral models, the results of such econometric exercises are likely to be sensitive to choices in model specification and data.[51] The serious questions that surround the reliability of food production as well as import and export data for many recipient countries (particularly sub-Saharan Africa) will continue to hamper all quantitative and qualitative analyses.

Some Current Recipients: A Provisional Stocktaking

The formal impact assessments of countries such as Brazil and India, which have ceased to be important recipients of cereals food aid in absolute or per capita terms, provide one form of evidence that is inconsistent with strongly negative disincentive critiques of food aid. In the case of these two countries, food aid has been a resource for growth, and relatively sophisticated management of agricultural systems has limited, if not eliminated, direct disincentive effects.[52] But to what extent is it appropriate to generalize from the experience of earlier decades to the low-income countries, particularly in sub-Saharan Africa, to which food aid now has been reallocated?[53] There have as yet been few systematic assessments of the impact of food aid for many currently important recipient countries.[54] But recent impact assessments for agency programs as well as independent research are beginning to suggest some important issues. These studies consider the implications of three important changes in food aid relationships since the early 1970s: a reduction in volumes of assistance, a reallocation between continents (to Africa) and between countries (from India to Bangladesh within Asia), and an increase in project and emergency uses at the expense of bilateral program assistance.

The impact assessment of PL-480 Title I concessional credits to five countries—Bangladesh, Egypt, Jamaica, Peru, and Sri Lanka—indicates the reduced significance of what historically has been the most important food aid channel and the most researched in terms of economic impact.[55] With the possible exception of Bangladesh, the scale of food transfers has been modest in relation to food imports and public food system operations for all five countries. But in the low-income African countries, food aid has been increasing in relation to food imports.[56] This raises a question about the relevance of the historical experience. To what extent is the debate on disincentives and the macroeconomic growth implications of food aid out of proportion to the current scale of transfers to many recipient countries?

These evaluations, studies of the EEC program, and some other country case studies reconfirm earlier findings that program food aid acts as a source of balance-of-payments support.[57] An expected corollary of this result is that the exact magnitude of any production disincentive effect that can be traced directly to food aid has proved difficult to determine. Evaluators therefore have emphasized the critical role of domestic food policy in their prescriptive conclusions.[58] Food aid can provide a recipient government with food resources to withstand pressure to alter food policies that imply disincentives to producers. This also may bring significant positive and widespread nutritional and income benefits to consumers, as noted in the AID evaluation for Egypt.[59] But by implication such policies only are sustainable while food imports are concessional. Alternatively, a food aid agreement can contribute to an overall food import policy that provides appropriate incentives to general policy reform, as in Jamaica,[60] Mali,[61] and possibly Bangladesh.[62] There is growing interest in such models in staple food import-dependent economies such as Madagascar, Mauritania, and Senegal.

Consumer Tastes and Dietary Patterns

Changes in consumer preferences, particularly the acquisition of tastes for imported foods to the disadvantage of locally produced commodities, have been widely identified as a potentially serious long-run disincentive effect of food aid.[63] The analysis of this issue has distinguished between observed changes brought about by rising incomes, urbanization and socioeconomic change and the effects of changes in relative prices.[64] As rising food imports are associated with economic growth, urbanization, and the expansion of the secondary and tertiary sector throughout almost the whole developing world, a separate effect of food aid has proved difficult to isolate.[65] However, in the short run, food aid has been observed in cross-section to be positively correlated with differences in levels of cereal imports,[66] largely wheat and rice, especially by low-income countries.[67] To the extent that these imports are additional, there would be some opportunity for impact, depending on importing country pricing and distribution policies or dietary patterns.

For example, food pricing policies have contributed to steadily increased per capita consumption of imported wheat in Bangladesh, Indonesia, and Sri Lanka, where little was consumed previously. Without differential pricing, wheat consumption would not have expanded at the expense of the major staple, rice, as well as various coarse grains and tubers.[68] In general, overvalued exchange rates supported by food aid may favor increased consumption of imported commodities even where there is no explicit policy of subsidizing consumption.[69]

There is wider evidence that socioeconomic change, urbanization, and rising energy costs have favored increased consumption of convenience foods.[70] Myriad factors contribute to the growth in consumption of processed foods using imported cereals. The accidents of colonial history and trade explain the relative significance of different bread wheat, durum wheat products, and rice types in particular countries.[71] Food processing technologies transferred from developed countries are specific to particular products and raw materials.[72] The evidence from country case studies is consistent with the view of critics that the availability of surplus bread wheat, rice, soybean oil, and dairy products on highly concessional terms has encouraged imports and increased consumer acceptance of these specific commodities.[73] Market development, long an objective of food aid policy, implies a higher level of demand than does the absence of such measures.[74]

Some analysts suggest that the growth in imports of food is an inevitable part of industrialization and tertiary sector and urban growth.[75] According to this view, local agriculture in the early phase of development has a low overall short-run elasticity of supply. The growth in effective demand for marketed staples and, with real income growth, demand for animal products, edible oils, and so on therefore will outpace the capacity of local agriculture to respond in the short run unless the intersectoral terms of trade rise to levels that directly choke off the transformation process or induce political and economic instability. What is at issue, therefore, is the extent to which import, price, and investment policies for the food sector have increased import dependence and reduced the positive intersectoral linkage effects of a growing domestic food market. This is illustrated most clearly in the controversy about appropriate patterns of investment in the food industry and food sector infrastructure. Is the observed low elasticity of supply partially a consequence of failure to invest in infrastructure and the integration of local markets?

Food Marketing, Storage, and Processing

The growth of food imports, which are financed in part by food aid and which create a set of food system linkages, has been identified in a number of recent country studies as having far-reaching negative development implications. The growth of large-scale, capital-intensive, centralized storage and processing can lead—as in Bangladesh,[76] Egypt,[77] and Indonesia[78]—to an absolute decline in food industry employment and to the redistribution of income from wage labor to capital and from rural to urban areas. These technical changes concern domestically produced staples as well as imports. Once made, the opportunity for profits on such investments linked to imported supplies, as in the case of wheat processing in Egypt and Sri Lanka, can shift the balance of private and public sector financial (but not necessarily social) return toward continued reliance on imports.

An asymmetrical set of food system linkages frequently has been observed even in least-developed countries. These linkages involve an efficient import sector, large relative to total market supply, able to handle a high inflow of commodities and stocks, which exists side by side with a poorly articulated food marketing, storage, and processing system for domestically produced food. This asymmetry has various negative developmental implications. Development is inhibited in peripheral regions.[79] The poor internal infrastructure contributes to the inelasticity of domestic marketed supply.[80] Large-scale imports that stabilize consumer prices, especially in urban areas, force adjustment effects of production instability onto domestic producers and rural consumers (who are not integrated into national markets) and intensify disincentive effects and rural food insecurity.[81] Systems that are well geared to handle imports, and even the marketing and processing of domestically produced food, typically do not readily allow exports.[82] This set of concerns about the longer-term implications of developments in the food industry are stated succinctly by Dunlop and others in an overview of the five country impact assessments of PL-480 Title I program food aid—where food processing, storage, and distribution are uncoupled gradually from the agricultural sector, the backward and forward linkages critical to development fail to grow.[83]

Food Assistance and U.S. Agricultural Exports

There is a long tradition of separating the policy discussion of aid as an instrument of development (and its foreign policy and trade environment) from questions of aid as an instrument of donor country export policy. Characteristically, the analysis of aid policies takes as given the scale, the commodity composition, and the terms on which resources are available.

Table 7.1   World and U.S. Trade and Aid in Cereals, 1983/84
(million tons)

	Wheat/ Products	Rice/ Products	Coarse Grains/ Products	Total Cereals
Trade				
World trade	103.3	12.5	92.5	208.3
U.S. exports	38.3	2.1	55.8	96.2
(%)	(37%)	(8%)	(60%)	(46%)
Food Aid				
World Total	7.433	1.134	1.265	9.832
(% Total)	(7%)	(9%)	(1.4%)	(5%)
U.S. (PL-480)	4.375	0.223	0.792	5.390
(% Food Aid)	(59%)	(20%)	(73%)	(55%)

Sources: FAO (data); White et al. in this volume.

But in asking what margin of maneuverability exists for making food aid a more effective developmental resource, it is critical to take account of the evolving trade policy context. Food aid continues to represent a significant resource transfer in kind to developing countries because of the existence of large-scale exportable surpluses in the major donor countries (the United States, Australia, Canada, and the EEC). In the context of this chapter, which is also concerned with the prospects for U.S. agricultural trade to developing countries, four issues regarding food aid and trade policy are considered: (1) the changing relationship between food aid and trade policy, a historical perspective necessary because of the lag in perceptions among those outside the small professional community of aid and trade analysts; (2) a brief review of the significance of PL-480 food aid in the 1980s, including recent legislative changes; (3) the potential tension between the developmental and trade promotion objectives of food aid, particularly the import-substitution versus additionality and commodity composition issues (attention is focused on food aid as conventionally defined by the OECD Development Assistance Committee, which in effect means transfers under Public Law 480); and (4) the projection of food aid requirements.

The Changing Relationship of PL-480 to U.S. Trade Policy
After a cursory glance at the trade and aid statistics (Table 7.1), it is legitimate to ask why give much attention to food aid in a discussion of agricultural trade policy. Food aid on a large scale began primarily as a surplus disposal operation in the 1950s following the Marshall Plan aid to postwar Europe. From that time until the mid-1960s, PL-480 exports amounted to some 25 percent or more of all U.S. agricultural exports, and about two-thirds of all U.S. wheat exports and nearly one-half of all U.S. rice exports were shipped

Table 7.2   Shipments of Food Aid in Cereals by Donor Country[a]

Donors	1975/76	1976/77	1977/78	1978/79	1979/80	1980/81	1981/82	1982/83	1983/84	1984/85	1985/86[b]
Argentina	—	15	32	30	38	67	20	33	30	51	35
Australia	261	230	252	329	315	370	485	349	460	482	400
Austria	—	—	—	—	—	32	20	34	11	13	20
Canada	1,034	1,176	884	735	730	600	600	843	817	943	900
China	64	12	68	3	25	2	6	6	31	92	—
EEC	928	1,131	1,374	1,159	1,206	1,278	1,580	1,571	1,890	2,468	1,580
Finland	25	33	47	8	19	29	9	28	40	20	20
India	—	—	100	295	80	51	1	10	—	100	—
Indonesia	—	—	—	—	—	—	—	—	5	—	68
Japan	33	47	135	352	688	914	507	517	445	330	300
Norway	10	10	10	10	11	40	36	36	17	43	30
OPEC special fund	—	—	—	—	—	—	37	30	14	—	—
Saudi Arabia	10	—	—	26	10	31	32	14	29	71	20
Spain	—	—	—	—	—	14	22	25	27	31	80
Sweden	47	122	104	104	98	94	119	87	83	88	80
Switzerland	36	33	32	32	32	16	22	29	30	39	27
Turkey	—	20	14	5	5	15	4	5	5	—	—
United States	4,273	6,063	5,992	6,238	5,339	5,212	5,341	5,375	5,655	7,536	7,200
WFP purchases	22	63	56	72	21	13	24	4	16	17	30
Others[c]	103	62	116	103	270	165	275	198	226	200	200
Total	6,846	9,017	9,216	9,501	8,887	8,943	9,140	9,194	9,831	12,524	10,910

Source: Compiled by FAO from data provided by donors, the International Wheat Council, the World Food Program, and other international organizations.

[a]Calculated in thousand tons, grain equivalent, July/June. To express cereal food aid in grain equivalent, wheat, rice, and coarse grains are counted on a one-to-one basis.

[b]Estimated on the basis of minimum commitments under the Food Aid Convention 1980, budgetary allocations, and other sources.

[c]In addition, according to unofficial reports, the USSR provided emergency aid to Asian countries amounting to 200,000 tons in 1977/78 and 1979/80 each and 400,000 tons in 1978/79.

Table 7.3   U.S. Food Aid Flows by Channel (in million dollars/% of total)

Year	Bilateral Grant	Bilateral Loan	Multilateral	Total	Total as percentage of ODA from OECD Countries	Total as percentage of ODA from U.S.
1970	360	n.a.	1	n.a.	n.a.	n.a.
1971	373	430	2	805	10.7	25.9
	(46.3)	(53.4)	(0.3)	(100.0)		
1972	360	494	124	978	10.6	24.7
	(36.8)	(50.5)	(12.7)	(100.0)		
1973	251	313	54	618	6.8	23.3
	(40.6)	(50.7)	(8.7)	(100.0)		
1974	238	400	90	728	6.3	19.8
	(32.7)	(55.0)	(12.3)	(100.0)		
1975	375	800	91	1,266	9.1	30.4
	(29.6)	(63.2)	(7.2)	(100.0)		
1976	565	600	45	1,210	8.7	27.8
	(46.7)	(49.6)	(3.7)	(100.0)		
1977	432	700	78	1,210	7.7	25.8
	(35.7)	(57.9)	(6.4)	(100.0)		
1978	406	637	75	1,118	5.6	19.7
	(36.3)	(57.0)	(6.7)	(100.0)		
1979	480	745	77	1,302	5.7	27.8
	(36.9)	(57.2)	(5.9)	(100.0)		
1980	471	687	149	1,307	4.8	18.3
	(36.0)	(52.6)	(11.4)	(100.0)		
1981	430	693	139	1,262	4.9	21.8
	(34.1)	(54.9)	(11.0)	(100.0)		
1982	387	628	119	1,134	3.8	12.8
	(34.1)	(55.4)	(10.5)	(100.0)		
1983	557	656	137	1,350	4.5	15.5
	(41.3)	(48.6)	(10.1)	(100.0)		
1984	651	733	158	1,542	4.9	16.4
	(42.2)	(47.5)	(10.2)	(100.0)		

Source: OEDC (data).

under PL-480. A decade later PL-480 exports represented only 5 percent of total farm exports.[84] In the early 1980s, PL-480 represented only 5 percent of U.S. grain exports, 11 percent of wheat and rice, and a little more than 1.4 percent of coarse grains, the growth area in cereal trade of recent years. The African food crisis has resulted in a large but possibly temporary increase in total aid flows (Table 7.2). Food aid also has steadily declined in significance as a proportion of development assistance since the early 1970s (Table 7.3).

Other legislative and internationally agreed regulatory changes have led a number of analysts to suggest that food aid is now more a resource of humanitarian and developmental aid policy than a resource of foreign policy.[85] These changes are paralleled by the declining significance of the United States as a provider of food aid. Before 1970, the United States was in effect the only significant provider of food aid. Following the establishment of the World Food Program (WFP), there was an informal understanding that the United States would provide one-quarter of the resources to this program of wholly grant food aid, including shipping costs, for projects and emergencies. Following the 1967 Food Aid Convention, a broad group of donors also agreed to minimum contributions of cereals food aid.[86]

In the decade following the World Food Conference of 1974, food aid flows were quite stable at 9 million tons of cereals and 500,000 tons of other commodities. At the 1980 Food Aid Convention, minimum commitments close to recent, expected programmed levels of cereals were made by most donors. The United States contributed more than one-half of all commodities. Only the United States and Japan provided food aid on a concessional credit basis. All other donors provided aid on a grant basis, and some included all associated costs, so that the overall U.S. contribution, when calculating commodity costs at national world market prices, was closer to 40 percent of the aid transfer.[87]

The implication of these changes is that officially designated aid under PL-480 and other donor programs ceased to be a policy instrument for managing the changing export surplus situation for the most important commodity groups, particularly wheat, maize, and oilseeds.[88] Rather, from the point of view of export trade managers in the USDA and other exporting countries, official food aid is a relatively more predictable, intramarginal element in their market management strategy. A fuller understanding of this role requires an examination of commodity determination. But prior to reviewing this question it is important to ask why the role of food aid has changed so significantly.

The changing role of food aid, not only for the United States but also for other donors, probably lies in the multiplicity of food aid objectives and the decreasing flexibility from a market management viewpoint that this aid eventually produced. Food aid flows increasingly have become institutionalized. The establishment of the World Food Program and other smaller-scale multilateral programs has resulted in what are in effect politically mandated commitments of resources to agency programs and the channelling of aid into project uses. The voluntary agency program under Title II probably has undergone a similar institutionalization. There are powerful developmental, programmatic, efficiency arguments for making forward commitments on a multiannual basis; even where these are not formalized, strong informal pressures exist to maintain annually programmed commitments in relation to past levels.

The 1975 Foreign Assistance Act was an important landmark in mandating food aid; according to the act, the larger share of such aid was to be used for developmental purposes.[89] A minimum level of resources was to be committed to the Title II Nongovernmental Organization (NGO) multilateral and emergency program. In addition, a minimum share of Title I agricultural credits was to be programmed to the World Bank's International Development Association (IDA)-defined low-income countries. The subsequent development of the Title III food-for-development legislation further mandated the flow of Title I commodities.[90] Program management also was required to take account of "self-help" legislative requirements and, subsequently, the Bellmon determination of avoidance of recipient country agricultural disincentive effects.[91]

The cargo preference sections of the legislation and the associated Merchant Marine Act mandating a share of gross tonnage for U.S. bottoms further decreased the flexibility of food aid as an agricultural trade policy instrument. The implications of those provisions may be more serious in the highly competitive dry cargo shipping markets of recent years.

Since the mid-1970s, side by side with the broad stability in PL-480 flows, there has been a significant increase in other purely agricultural, "soft" credit measures to manage markets.[92] More recently, Section 416 of the Agricultural Act of 1949 has been employed at the margin in preference to PL-480 for the use of surplus commodities in international programs. The subsequent administrative issues raised by this add-on tactic are reflected in the extensive legislative provisions of the 1985 Food Security Act (Section 1109 of PL99-198) concerned with S416 donations.

The evolution of agricultural export policy and aid policy practice in light of legislative and other regulatory action since the 1960s suggests an important lesson for the legislature and for aid lobbyists. The original legislation reflected not easily reconcilable trade and foreign policy as well as developmental objectives. The progressive introduction of regulatory constraints intended to prevent a repetition of Vietnam War–style foreign policy abuse and damaging (to low-income countries) short-run, trade-motivated behavior (1971–1974) has encouraged a multiplication of policy instruments. An important question for policy analysis is whether giving increased priority to developmental and humanitarian goals within the official food aid program (i.e., PL-480) is justified by the significantly lower level of food surpluses moving through this channel. What are the developmental implications of a larger share of subsidized exports flowing through agricultural channels? During the period in which world markets for temperate zone commodities are overhung by surpluses, this question concerns the United States as well as food aid policy more generally.

PL-480 and U.S. Agricultural Exports in the 1980s
The scope for short-run programming flexibility of food aid has been very substantially reduced under the 1980 Food Aid Convention (Table 7.4).[93] This convention is likely to be extended until the end of the decade, at least at existing levels. The experience of the years since 1980 has shown that a capacity also exists to increase commodity flows substantially beyond these

Table 7.4   Total U.S. Cereals Food Aid and Contributions Through
the Food Aid Convention

Year	FAC Minimum Contribution (000 tons)	Total Cereals (000 tons)	Food Aid as % of Minimum FAC Contribution
1970/71	1890	9039	478
1971/72	1890	9220	488
1972/73	1890	6948	368
1973/74	1890	3186	168
1974/75	1890	4722	250
1975/76	1890	4273	226
1976/77	1890	6068	321
1977/78	1890	5992	317
1978/79	1890	6238	330
1979/80	1890	5339	283
1980/81	4470	5242	117
1981/82	4470	4791	107
1982/83	4470	5862	131
1983/84	4470	6453	144
1984/85	4470	6976	156

Sources: FAO, Food Aid in Figures; International Wheat Council.

"normal" levels in response to emergency conditions. Whether or not the scale, direction, and timing of the response was strongly countercyclical (thereby dampening the short-run effects of reduced production in sub-Saharan Africa) is an issue for review.

The establishment of a food aid wheat reserve of 4 million tons by the Carter administration represented another form of commitment to making food aid a more stable element of foreign assistance and global food security. The reserve was created in a weakening market as stocks accumulated in 1979 following the restriction on sales to the Soviet Union. The practical significance of earmarking wheat to sustain commitments and to allow for high levels of shipments in food crisis in weaker market conditions generated some initial skepticism. But this move appears justified retrospectively by the comparative ease with which the United States could expand emergency food aid levels during the African emergency (see Table 7.2). This measure, which in many ways could have been a model for other donors in establishing exporter-managed food security stocks, underscores an important lesson. It is precisely in a weaker market that conditions favor such forward-looking measures.

There have been no significant changes in the procedures and practices for determining the commodity composition of either credit sale Title I or the grant Title II program. The programs continue to depend on USDA determination of "available" commodities. The practical consequence of these procedures is apparent in the lack of any significant trend prior to the African emergency in the pattern of cereals and the buildup of milk powder aid. There has been substantial short-term fluctuation in the level of individual commodities "made available" and programmed under both grant and credit programs (Tables 7.5 and 7.6).

Within the cereals group, the most significant fluctuations have been in rice (Table 7.5). A more detailed breakdown of other cereals that distinguishes types of wheat and coarse grains probably would reveal similar short-term movements. These fluctuations indicate a possible tension between short-run export market and surplus management objectives and tighter and predictable medium-term programming in relation to developmental criteria. If allowance is made for a few large, more predictable country programs, especially to Egypt, the year-to-year fluctuations imply that many marginal countries and projects do not know with any certainty whether they will get assistance and what commodities will be available. As discussed earlier, this cannot foster constructive programming.

The cereals part of the program is also significant for particular producer, processor, and trader interests. For example, the proportion of agricultural exports in fiscal year (FY) 1981 accounted for by food aid ranged from less than 2 percent of coarse grains to 68 percent of wheat flour and 76 percent of bulgar wheat exports (Table 7.7).

Vegetable oils have remained the most important noncereal commodity group. Shipment again has fluctuated as availabilities have been determined by changing internal market conditions and stock levels (see Table 7.6). There apparently has been little investigation of the consequence of this

Table 7.5   Commodity Composition of U.S. Cereals Food Aid (000 tons)

Year	Wheat	Coarse Grains	Rice	Total Cereals
1970/71	6,566	1,550	923	9,039
1971/72	6,408	1,750	1,062	9,220
1972/73	4,071	1,828	1,050	6,948
1973/74	1,421	1,124	641	3,186
1974/75	3,473	501	747	4,722
1975/76	3,321	442	511	4,273
1976/77	4,737	486	845	6,068
1977/78	4,284	1,007	702	5,992
1978/79	4,806	950	481	6,238
1979/80	3,879	967	494	5,339
1980/81	3,402	1,382	429	5,212
1981/82	4,077	1,042	223	5,341
1982/83	4,121	594	492	5,375
1983/84	4,375[a]	792[b]	488	5,655

Sources: FAO, *Food Aid in Figures*; International Wheat Council.

[a]Includes 209,000 tons of bulgar wheat.
[b]Includes 158,000 tons of cereal component of blended foods.

Table 7.6   Commodity Composition of U.S. Noncereal Food Aid (tons)

Year	Solid Milk Products	Other Dairy Products [a]	Butter Oil	Vegetable Oil
1977	57,041	14,726	—	171,679
1978	74,443	17,541	—	229,955
1979	63,315	10,050	—	150,678
1980	63,634	26,320	—	234,350
1981	98,158	24,450	—	275,347
1982	111,676	15,095	2,460	299,722
1983	126,206	41,709	—	290,108
1984	163,341	33,133	64	270,593

Sources: FAO, *Food Aid in Figures*; International Wheat Council.

[a]Includes the dairy component of blended foods.

fluctuating supply for either credit sales or project use.[94]

After a sharp drop in levels of dairy products aid by the early 1970s, there has again been a gradual buildup of supplies, especially of dried skimmed milk, or DSM (see Table 7.6). This is one of the few apparent, sustained movements in the commodity composition of the program. In FY 1981, shipments under PL-480 accounted for 90 percent of U.S. exports of DSM (see Table 7.7). The use of aid channels to dispose of surpluses subsequently has been carried further by provision for donations under Section 416 of the Agricultural Trade Act of 1949. Some processed products, such as soya-sorghum grits, that have export outlets and, indeed, are only marketed through Title II have been among the most stable elements in the program. Yet it is important to recall that the introduction of these blended products resulted from the search for substitutes (in nutritional projects) for shrinking supplies of milk powder in the 1960s.

When the commodity composition of the program is considered in cross-section, in FY 1981 for example, a clear relationship emerges between channels and commodity types (Table 7.8). The credit sales under Title I are heavily concentrated in widely traded wheat and coarse grains, although these form a relatively small proportion of the market in commodities. For wheat in particular, year-to-year movements are small in relation to total quantities programmed for export. However, where food aid represents a more important segment of the market, as in the case of rice or soybean oil, then the relative scale of annual fluctuations has been much larger. The program is much more sensitive to, and perhaps plays a more important role in, market management.

The grant program Title II is disproportionately significant in comparison with Title I for less widely traded commodities, such as DSM, bulgar wheat, and blended foods, where the United States has had no significant commercial export trade. Wheat flour and vegetable oils appear to be intermediate cases, important in both programs and relatively significant within

Table 7.7   U.S. Commodity Composition of PL-480 and Multilateral Aid Programs, Fiscal Year 1981 (000 tons)

Commodity	PL-480 Title I	PL-480 Title II	PL-480 Total	AID (Mutual Security)	PL-480 Percentage of Total Agricultural Exports	PL-480 + Aid Percentage of Total Agricultural Exports
Animals and Products	—	91.4	91.4	103.8	5.0	10.6
Inedible tallow	—	—	—	88.8	—	6.6
Poultry meats fresh/frozen	—	—	—	15.0	—	3.9
Nonfat dry milk	—	91.4	91.4	—	90.0	90.0
Grains and Products	3,663.4	1,473.6	5,137.0	448.0	4.4	4.8
Wheat	2,203.0	266.5	2,469.5	4.2	5.8	5.9
Wheat flour	664.8	217.5	882.3	—	68.1	68.1
Bulgar wheat	0.5	354.4	354.9	—	75.7	75.7
Rice	242.0	104.6	346.6	—	10.9	10.9
Coarse grains and products[a]	553.1	325.2	878.3	443.8	1.3	1.9
Blended food products	—	185.1	185.1	—	90.9	90.9
Soya-sorghum grits	—	20.3	20.3	—	100.0	100.0
Oilseeds and Products	130.4	121.7	252.1	—	0.8	0.8
Soybean oil	126.7	121.4	248.1	—	33.6	33.6
Cottonseed oil	3.7	—	3.7	—	1.2	1.2
Pulses	—	8.0	8.0	15.5	1.0	2.7
Cotton	4.2	—	4.2	—	0.4	0.4
Tobacco	—	—	—	3.6	—	1.4
Other	—	—	—	0.6	—	b

Source: USDA, *Report on Food For Peace* (Washington, D.C.: USDA, 1981).

[a]Includes maize, sorghum, and products.
[b]Negative commercial exports.

U.S. agricultural trade. There is a large international market for flour, but the United States has faced severe competition, especially from the EEC, and thus the relative share of food aid in total flour exports probably fluctuates sharply from year to year. Flour and oil also have an important role in emergency assistance and direct distribution projects so that large allocations would be required for Title II. Broadly, where recipient countries are contributing directly to commodity and associated costs of credit sales under Title I, they show a revealed preference for widely traded commodities. Where, as under Title II, commodities are made freely available, then less widely traded commodities and, indeed, some commodities that have found a niche only in the food aid program are much more significant. This discrepancy between the outcome of decisions reflecting the greater influence of recipients and suppliers on commodity selection is suggestive of a tension between recipient/developmental and supplier/internal agricultural interests. From the donor viewpoint this raises questions about the cost effectiveness of the aid transfer.[95]

Tensions Between Developmental and Agricultural Trade Concerns
In the first fifteen years of PL-480, the United States in effect could act almost

Table 7.8   U.S. Cereals Food Aid by Country, 1981/82

Country	Quantity (000 t)	As Percentage of Total Cereals Aid	Country	Quantity (000 t)	As Percentage of Total Cereals Aid
Angola	14.4	19.3	Kampuchea	17.3	34.7
Bangladesh	453.6	45.1	Kenya	50.3	39.5
Barbados	0.2	100.0	Korea, Rep. of	160.3	37.3
Benin	2.4	28.9	Lesotho	28.3	82.7
Bhutan	1.1	100.0	Liberia	40.9	96.5
Bolivia	14.2	32.1	Madagascar	87.1	40.4
Botswana	6.3	96.9	Malawi	0.9	45.0
Brazil	1.0	33.3	Mali	5.9	8.9
Burundi	7.2	80.0	Mauritania	24.9	28.8
Cameroon	6.7	63.8	Mauritius	32.5	76.5
Cape Verde	25.3	47.0	Morocco	414.1	86.7
C.A.R.	0.3	15.0	Mozambique	22.0	14.8
Chad	11.2	39.2	Nepal	9.8	42.2
Chile	8.3	45.4	Nicaragua	1.5	1.4
China	10.3	13.1	Niger	19.3	27.0
Comoros	2.0	25.3	Pakistan	131.6	37.9
Congo	0.1	25.0	Panama	3.1	100.0
Costa Rica	43.2	95.6	Paraguay	1.1	100.0
Djibouti	5.2	46.0	Peru	61.2	50.3
Dominican Rep.	57.1	100.0	Philippines	49.0	89.9
Ecuador	5.3	63.9	Poland	397.3	95.2
Egypt	1,695.4	86.7	Rwanda	6.2	49.2
El Salvador	125.2	97.0	Sao Tome	0.1	3.2
Ethiopia	7.6	4.0	Senegal	31.8	38.5
Gambia	4.4	21.0	Seychelles	0.5	38.0
Gaza Strip	4.7	79.7	Sierra Leone	5.6	19.4
Ghana	31.1	72.2	Somalia	63.2	34.0
Guatemala	10.6	100.0	Sri Lanka	116.4	57.5
Guinea	17.3	44.8	Sudan	111.8	57.6
Guinea Bissau	6.6	21.8	Tanzania	39.9	13.0
Guyana	0.3	23.1	Togo	4.6	100.0
Haiti	84.4	93.9	Tunisia	66.0	68.8
Honduras	24.9	73.7	Turkey	0.3	100.0
India	310.0	91.8	Uganda	26.0	53.6
Indonesia	90.6	85.0	Upper Volta	44.6	55.1
Jamaica	71.5	86.4	Zaire	79.5	100.0
Jordan	5.2	7.2	Zambia	73.2	73.2
			Total	5,393.3	58.4

Sources: FAO, *Food Aid in Figures*; International Wheat Council.

Note: Includes indirect U.S. contributions through multilateral programs and NGO activities.

as a discriminating monopolist operating on the demand for agricultural export commodities, particularly wheat. In retrospect, there was some significant consistency of interest between the United States as an exporter and
developing countries with a growth potential. Overhanging surpluses with
little value were disposed. The extent to which imports were truly additional, or involved substitution of concession for hard currency imports, is a
matter for speculation. The scarcity of hard currency probably implied that
a high proportion of such imports were additional, especially in the case of
the largest recipient, India,[96] and at least to some extent in the case of the
now middle-income countries in East Asia and Latin America. Where food
aid provided balance-of-payments support, the transfers promoted the
growth process and indirectly promoted the market for imported cereals.
South Korea was such a case.[97] The global distributional impact may have
been higher prices to commercial importing countries. Since the collapse
of that trade regime, food aid, it is argued, has come to play a different role.

Flows are more predictable overall, but in quantitative terms they are
smaller. The higher share of aid from non-U.S. sources implies a higher degree of concessionality; thus, assessing the changing value of the total resource transfer is less clearcut. Official food aid has been reallocated toward
the least-developed countries in sub-Saharan Africa and to Bangladesh.
Egypt, not a least-developed country but the largest recipient, is the outstanding exception (see Table 7.8). The fragmentary evidence suggests that
most program food aid is only partially additional to commercial imports.[98]
A balance of unfavorable factors beyond the control of low-income countries, particularly the world recession since 1979, have put all these countries under severe economic stress. In these circumstances food aid flows
have represented an income transfer in kind. The considerable degree of
fungibility implies support for policies both good and bad. The chapters on
food strategies and agricultural policy reform in this volume reflect these
issues.[99] Yet food aid remains an inherently second-best way of providing
such support. The long-standing justification for such aid always has been
that at least part of the food aid is an additional resource transfer reflecting
the strength of agricultural support. But clearly, the tension still remains between developmental and agricultural influences on food aid flows.

In an aggregate sense official food aid has become a more predictable
resource. There is an opportunity for a greater degree of predictability at a
country level through programmatic innovations, such as Title III, that offered multiyear commitments. There is greater concessionality, again exemplified by Title III, larger-scale emergency aid, and significant government-to-
government aid under Section 206 of Title II to Africa. Yet in contrast to other
aid, the complexities of controls and commodity timing that reflect exporter
agricultural interests are more severe. The process of commodity selection,
which is strongly sensitive to short-run surplus disposal considerations, in-

volves the acceptance of a potentially significant tradeoff between developmental and market management concerns. This issue is exemplified by the rapid expansion of DSM exports through PL-480 and subsequently under S416 as well. Since the early 1970s until 1985, the EEC has been the most important source of food aid in dairy products, directly and through the WFP. The record does not justify the United States becoming a significant supplier of DSM as food aid.

Dairy Food Aid

World markets of dairy products are depressed by large, overhanging surpluses. Most developed country producers are dumping into developing country markets. Food aid has been used to facilitate the development of local dairy production (this is called "project food aid"). The best-known example is Operation Flood in India, and there have been other projects in Kenya and Tanzania. More recently, the United States has supported a similar "project" in Sri Lanka. Other aid resources have been used to support dairy development through complementary capital investments and technical cooperation.

With seasonally fluctuating local supply, dairy production in most tropical and semitropical developing countries typically depends for at least a proportion of its inputs on imported dairy products for reconstitution. Food aid therefore can facilitate the development of local production by financing the import of such inputs. Attention always has focused on the local generation of revenue, called counterpart funds. These funds can be used for local dairy development or for subsidizing local processing capacity. With markets overhung by surpluses, the profitable reconstitution of commercially acquired inputs may be difficult at import parity prices for full-cream milk powder. What is at issue is not just the prices at which domestic producers can be encouraged to supply milk, but also the operating costs of the local dairy processing industry. Are local prices to final consumers set at a level that ultimately allows the profitable expansion of local dairy production? In present market circumstances tariffs or other restrictions may be required on commercial inputs of products in a form readily salable to the final consumer. The real danger is that food aid will be used to subsidize both consumer and local processing capacity by making possible sales of locally reprocessed commodities at or less than input parity levels established by dumping.

Dairy aid is meeting the balance-of-payments costs by providing more materials to a local industry. Consumers are being subsidized. But are these desirable beneficiary groups or middle- and upper-income urban households? More importantly, is the aid being provided in a context in which a local production capacity will develop that can be based on local milk production or efficiently can utilize commercially purchased imports in the future? Evaluation of EEC-supported projects was pessimistic as to the developmental value of most such programs (except Operation Flood).[100] With dairy products, the scope for policy dialogue is far less than is the case of cereals that have macroeconomic significance. The donor of course can withdraw, but this is a difficult decision when larger levels of commodities are being programmed.

The other common use of dairy aid is in supplemental nutrition programs. This again is a highly controversial area. There are lactose intolerance problems. The desirability of organizing nutritional programs around commodities that are not widely consumed locally by poor, vulnerable groups has been questioned. Except where these commodities are widely consumed among potential beneficiary groups or have a local market resale value approximate to import parity prices, the use of such commodities may not be cost effective. Finally, these are more difficult commodities than grains to store and distribute. The EEC, in part bowing to the considerable weight of criticism, progressively has been reducing the scale of dairy aid. An EEC Commission policy paper on food aid described DSM as a "difficult" commodity and proposed a reduction in the levels at which it can be used effectively.[101] From a developmental point of view it would probably be more cost effective for the EEC to dispose of these commodities in some other way and substitute other, more appropriate commodities or nonfood aid.[102] What then is the developmental rationale for U.S. intervention on a large scale?

The Additionality Issue

A long-standing concern of agricultural interests has been to safeguard the sale through commercial sources of all transfers less concessional ones. This concern was reflected in the strict requirement that commodities provided through NGOs or international programs under Title II would not be sold on local markets. In circumstances where practically no other external resources were provided to support local projects, this imposed a severe restriction on project design and finance. The whole evaluative experience is that project food aid, both food for work and nutritional programs, has been constrained severely in its effectiveness by a lack of complementary resources, including finance for the local movement of commodities, payment of staff, purchase of equipment, maintenance, and the like. Of course, any local sale of commodities raises difficult management and accounting issues, which could be handled on a case-by-case basis. Blanket restrictions reflect an overwhelming concern for agricultural trade interests that severely reduce the developmental possibilities of food aid as a resource. It is encouraging that this has been recognized in recent years, and there is more willingness to allow the monetization of a proportion of commodities to meet local costs. A positive feature of the 1985 Food Security Act is the requirement that monetization must become a normal feature of voluntary agency nonemergency projects (Section 1104).

However, PL-480 budgetary practice still falls short of the flexibility of some other donors in terms of their capacity to program locally available commodities into emergency or developmental action (local purchase) and swap arrangements (exchange of imported for local food). Little attempt is being made to utilize triangular actions (importing food from another developing country). This issue of flexibility is highlighted by the recent experience in sub-Saharan Africa. As noted previously, local staples, such as white maize and indigenous varieties of sorghum and millet, often are preferable, particularly for rural projects and relief operations. Where projects are funded on an annual basis, local purchase and swaps offer the opportunity to respond to fluctuating local food supplies. For example, the WFP is currently purchasing grain in Burkina Faso—which has recently been in serious food deficit—for local projects. Maize surpluses in Kenya, Malawi, and Zimbabwe might be similarly utilized in-country (in the case of Kenya) or to meet the food requirements of neighboring countries. The budgetary framework and policy practices of PL-480 are in this respect apparently less flexible than those of other food aid donors such as Australia, Canada, Japan, and most European countries. The multiplication of policy instruments to manage agricultural markets has not reduced the tension between developmental and agricultural trade objectives in the budgetary and policy framework of PL-480. Is this because other donors characteristically fund food aid as part of their aid programs?

Future Requirements for Food Aid

Globally, the projection of recent trends indicates a continually rapid increase in the demand for imported cereals by developing countries.[103] Such projection exercises are fraught with difficulties. More recently, rates of growth have declined, and many developing countries have experienced a sharp fall in per capita national income levels. Consequently, income-related expansion in demand may be less than implied by projections reflecting trends since the mid-1960s. The most recent movements in oil prices and currency rates are a reminder that the international distribution of growth in demand in the Third World may be different from that of the past decade or so. Exercises in projections into the future are difficult, and the estimation of food aid requirements is no exception. Nevertheless, in the context of a volume looking at prospects for development and agricultural trade, these questions require consideration.

In reviewing projection exercises by FAO, the International Food Policy Research Institute (IFPRI), WFP, and USDA, two general results were noted.[104] First, food aid requirements reflecting various assessments of capacity to finance imports are typically in excess of current levels and are expanding. Second, estimates based on World Health Organization (WHO)/ FAO nutritional guidelines—which are a reminder of the urgent need to improve nutritional status in many countries beyond current abysmal levels— produce far higher requirements than projections reflecting demand, whether based on past trends or improved growth scenarios.

Some analysts are much more optimistic about the future. For example, Bale and Duncan, using the dictum that "we know that the future will be similar to the past because in the past the future has been similar to the past," argue that the trend has been for agricultural prices to decline and crop yields to increase in developing countries and that there is no reason why these trends should be suddenly reversed.[105] Indeed, if developing countries have "pricing policies that remove the existing distortion under which agricultural production labors," then the positive trend in food consumption they observe would be accelerated. In this optimistic, highly aggregated view, no mention is made of aid requirements, although the authors' implicit view is that food aid would be temporary, which does not accord with the various projection estimates on the need for greatly increased allocations in the future.

Such highly aggregated assessments are not consistent with the results of FAO's disaggregated exploration of greater-than-trend growth scenarios.[106] Other analysts also stress that although short- to medium-run projections of food production may not look too bad for many countries, longer-run projections show the importance of continued attention to sustain supply increases.[107] It also has been suggested that optimistic assessments confuse the micro and macro question. Some countries will succeed in being less dependent on food transfers, if not on food imports more generally, but many others will fail to do so. This is not readily apparent with aggregate figures, but it means that in terms of actuarial risk increased concessional financing for food imports probably will be required and should be taken into account in planning U.S. food aid policy. The onus is upon those who argue for maintaining or reducing levels of food aid to ensure that alternative financial mechanisms exist to meet the unavoidable food import bill of low-income countries. The notional actuarial risk provides a useful metaphor for the problem. Just as insurance companies do not know exactly who will be making claims, they nevertheless can anticipate that the level of claims during several years will be such that adequate resources must be set aside to meet these as they arise. Some projections made in the early 1980s for food aid requirements in sub-Saharan Africa in 1990 already have been exceeded in the crisis period of 1984/85.

The record on the recipient and donor side indicates that there are not only choices but constraints on what is institutionally and politically possible in the foreseeable future. The requirements estimates should be interpreted, therefore, as an upper limit to the amount of food aid that can be used effectively. Food aid is a resource with the potential for powerful positive and negative impacts on recipient countries. To grasp the opportunity to use food aid positively requires not just the political will to follow difficult policies, but considerable planning and management sophistication in recipient countries. The evidence is that development will create significant markets for agricultural exports. But there are risks, especially when agriculture generally or particular agricultural sectors are under pressure. In these situations the shortsighted assertion of narrow interests over developmental and humanitarian concerns can undermine the credibility of an aid resource that requires flexibility and sensitivity on the donor side.

Notes

1. For example, within the EEC, food aid policy involves a sharing of responsibility between DG6 (agriculture) and DG8 (development). DG6 is represented in the aforementioned international agreements. There is a Food Aid Management Committee chaired by the commission, but many representatives of member governments are from the Ministries of Agriculture. The rule of DG6, Ministries of Agriculture, and members of the European Parliament who represent agricultural areas in the formation of policy (in particular, the size of the food aid program and the balance of commodities and noncommodity resources) is far from clear but widely acknowledged as very powerful. A review of other donor programs would show similar influences, except perhaps for the few small food aid donors that do not have agricultural commodities for export. See E. J. Clay, *Review of Food Aid Policy Changes Since 1978,* Occasional Paper no. 1 (Rome: World Food Program, Public Affairs and Information Unit, 1985).

2. Ibid., Chapter 6.

3. E. J. Clay, "Sri Lanka: Food Aid as a Resource Transfer," *Food Policy* 8, no. 3 (August 1983a).

4. See S. J. Maxwell and Hans Singer, "Food Aid to Developing Countries: A Survey," *World Development* 7 (1979):225–247.

5. T. W. Schultz, "Value of U.S. Farm Surpluses to Underdeveloped Countries," *Journal of Farm Economics* 42, no. 5 (December 1960):1019–1030. Much of the import literature continues to look for evidence of such direct price effects that occur locally. See T. Jackson, *Against the Grains* (Oxford: Oxfam, 1982). For literature concerned with evidence of direct price effects that occur nationally, see D. W. Dunlop and C. Adamczyk, *A Comparative Analysis of Five PL 480 Title I Impact Evaluation Studies,* Aid Impact Evaluation Discussion Paper no. 19 (Washington, D.C.: AID, 1983).

6. See P. J. Isenman and H. W. Singer, "Food Aid: Disincentive Effects and Their Policy Implications," *Economic Development and Cultural Change* 25, no. 2 (January 1977).

7. Lower cereal prices might favor poor landless rural households at the expense of richer surplus producers in Bangladesh (interhousehold distribution). See R. Ahmed, *Agricultural Price Policies Under Complex Socioeconomic and Natural Constraints: The Case of Bangladesh,* Research Report no. 27 (Washington, D.C.:

IFPRI, October 1981). For a discussion on urban consumers gaining at the expense of rural small-scale producers in Zambia (sectoral distribution), see R. Chambers and H. W. Singer, *Poverty, Malnutrition and Food Insecurity in Zambia,* Staff Working Paper no. 473 (Washington, D.C.: World Bank, August 1981).

8. D. Steinberg et al., *Sri Lanka: The Impact of PL 480 Title I Food Assistance,* AID Impact Evaluation no. 39 (Washington, D.C.: AID, October 1982). Also see H. Alderman and C. P. Timmer, "Consumption Parameters for Sri Lankan Food Policy Analysis," *Sri Lankan Journal of Agrarian Studies* (January 1981).

9. There is widespread concern that food aid will encourage a special, technical pattern of investments in food handling, processing, and storage that is geared to bulk imports rather than to more widely dispersed, domestic production. See, for example, Dunlop, *A Comparative Analysis.* Also see E. J. Clay, "Food Aid and Food Policy in Bangladesh," *Bangladesh Journal of Agricultural Economics* 1, no. 2 (1979):107–120.

10. Relatively lower food prices dependent on targeting have been seen as reducing (rural) employment opportunities by encouraging relatively capital-intensive, urban industrial employment. See M. Lipton, *Why Poor People Stay Poor* (London: Croom Helm, 1977). Alternatively, there is a positive employment opportunity offered if lower food prices, especially direct use of food as wage goods, can favor relatively labor-intensive production throughout the economy and especially labor-intensive rural works. See Isenman, "Food Aid."

11. For example, Clay, "Food Aid and Food Policy," and J. R. Stepanek, *Bangladesh—Equitable Growth?* (New York: Pergaman Press, 1979), were concerned about the fiscal dependency of Bangladesh on food aid.

12. For example, contrast the negative assessments of C. P. Timmer, "The Political Economy of Rice in Asia: Lessons and Implications," *Food Research Institute Studies* 14 (1975):419–432; R. Blue et al., *PL 480 Title I: The Egyptian Case* (Washington, D.C.: AID, February 1983); Clay, "Food Aid and Food Policy"; Stepanek, *Bangladesh*; and Q. K. Ahmed, *Contribution of Food Aid to Equitable Growth: The Case of Bangladesh* (Amsterdam: WFP/Government of Netherlands, 1983), with the more positive view of G. O. Nelson, "Food Aid and Agricultural Production in Bangladesh," *IDS Bulletin* 14, no. 20 (1983) Institute of Development Studies, University of Sussex; and B. C. Richardson et al., *Bangladesh: Food Aid: PL 480 Title I and Title III,* Project Impact Evaluation (draft) (Washington, D.C.: AID, January–February 1983).

13. See review by Isenman, "Food Aid"; and J. W. Mellor, "Food, Employment and Growth Interactions," *American Journal of Agricultural Economics* 64, no. 2 (1982):304–311.

14. See, for example, T. W. Schultz, "Effects of the International Donor Community on Farm People," *American Journal of Agricultural Economics* 62, no. 5 (December 1980):873–878; and G. E. Schuh, "Food Aid as a Component of General Economic and Development Policy," in ADC, *The Developmental Effectiveness of Food Aid in Africa* (New York: ADC, 1982).

15. For example, striking contrasts in the interpretation of the impact of food aid on the Bangladesh economy are noted in notes 5-10.

16. See S. J. Maxwell, ed., *An Evaluation of the EEC Food Aid Programme,* Commissioned Study no. 4 (Sussex: IDS, University of Sussex, 1982); and E. J. Clay

and H. W. Singer, *Food Aid and Development: The Impact and Effectiveness of Bilateral PL 480 Title I Type Assistance* (IDS, University of Sussex, Brighton, February 1982); B. Huddleston, *Closing the Cereals Gap With Trade and Food Aid,* Research Report no. 43, (Washington, D.C.: IFPRI, 1984); and C. Stevens, Food Aid and the Developing World: Four African Case Studies (London: Croom Helm, 1979).

17. H. W. Singer, *Food Aid Policies and Programmes: A Survey of Studies of Food Aid* (Rome: FAO, 1978).

18. See P. C. Abbott and F. D. McCarthy, "The Welfare Costs of Tied Food Aid," *Journal of Development Economics* 11, no. 1 (1982); Huddleston, *Closing the Cereals Gap*; Isenman "Food Aid"; J. W. Mellor, "Food Aid and Nutrition," *American Journal of Agricultural Economics* 62, no. 5 (December 1980); and Nelson, "Macro-Economic Dimensions."

19. Abbott "The Welfare Costs"; and Huddleston, ibid. Formally this approximates a closed economy into which food aid is introduced without any direct repercussions on agricultural imports or exports. Despite the unrealism of this case, many models—for example, those for India—chose to assume away any trade effects. See D. Blandford and J. Plocki, "Evaluating the Disincentive Effect of PL 480 Food Aid: The Indian Case Reconsidered" (Ithaca: Dept. of Economics, Cornell University, New York, July 1977).

20. See S. Reutlinger and J. Katona-Apte, *The Nutritional Impact of Food Aid: Criteria for the Selection of Cost-Effective Foods,* Discussion Paper no. 12 (Washington, D.C.: Research Unit, Agricultural and Rural Development Department, World Bank, September 1983). These authors provide the most systematic analysis of income effectiveness of food transfers, although they are concerned primarily with supplementary feeding and food-for-work projects. The choice of commodity is critical because the cost effectiveness of the income transfer is maximized at local prices and, for a given level of costs, only where the food aid substitutes directly for purchases or home-produced food of similar unit value. The transfer is reduced where households incur transaction costs in resale or consume or otherwise substitute in use for lower-cost commodities (e.g., animal feed).

21. Schuh, *Food Aid as a Component;* and Schuh, "Increasing the Effectiveness of Food Aid: Offsetting the Opportunity Costs of Schooling" (Paper for the WFP/Government of the Netherlands Seminar on Food Aid, The Hague, October 2–5, 1983).

22. Mellor, "Food, Employment and Growth Interactions."

23. See Stevens, *Food Aid and the Developing World.* The author argues in the case of four African countries that if food aid were distributed freely—for example, as meals or take-home food in schools where government would otherwise have made provision—then this also would give budgetary support.

24. S. Reutlinger, *Project Food Aid and Equitable Growth: Income Transfer Efficiency First,* Report no. 13 (Washington, D.C.: Research Unit, Agriculture and Rural Development Department, World Bank, 1983).

25. H. W. Singer, "Use and Abuse of Local Counterpart Funds," *International Development Review* 3, no. 3 (October 1961).

26. See Canadian International Development Agency, *A Review of CIDA's Counterpart Fund Policy and Practices* (Ottawa: CIDA 1984). The practice of requiring the recipient countries to account separately for revenue from sales proceeds of

commodity aid has its origins in the Marshall Plan. Such revenues were supposed to be used for reconstruction and development. Other developed country donors also adopted this practice; as early as 1951/52 Canada employed this practice in making grants under the Colombo Plan.

27. Abbot, "The Welfare Costs"; Huddleston, *Closing the Cereals Gap*; and Nelson, "Macro-Economic Dimensions."

28. For example, the scope of work for the five evaluations of PL 480 Title I country programs asked for sequential consideration of the balance-of-payments effect and uses of local currency sales without linking discussion of these questions. See Dunlop, *A Comparative Analysis*, Appendix A.

29. Nelson, "Macro-Economic Dimensions"; and Huddleston, *Closing the Cereals Gap*.

30. Huddleston, ibid.

31. For a critical analysis of interventions in agriculture, see T. W. Schultz, "Effects of the International Donor Community on Farm People," *American Journal of Agricultural Economics* 62, no. 5 (December 1980):873–878; and T. W. Schultz, ed., *Distortion of Agricultural Incentives* (Bloomington: Indiana University Press, 1978). A survey of the agricultural price policy literature may be found in FAO, *Expert Consultation on Agricultural Price Policies,* (Rome: FAO, 1983).

32. See Isenman, "Food Aid"; Mellor, "Food Aid and Nutrition," and "Food, Employment and Growth Interactions"; and Nelson, "Macro-Economic Dimensions."

33. See, for example, the country impact assessments undertaken since 1980 by various bilateral donors such as those for PL-480 Title I in Dunlop, *A Comparative Analysis.* For an examination of the EEC action program, see S. J. Maxwell, ed., *An Evaluation of the EEC Food Aid Programme,* Commissioned Study no. 4 (Sussex: IDS, University of Sussex, 1982). For a country impact assessment of Australian aid, see Australian Development Assistance Bureau, *Food Aid to Bangladesh: A Review of the Australian Programme* (Canberra: ADA, 1983).

34. This section draws heavily on unpublished doctoral research by Nelson and the survey article of models for India in Blandford, *Evaluating the Disincentive Effect.*

35. Opponents of food aid have cited less-favorable results. See, for example, F. M. Lappé et al., *Aid as Obstacle: Twenty Questions About Our Foreign Aid and the Hungry* (San Francisco: IFDP, 1980).

36. Blandford, *Evaluating the Disincentive Effect.*

37. T. J. Goering, "PL 480 in Colombia," *Journal of Farm Economics* 44 (1962).

38. L. Dudley and R. J. Sandilands, "The Side Effects of Foreign Aid: The Case of PL 480 Wheat in Colombia," *Economic Development and Cultural Change* 23, no. 2 (January 1975).

39. L. Hall, *The Effects of PL 480 Wheat in Latin American Countries,* Working Paper no. 62 (Berkeley: Giannini Foundation of Agricultural Economics, University of California, 1978).

40. L. Hall, "Evaluating the Effects of PL 480 Wheat Imports on Brazil's Grain Sector," *American Journal of Agricultural Economics* 62, no. 1 (February 1980). Also see G. C. Williamson, *Food Consumption Parameter for Brazil and Their Application to Food Policy,* Research Report no. 32 (Washington, D.C.: IFPRI, 1982).

41. M. Bezunch and B. J. Deaton, *Food Aid Disincentives: The Tunisian Experience* (Richmond, VA: Virginia Polytechnic Institute and State University, 1983). Also see Stevens, *Food Aid and the Developing World*; and *Reviews of Selected National Experiences With Food Aid Programmes and Policies: The Tunisian Experience* (Rome: WFP/CFA, September 1983).

42. Isenman, "Food Aid"; and Mellor, "Food, Employment and Growth Interactions."

43. Nelson, "Macro-Economic Decisions."

44. Mellor, "Food Aid and Nutrition."

45. Nelson, "Food Aid and Agricultural Production."

46. For Egypt, contrast the conclusions of Blue, *PL 480 Title I,* which identifies serious negative disincentive effects of food import policy sustained by food aid on wheat production, with the inconclusive results of G. M. Scobie, *Government Policy and Food Imports: The Case of Wheat in Egypt,* Research Report no. 29, (Washington, D.C.: IFPRI, 1981); G. M. Scobie, *Food Subsidies in Egypt: Their Impact on Foreign Exchange and Trade,* Research Report no. 40 (Washington, D.C.: IFPRI, 1983); and J. Van Braun and H. de Haen, *The Effects of Food Price and Subsidy Policies on Egyptian Agriculture,* Research Report no. 42 (Washington, D.C.: IFPRI, 1983). See Nelson, "Food Aid and Agricultural Production," for positive conclusions in the pre-1971 period in Bangladesh. For negative assessments of the period 1972–1978, see Clay, "Food Aid and Food Policy"; and Stepanek, *Bangladesh.* See Richardson, *Bangladesh: Food Aid,* for positive results since 1978.

47. Clay, *Food Aid and Development,* Chapter 3.

48. See I. J. Ahluwalia, "An Analysis of Price and Output Behavior in the Indian Economy: 1951–1973, *Journal of Development Economics* 6, no. 3 (1979). The earlier sectoral studies were concerned only with the cereals sector, including any crossprice effects between commodity sectors in agriculture. This probably contributed to the overestimation of the overall disincentive effect. The Green Revolution technology, which reduced unit costs, and associated positive pricing policies, which favored wheat relative to pulses and oil seeds, resulted in significant substitution of wheat for these crops. See J. G. Ryan and M. Asokan, "Effect of Green Revolution in Wheat on Production of Pulses and Nutrients in India," *Economic Programme* Occasional Paper no. 18 (Hyderabad, India: ICRISAT, 1977). Presumably, higher relative prices for cereals in the years 1950–1965 would have had a similar substitution effect, excluded by the assumption from sectoral models of the impact of cereal (food aid) imports on agricultural production.

49. A series of modeling studies for Egypt are being developed at IFPRI relating to different facets of the food system. For trade, see Scobie, *Government Policy,* and *Food Subsidies;* for consumption, see H. J. Alderman et al., *Egypt's Food Subsidy and Rationing System: A Description,* Research Report no. 34 (Washington, D.C.: IFPRI, 1982); and H. Alderman and J. Van Braun, *Welfare and Distributional Impact of the Egyptian Food Ration and Subsidy System* (Washington, D.C.: IFPRI, forthcoming); for agriculture, see Van Braun, *The Effects of Food Price.* For a useful guide to such macro models, including an illustrative model for the Egyptian food system, see L. Taylor, *Macro-models for Developing Countries* (New York: McGraw Hill, 1970).

50. On Sri Lanka, see Steinberg, *Sri Lanka: The Impact of PL 480*; Clay, "Sri

Lanka"; and P. A. S. Dahanyake, "Disincentive Effects of Food Aid on Food Production in Sri Lanka," Central Bank of Ceylon Occasional Papers 1978–79 (Colombo: Central Bank of Ceylon, 1978).

51. Blanford, *Evaluating the Disincentive Effect.*

52. See Agricultural Development Council, *Implementation of United States Food Aid—Title III,* Seminar Report no. 20 (New York: ADC, August 1979); ADC, *The Developmental Effectiveness of Food Aid*; E. J. Clay, "The Changing World Food Aid System: Some Implications of the Proliferation of Donors and Recipients," *IDS Bulletin* 14, no. 2 (April 1983b); and Isenman, "Food Aid."

53. See C. Christensen and E. Hogan, "Food Aid as an Instrument of Development: A Seminar Report," in ADC, *The Developmental Effectiveness of Food Aid in Africa* (New York: ADC, 1982); Clay, ibid.; and H. W. Singer and S. J. Maxwell, "Development Through Food: Twenty Years' Experience" (Paper for the Twentieth Anniversary Conference of the World Food Program, The Hague, October 1983).

54. See ADC, ibid. Concern about the political as well as economic implications of food aid dependency are exemplified by R. Vengroff, "Food Aid Dependency: PL 480 to Black Africa," *Journal of Modern African Studies* 20, no. 1 (March 1982): 27–44. For case studies of Botswana, Lesotho, and Upper Volta, see Stevens, *Food Aid and the Developing World.* For other examples of exploratory analysis of food aid's macroeconomic role and the effect in other important recipient countries in Africa, see J. F. J. Holt, "Ethiopia: Food for Work or Food for Relief," *Food Policy* 8, no. 3 (August 1983); M. Mitchell and C. Stevens, "Mauritania: The Cost-Effectiveness of EEC Food Aid," *Food Policy* 8, no. 3 (August 1983); and A. M. Thomson, "Somalia: Food Aid in a Long-Term Emergency," *Food Policy* 8, no. 3 (August 1983). The growth of interest in food strategies can be expected to affect the interrelationships between food policy and food imports including food aid.

55. Summarized in Dunlop, *A Comparative Analysis.*

56. Clay, "The Changing World Food Aid System," Table 3.

57. See IDS/CEAS, *The European Community's Cost of Food Aid Study,* vols. 1 and 2 (Sussex: IDS, University of Sussex/CEAS, University of London, 1982); Clay, "Sri Lanka"; and Scobie, *Government Policy* and *Food Subsidies.*

58. Dunlop, *A Comparative Analysis*; Maxwell, *An Evaluation of the EEC Food Aid Program.*

59. Blue, *PL 480 Title I*; and A. M. Thomson, "Egypt: Food Security and Food Aid," *Food Policy* 8, no. 3 (August 1983).

60. Sidman et al., *Jamaica: The Impact and Effectiveness of the PL 480 Title I Program,* AID Project Impact Evaluation Report no. 51 (Washington, D.C.: AID, 1984).

61. "The Lesotho Experience," *Review of Selected National Experiences With Food Aid Programs and Policies* (Rome: WFP, 1984).

62. Richardson, *Bangladesh: Food Aid.*

63. See, for example, Maxwell, "Food Aid to Developing Countries"; Clay, *Food Aid and Development*; and Jackson, *Against the Grains.*

64. Dunlop, *A Comparative Analysis.*

65. See FAO, *Agriculture Towards 2000,* Economic and Social Development Series no. 23 (Rome: FAO, 1981).

66. For an analysis of the factors associated in cross-section with levels of

cereal import dependence, see T. K. Morrison, "Cereal Imports by Developing Countries: Trends and Determinants," *Food Policy* 9, no. 1 (1984):13–26.

67. Huddleston, *Closing the Cereals Gap.*

68. For example, Ahmed, *Agricultural Price Policies*; C. P. Timmer, "Food Prices and Food Policy Analysis in LDCs," *Food Policy* 5, no. 3 (August 1980); Alderman, "Consumption Parameters"; and Steinberg, *Sri Lanka: The Impact of PL 480.*

69. Schuh, "Food Aid as a Component"; and Schultz, "Effects of the International Donor Community."

70. Mellor, "Food, Employment and Growth Interactions."

71. See, for example Thomson, "Somalia."

72. J. James and F. Stewart, "New Products: A Discussion of the Welfare Effects of 16 Introductions of New Products in Developing Countries," in F. Stewart and J. Jones, eds., *The Economics of New Technology in Developing Countries* (London: Frances Pinter, 1982), 225–255.

73. For example, F. M. Lappé and J. Collins, *Food First—Beyond the Myth of Scarcity* (Boston: Houghton Mifflin, 1979); S. George, *How the Other Half Dies* (New York: Penguin, 1970); and C. Tudge, *The Famine Business* (New York: Penguin, 1977).

74. For a historical review of market development as a food aid policy objective, see M. B. Wallerstein, *Food for War—Food for Peace: United States Food Aid in a Global Context* (Cambridge, Mass.: MIT Press, 1980); and J. Cathie, *The Political Economy of Food Aid* (Aldershot: Gower, 1982).

75. See Mellor, "Food, Employment and Growth Interactions"; and P. A. Yotopoulos, *Middle Income Classes and Food Crisis: The Food-Feed Competition,* Food Research Institute Discussion Paper no. 3 (Palo Alto, Calif.: Stanford University, 1983).

76. See B. Harris, "Appraisal of Rice Processing Projects in Bangladesh," *Bangladesh Journal of Agricultural Economics* 1, no. 2 (1978); and *Bangladesh: Selected Issues in Rural Employment* (Washington, D.C.: World Bank, March 1983).

77. Blue, *PL 480 Title I*; and Alderman, *Egypt's Food Subsidy.*

78. C. P. Timmer, "Choice of Technique in Rice Milling in Java," *Bulletin of Indonesian Economic Studies* 9, no. 2:57–76.

79. See T. Johnson et al., *The Impact of PL 480 Title I in Peru: Food Aid as an Effective Development Resource,* Projects Impact Evaluation no. 47 (Washington, D.C.: AID March 1983).

80. The limited responsiveness of domestic food supply to prices in many African countries is attributable in part to the lack of infrastructure and consequently poor integration of markets. See C. Christensen et al., *Food Problems and Prospects in Sub-Saharan Africa,* Foreign Agricultural Research Report no. 166 (Washington, D.C.: USDA, 1981); and C. Christensen and L. Witucki, "Food Problems and Emerging Policy Responses in Sub-Saharan Africa," *American Journal of Agricultural Economics* 64, no. 5 (December 1982).

81. See, for example, Zimbabwe Maize Train Operations: An Information Note (Rome: WFP, October 7, 1981). Also see Chambers, *Poverty.*

82. Dunlop, *A Comparative Analysis.*

83. Ibid.; ADC, *Implementation, The Developmental Effectiveness of Food Aid*; WFP/Government of the Netherlands, "Report of the Netherlands Seminar on Food

Aid" (The Hague, October 3–5, 1983); Maxwell, *An Evaluation of the EEC*; and World Food Council, *The World Food and Hunger Problem: Changing Perspective and Possibilities: 1974–84* (draft) (Rome: World Food Council, 1983).

84. Wallerstein, *Food For War*.

85. See R. F. Hopkins, "What More Can You Say About Food Aid?" *Food Policy* 8, no. 3 (1983); and Schuh, "Food Aid as a Component."

86. J. H. Parotte, "The Food Aid Convention: Its History and Scope," *IDS Bulletin* 14, no. 2 (1983).

87. Clay, *Review of Food Aid*; and Huddleston, *Closing the Cereals Gap*.

88. Food aid as officially defined by the DAC as part of official development assistance involves commodity assistance with concessionality of at least 25 percent, the programming of aid in relation to explicit developmental or humanitarian objectives, and the involvement of official channels.

89. Schuh, "Food Aid as a Component"; and Clay, *Food Aid and Development*.

90. J. M. Garzon, "Food Aid as a Tool of Development: The Experience of PL 480, Title III," *Food Policy* 9, no. 3 (1984).

91. AID, *Background Paper and Guide to Addressing Bellmon Amendment Concerns on Potential Food Aid Disincentives and Storage* (Washington, D.C.: Office of Food for Peace, 1985).

92. See Chapter 6 of this volume.

93. Clay, *Review of Food Aid*.

94. For example, the Title I evaluations undertaken in 1981/82 focused almost exclusively on cereals, and so Dunlop, *A Comparative Analysis,* has little to say on vegetable oil credits.

95. For a general theoretical framework on the costs of tied food aid, see Abbott, "The Welfare Costs." The issue of cost-effective resource transfers for EEC dairy aid is explored in E. J. Clay and M. Mitchell, "Is European Community Food Aid in Dairy Products Cost-Effective?" *European Review of Agricultural Economics* 10, no. 2 (1983). Also see National Science Foundation, *Nutritional Analysis of Public Law 480 Title II Commodities* (Washington, D.C.: National Academy Press, 1982); and Reutlinger, *The Nutritional Impact*.

96. J. W. Mellor, *The New Economics of Growth: A Strategy for India and the Developing World* (Ithaca, N.Y.: Cornell University Press, 1976).

97. Cathie, *Political Economy*.

98. See Clay, *Food Aid and Development*; and Maxwell, *An Evaluation of the EEC*.

99. See Chapter 2 in this volume.

100. Clay, "Is European Community Food Aid Cost Effective?"; and Maxwell, *An Evaluation of the EEC*.

101. European Communities Commission, "Food Aid for Development," COM (83) 141 final (Brussels: EEC, April 6, 1983).

102. Clay, "Is European Community Food Aid Cost Effective?"; and A. Mathews, "EC Food Stocks and African Hunger" (Paper prepared for the Irish Council of European Movement Seminar, Dublin, March 21, 1986), provide empirical substance for the theoretical argument of Abbot, "The Welfare Costs."

103. See Chapter 1 in this volume.

104. E. J. Clay, "Food Aid Forecasting: The Literature on Needs and Requirements," *Food Policy* 11, no. 1 (1986).

105. M. D. Bale and R. C. Duncan, "Food Prospects in the Developing Countries: A Qualified Optimistic View," *American Economic Review* 73, no. 2 (1983).

106. FAO, *Agriculture Towards 2000.*

107. G. Fox and V. W. Rultan, "A Guide to LDC Food Balance Projections," *European Review of Agricultural Economics* 10, no. 4 (1984).

Commentary

Daniel E. Shaughnessy

International food aid exists because donors have more food than they require for domestic consumption and commercial sale. Food aid is not motivated primarily by a burning desire to use food for economic development purposes. Donor countries do favor the general use of food aid for humanitarian purposes, but this desire may not be enough to sustain large, continued flows of food aid given the cyclical nature of supply, the changing needs for outright famine relief, and the on again, off again, attendant fluctuations in public interest.

Further, it is no accident that food aid (certainly in the United States) is an outgrowth of domestic farm and agricultural policies. Nor is it an accident that the PL-480 legislation is part of the U.S. farm bill; and it is not surprising that the financial control of PL-480 resides with the Commodity Credit Corporation (CCC). Although the Agency for International Development has authority for certain activities in the area of food aid, the ultimate responsibility for reporting to and dealing with Congress on PL-480 appropriations resides with the U.S. Department of Agriculture. Consequently, U.S. domestic farm, agricultural, and trade issues, together with related foreign policy concerns, often overshadow the debate about the developmental or humanitarian impact of food aid.

For the most part then, the U.S. food aid program is an outgrowth of domestic agricultural policies; this always has been the case in the thirty-plus year history of PL-480, and there is no indication that this situation will change. Although there have been different emphases on PL-480 during the years, which ranged from disposing surplus to meeting political, foreign policy, or humanitarian objectives, the fact remains that PL-480 exists because domestic agricultural policies assure a large supply of food. Given this underlying rationale for the existence of a food aid program, those interested in the application of food aid for developmental and humanitarian purposes must remember the genesis of political and financial support that sustains the supply of commodities for food aid purposes.

It is in this context that I wish to comment on Clay's chapter. I would like to note that I approach this effect as a "practitioner" of food aid. I do not attempt to add analytically to what is already a very thorough, excellent analysis. To begin, I would like briefly to reiterate some features of Clay's paper that struck me as particularly appropriate for this discussion.

Case Studies

In the effort to determine to what extent food aid has been and can be a significant resource for development and an important instrument of agricultural trade policy, the record of specific examples and case studies can lead to a variety of conclusions. Indeed, in his section entitled "Trade Case Studies," Clay notes that the debate on these issues, based upon a review of case studies, is "intrinsically indeterminate." That also has been my experience. Reviewing case studies can lead to whatever conclusion one wished to draw in the first place. Furthermore, it always is possible to find both favorable and unfavorable examples of food aid, such as those dealing with disincentives or those that may have helped to provide a stable supply of agricultural products at reasonable prices while other forms of development began.

Targeted Food Aid

Clay notes that the highest real income effect resulting from the transfer of resources to final recipients can be achieved most readily by targeting distributed food directly to the poorest households. It has been my experience that the only way to really assure the desired effects of food aid is through targeted food aid activities. In the case of the United States this almost always involves targeted project activities under PL-480's Title II program, either through U.S. voluntary agencies or the World Food Program. In short, the only way to be absolutely sure of achieving the desired effects is through extremely close management and supervision, and this usually can be done only in project food aid and on a relatively small-scale basis.

Changing Patterns of Food Aid

There is a changing pattern in both food aid flows and in the nature of recipients of food aid. As Clay accurately points out, the large food aid transfers to Asia that characterized prior years are no longer the norm. Now the trend is moving decidedly in the direction of both concessional and project aid to Africa. The nature of these food aid recipients, the conditions attached to such aid, and the potential involvement of such countries in further agricultural trade activities all provide evidence of a changing scene that has major implications for donors and recipients alike.

Agricultural Marketing

Clay notes that government interventions in domestic agricultural markets are pervasive, with or without food aid. This is certainly the case in both developed and developing countries. Certainly, the experience in the United States of attempts at government intervention into agricultural marketing and farm programs is a mixed record at best. In the case of developing countries, including those with aspirations of involvement in agricultural trade, the potential involvement of government is almost a certainty. For donors, having some influence on that involvement becomes a major objective.

Effects of Food Aid

On the continuing debate regarding disincentives and other effects (both positive and negative) of food aid, Clay's statement that "the overall impact of food aid is a priori indeterminate" needs no elaboration. Obviously, food aid exists because resources are available. Just as obviously, what is done with those resources depends very much on donor management, recipient country policies, and actual implementation of programs and projects. Clay's case study review demonstrates this very clearly.

A Question of Perspective

Given the changing patterns of food aid, there is a real question about how important the debate about market intervention and disincentives really is. Clay correctly questions the extent to which the debate on disincentives and the macroeconomic growth implications of food aid is out of proportion to the current scale of transfers. Is it worth engaging in extended debate about the possible effects of a program whose levels may not be worth the effort? This is particularly true concerning countries where food aid flows are small, both in proportion to the donor program and in proportion to the recipient country's overall agricultural situation.

Food Aid and the Transition to Exports

As a prelude to commenting on the relationships between agricultural trade and food aid, I note here that I agree with Clay's assertion that "systems that are well geared to handle imports, and even the marketing and processing of domestically produced food, typically do not readily allow exports." Consequently, the transition from food aid participation to commercial trading and marketing can be a difficult one for a country that has been a basic importer of agricultural products, even when that country's agricultural economy is developing to the point where exports are possible.

It is in the section dealing with trade that Clay clearly articulates several issues that are of particular importance. First, he correctly raises the question, Why give much attention to food aid in a discussion of agricultural trade policy? As he notes, there have been a number of legislative and regulatory changes that have led commentators and analysts to suggest that food aid is now increasingly a resource for humanitarian, developmental, and foreign policy activities. With declining flows of food aid from the United States these changes have diminished perhaps the role of food aid in agricultural trade policy.

Nevertheless, in the current context food aid can still be regarded as an important component of agricultural trade policy. Consider the following:

1. Although overall levels of PL-480 are no longer as high as they were in the 1960s, PL-480 still represents a major avenue for agricultural export and trade in certain commodities. Indeed, worldwide commercial market conditions for U.S. wheat flour, soybean oil, and rice may make PL-480 or other government export programs "the only game in town."

2. For the shipping industry, carrying food aid cargoes has become a priority objective. In the liner trades, the World Food Program is the largest single originator of liner parcel in the world. In the United States, PL-480 and Section 416 cargoes are so attractive that they will soon be subject to a 75 percent U.S. flag preference. In many cases, PL-480 cargoes are the only realistic sources of revenue for large U.S. bulk carriers.

3. For inland transportation interests such as railroads, port authorities, and elevator operators, handling food aid is a much sought after activity. Labor wage concessions, reduced terminal rates, lower stevedoring, reduced intermodal transport, and lower port costs all are characteristic of efforts employed to attract such business.

4. Provisions in the 1985 farm legislation demonstrate a clear intention on the part of the U.S. Congress to use U.S. agricultural supplies to enhance exports. PL-480 and Section 416 certainly play a role in any such action.

Even with these strong domestic export interests in place, PL-480 continues to be subject to other political initiatives. For example, in the summer 1985, PL-480 funding obligations were deliberately halted in order to "save" money for expenditures associated with the Central American "contra" aid package.

In view then of conflicting or competing food aid objectives, policies, and practices, where does the subject of this volume—U.S. agriculture and Third World development—fit in the context of the recipients of such aid? For guidance, I return to a section in Clay's chapter in which he reviews PL-480 and agricultural exports in the 1980s. Here he notes that weak market conditions brought about the establishment of the U.S. 4 million ton wheat reserve. He goes on to say that "it is precisely in a weaker market that conditions favor such forward-looking measures."

I agree, and certainly we are now experiencing "weak market conditions." But can this situation help bring about the assurances that are needed to reconcile donor export interests with recipient developmental concerns? I think not, at least not in any conclusive manner.

Is it really possible to control the "assertion of narrow interests over developmental and humanitarian concerns" in the administration of "an aid resource that requires flexibility and sensitivity on the donor side?"

part four

Policy Prescriptions

chapter eight

U.S. Agriculture and the Developing World: Partners or Competitors?

Robert L. Paarlberg

Agricultural development in the developing countries is sometimes described as a menace to U.S. agriculture. According to this view, every additional bushel of farm production in the Third World represents one less bushel of farm sales potential for the United States. A recent surge of farm production in poor countries, some believe, has been a major cause of the recent slump in U.S. farm trade.

The chapters in this volume have challenged some of these common assumptions. An even more direct challenge is made here. I review evidence that indicates that additional farm production in developing countries has not been an important contributor to the recent slump in U.S. farm trade. With the proper policies in place, in fact, additional farm production in developing countries actually can benefit U.S. farm trade. U.S. and Third World farmers ought not to view one another only as competitors. Under properly managed circumstances they often can operate as partners.

The Possibility of Partnership

The possibility of a partnership between U.S. and Third World farmers rests on the unique contribution farm production can make in poor countries to broad-based income growth and hence to dietary improvements and enlarged food consumption demands. Among wealthy, developed countries, to be sure, additional farm production may not make this contribution. In regions where citizens already are wealthy and where diets already are rich—such as the European Economic Community (EEC)—additional farm production is not likely to add much to broad-based income growth or to internal food consumption demands. Additional farm production in such regions more likely will replace trade or enter export markets. U.S. farm operators therefore have every reason to feel threatened by production subsidies in other rich, farming countries.

But an entirely different response to added farm production occurs among today's developing countries, where large numbers of poor people with poor diets are dependent directly upon farming for income and employment. In such countries, where most of the income gained from farm growth will go directly into additional food consumption, the paradoxical result of successful farm development can be larger farm import demands.

The process of rapid wealth creation cannot get underway in most poor countries without farm development. Successful farm development helps create a pool of savings. It stimulates effective consumption demands, and it releases a competent labor force needed to launch efficient urban industrial growth. Efficient industrial growth, in turn, pushes personal income still higher and turns loose still larger food consumption demands. These demands usually include a taste for diets that are rich in higher quality foodgrains and in animal products such as meat, milk, and eggs. Even for agriculturally successful developing countries, some of the agricultural inputs needed to satisfy these enriched dietary demands will be cheaper to purchase from abroad than to produce at home. Animal feedstuffs, in particular, often will be imported in ever larger volume in response to income growth originally turned loose in developing countries by farm sector prosperity. U.S. agriculture, which is the world's most efficient producer and largest exporter of high-quality foodgrains and animal feedstuffs, obviously is well positioned to prosper from such larger import demands.

Evidence of a Partnership

Can this sort of harmonious relationship between rapid farm development in the Third World and U.S. farm trade actually come into existence? The evidence that it can rests on the well-established fact that high-income developing countries do import more farm products than low-income developing countries. Note from Table 8.1 that the low-income developing countries (where Gross National Product per capita is less than $400) took only 11.4 million tons, or just 15 percent, of all free world developing country grain imports in 1982, despite the fact that most of the developing world's malnourished citizens live in these low-income countries. The upper-middle-income developing countries, because of their much greater purchasing power and despite their much smaller physical size, import almost three times as much.

Moreover, although low-income country grain imports grew by only 40 percent (from a small base) during the decade shown in Table 8.1, upper-middle-income countries increased their purchases by 102 percent, from a base one-half again as large. Imports of coarse grains increased among these more prosperous developing countries by roughly 300 percent, thus indicat-

Table 8.1 Grain Imports by the Developing Countries (million tons)

Country Grouping[a]	Imports in 1972/73 (July/June)				Imports in 1982/83 (July/June)				Increase 1972/73–1982/83
	Wheat	Coarse Grains	Rice	Total	Wheat	Coarse Grains	Rice	Total	Total Grains
Developing Countries[b]									
Low income	6.1	1.1	1.0	8.2	8.7	0.8	2.0	11.4	+40%
Lower-middle income	7.1	1.4	2.2	10.8	17.2	5.1	2.5	24.8	+130%
Upper-middle income	9.4	5.1	1.6	16.2	12.5	19.0	1.3	32.8	+102%
High-income oil exporters	0.7	0.2	0.4	1.3	1.7	2.6	0.8	5.2	+289%
Centrally planned LDCs	7.1	1.1	0.2	8.4	14.8	3.3	0.4	18.6	+121%
Total developing countries	30.4	8.9	5.4	44.9	54.9	30.8	7.0	92.8	+107%
Total world trade	67.6	57.8	8.0	133.4	96.1	86.4	11.8	194.3	+46%
Developing country share (%)	45	16	68	34	57	36	60	48	

Source: International Wheat Council (data).

[a]On the basis of 1982 income (GNP per capita) the groupings are as follows: low-income, less than $400; lower-middle income, $400–1,650; upper-middle income, more than $1,650. The high-income oil exporters were greater than $6,000. Centrally planned developing countries have not been included in these groupings and are shown separately.

[b]Figures include centrally planned developing countries (China, Mongolia, Vietnam, North Korea, and Cuba).

ing that a significant increase in animal feeding, driven by dietary diversification, was well underway. Among the low-income countries, coarse grain imports were not only low but actually in decline.

U.S. farm exporters, especially coarse grain exporters, therefore have an unmistakable interest in promoting income growth in the developing world. It is not the hunger of poor countries, or even their growing populations, that makes them better customers for U.S. farm producers. It is the purchasing power that comes from their growing wealth.

But what evidence is there that farm production contributes to this broad-based income growth that stimulates farm imports in developing countries? What evidence is there that farm production in developing countries and farm imports can increase simultaneously? Several recently completed studies have reached precisely these conclusions.

The first of these was a study done in 1979 for the International Food Policy Research Institute by Kenneth Bachman and Leonardo Paulino that examined the trade consequences of rapid food production growth in sixteen developing countries; Bachman and Paulino found that although the proportion of domestic food consumption satisfied by imports generally fell in these countries, net imports of staple foods nonetheless increased, to the presumed benefit of U.S. agriculture. The authors also found that annual net staple food imports in these agriculturally successful developing countries actually rose in volume by 133 percent between 1961–1965 and 1974–1976.[1]

In a second, more recent study by John Lee and Mathew Shane at the U.S. Department of Agriculture, similar results were found in two specific developing countries that are presumed by many U.S. agriculturalists to be among their most threatening competitors—Malaysia and Brazil. Lee and Shane found that both countries, despite rapid agricultural development between 1967 and 1983, increased farm imports along with farm exports. On a wheat equivalent basis, Malaysia's imports of food, feedgrains, and oilseeds (primarily U.S. soybeans) increased from 1 million tons to almost 2.4 million tons during this period. Brazil showed a similar pattern. In spite of Brazil's noteworthy success in boosting farm production and farm exports, it became a significant agricultural importer of grains. Lee and Shane concluded that "contrary to what seems to follow from common sense reasoning, economic development in the developing countries along comparative advantage lines is not competitive with [U.S.] export interests, but generally complementary to it."[2]

A 1985 study by Earl Kellogg of the Consortium for International Development in Arizona reached similar conclusions. This study examined per capita changes in agricultural imports in eighteen significant developing countries (out of ninety-two) that exhibited the most rapid growth in per capita food production during the period 1970–1980; the study compared these changes to those in thirteen countries that exhibited the least rapid food production growth. The data revealed that this first category of agriculturally successful developing countries increased its dollar value of per capita agricultural imports by 47 percent, compared to only a 37 percent increase among the second group of agriculturally unsuccessful countries. In other words, food imports went up faster when poor country farmers were doing well and making money than when they were doing poorly and losing money.

This same study also specifically compared the trade patterns of two agriculturally successful developing countries (Brazil and Korea) to those of a much less successful counterpart (Sierra Leone). It found that in the former case the volume of U.S. farm sales to Brazil and to Korea increased by an average of 8.7 percent and 6.7 percent per year respectively between 1970 and 1983; the volume of U.S. farm sales to Sierra Leone actually decreased at a 2.5 percent annual rate. Kellogg concluded that "in the intermediate term increases in agricultural production in developing countries do not have a negative impact on aggregate U.S. agricultural exports to these countries."[3]

Another 1985 study by Richard Kodl at the University of Illinois amplified Kellogg's findings. Using a regression analysis with time series and cross-sectional data on seventy-seven developing countries, Kodl found no significant negative correlation between per capita agricultural production in developing countries and their per capita imports of agricultural products. In six of thirteen equations, in fact, he found a significant positive correlation. Kodl's examination of Kellogg's same specific country cases further confirmed the aggregate tendency for farm growth in poor countries to stimulate food import growth.[4]

Further evidence to support this same conclusion also is found in a 1986 research note produced by James P. Houck at the University of Minnesota. Using a forty-four-nation sample and 1983 data, Houck found a relatively close association between agricultural productivity, per capita Gross Domestic Product (GDP), and per capita cereal imports. He concluded that "the burden of proof clearly rests with those who argue that agricultural assistance for low-income nations is usually a trade-stifling undertaking."[5]

These findings should not be taken to mean that in every individual case rapid farm growth in developing countries will produce an immediate gain for U.S. farm exports. We know that in some recent cases, for example India and China, record farm production gains have been accompanied by a decline rather than an increase in farm imports. We also know that in some other developing countries, for example Egypt, farm imports have grown rapidly in part because local farm production has not. In some oil-exporting developing countries—especially those that enjoyed windfall foreign exchange earnings during the 1970s—a sudden growth of farm imports was registered for reasons essentially unconnected to local farm production trends.

Even if these studies confirm that U.S. farmers and farmers in poor countries can prosper side by side, the studies do not demonstrate specifically that farm production gains in poor countries are the original cause of these joint gains. In some instances, successful industrial development may have come first, with agricultural production gains following rather than leading the all important step of income growth and dietary diversification.[6] If so, it will be the growth of income but not necessarily the prior growth of farm production that will bring gains to U.S. farm exporters.

In the complex world of development, many different paths can lead to the same outcome; the same path, when pursued by different countries in different circumstances, sometimes can lead to divergent outcomes. Those policymakers and development planners who want to find a path that consistently links developing country farm development to U.S. farm trade expansion therefore must be wary of generalizations. There is plenty of evidence to suggest that such linkages already have been widely formed. But it is essential to recognize the significant variety of cases in which mutual gains for U.S. farmers and Third World farmers have not been achieved; it also is essential to elaborate the reasons joint gains were not achieved, as a prelude to adopting suitable policy correctives.

Where a Partnership Does Not Exist

In several of the individual country cases examined in this volume, a satisfying link had not yet been formed between local farm development and U.S. farm export expansion. These cases instruct us in the many things that can prevent joint gains between U.S. and Third World country farm operators from being fully realized.

We notice immediately, in the case of China, that farm imports from the United States have fallen during the most recent period of remarkable local production gains (see Chapter 4). Since 1978, the value of farm production in China has risen by 50 percent, a rise due in large measure to price and incentive reforms. The result lately has been fewer Chinese purchases of U.S. wheat and a total halt to Chinese purchases of U.S. corn. In fact, by 1985 China was exporting corn, thus displacing U.S. sales in a variety of third country markets including Japan, South Korea, and the Soviet Union.

Farm production growth in China did lead, as expected, to rapid per capita income gains, but these gains did not result in the expected increase in demand for imported food and feedstuffs. This lack of increase was due, in part, to the fact that most of these income gains were registered in rural areas where local supplies were abundant and larger consumption demands were accommodated badly by the poorly integrated Chinese marketing system and by the slow-moving Chinese bureaucracy. If Chinese development planners can improve these markets and relax these internal controls and constraints, a significant upgrading of the still poor Chinese diet—to include more animal product consumption—could yet lead to larger farm import demands.

A highly conservative attitude inside the Chinese government toward the expenditure of foreign exchange, an attitude that was only temporarily relaxed between 1978 and 1984, also is standing in the path of larger Chinese farm imports. In order to repair a sagging overall trade balance the Chinese government has curtailed imports, including food imports, in recent years. China's internal farm production gains have not always been the decisive factor. For example, Chinese corn production fell by 13 percent in 1985; by 1986, noticeable feedgrain shortages had emerged in the southern part of China, but corn exports nonetheless were continued, no doubt for reasons linked to overall trade strategy. Until China becomes capable of earning more foreign exchange with exports and more comfortable using imports to boost consumption, it may not be joining the smaller states of East Asia as a permanently rewarding market for U.S. feedgrain exports.

India often is mentioned alongside China as a developing country that has recently stopped importing food because of internal farm production gains and instead has begun exporting. In fact, India's recent emergence as a small net exporter of wheat is not so unusual. India was also a net exporter of wheat in 1978–1980 and even for a brief time in 1972.[7] India did import large quantities of U.S. wheat in the 1960s, but in the form of food aid on concessional rather than commercial terms. India is exporting wheat today not because its internal food needs have all been met, but because low income within India restricts the purchasing power of the population. Because of this lack of effective internal demand, even small, localized production gains can result in commercial surpluses and a need to export. If India's several hundred million desperately poor, chronically undernourished citizens should ever gain the income needed to express their unsatisfied food demands, India's current trade posture in international foodgrain markets could be transformed quickly.

U.S. farm exporters also have had reason to be disappointed with the development of marketing opportunities in the Philippines because of the failure of sustained farm sector growth and rapid income growth to develop in the first instance. As noted in Chapter 5 by Clarete and Roumasset, rapid farm productivity gains elsewhere in Southeast Asia (a 35 percent increase since the mid-1970s) have helped bring to those countries rapid income growth and an equally rapid growth in consumption of meat and dairy products. This growth has resulted in increased imports of both livestock and feed products and increased business for U.S. farm exporters. But the Philippines "dropped out of the pack" of rapidly developing Association of Southeast Asian Nations (ASEAN) economies at least a decade ago, and so that country has not been able to offer U.S. agriculture comparable market opportunities. This disappointing growth performance is attributed largely to an inward-looking, import-substitution development strategy and to the rent-seeking policy stance (especially toward agriculture) embraced since 1949 by a succession of increasingly ineffective, sometimes corrupt, political leaders.

Valdés explains that similar difficulties have been encountered in many of the states of Latin America (see Chapter 3). Official policies biased to protect relatively inefficient urban industries and to serve politically powerful organized urban consumer interests have retarded farm sector development in Latin America. Joint gains between U.S. and Latin farmers also have been blocked because agriculture in Latin America has been oriented more toward earning foreign exchange through exports and less toward producing domestic employment and income growth. From nations such as Argentina and Brazil, for example, U.S. farm operators often encounter stiff competition in international farm markets. The Latin farm sector also is less likely to generate broad-based income and hence larger farm imports because Latin American peasants are smaller in relative numbers than in Asia, they are less secure in their access to land, and in most instances they lack the political power to ensure that income from farming will be shared widely. Also, the greater availability of underutilized land resources in Latin America has encouraged a pattern of livestock production based more on the expansion of pasture area and less on the use of imported feedstuffs.

For all these reasons, rapid farm production gains in Latin America will less often stimulate an immediate demand for larger farm imports. In Mexico, for example, the extended period of rapid farm production gains (especially in wheat and corn) that began during World War II and lasted through the mid-1960s only lessened Mexico's need to import food. Mexico's grain purchases from the United States were later revived during the 1970s, but these purchases were not really made in response to income or foreign exchange gains generated from farm production. By the 1970s, Mexico was earning foreign exchange from oil, and its farm sector (especially its grain sector) was no longer experiencing rapid growth. In fact, the restoration of swift farm sector growth, which briefly came thanks to good weather and heavy production subsidies after 1980, only reduced Mexico's need to import from the United States.[8]

In their chapter on Kenya and Tanzania, Christensen, Lofchie, and Witucki provide another example of an unsatisfying linkage between farm sector development in the Third World and farm export opportunities for developed countries (see Chapter 2). Kenya and Tanzania have embraced radically different development policies. Kenya has pursued a less-regulated, more trade-dependent strategy that favors the production of cash crops for export; and Tanzania has promulgated a highly regulated, highly insular strategy (which has done little, despite abundant land resources, to boost either domestic cash crop or food crop farm production). But neither country has yet reached the level of income or has gained the international purchasing power necessary to emerge as a significant, dependable commercial farm market for the United States. Kenya periodically imports maize, but primarily in response to cycles of drought rather than in response to any farm income–driven pattern of advanced dietary diversification. Some foresee that Kenya might emerge as a more regular cereal importer in the future, which probably results from the country's inability to keep up with the basic food requirements of such a rapidly growing population. Tanzania's food imports, most of which are arranged on a concessional basis, already have this disappointing quality.

Thus, even the briefest review of individual country cases reveals that not every developing country is on its way to farm sector prosperity and not every agriculturally prosperous developing country automatically becomes a better customer for U.S. farm exports. Opportunities may exist for Third World country farmers and U.S. farm exporters to prosper side by side, but in many instances and for many reasons those opportunities are going to waste. What policy steps, then, might be taken by the United States to recover some of these wasted opportunities?

Policies to Promote Partnership

Our prescriptive efforts might begin with a critical review of some recent U.S. farm trade policies that have *not* been making a positive contribution toward harmonious farm relations between the United States and the Third World. Most of the trade interventions used by the United States either to push surplus farm production into developing country markets or to keep developing country farm production out of the U.S. market must fall into this category.

Farm export credits, export credit guarantees, and export subsidies (including the $1 billion worth of payment-in-kind export subsidies that are being offered now under the 1985 Export Enhancement Program) are an expensive proposition for U.S. taxpayers. These interventions also can be harmful to long-term development prospects in targeted developing countries where farm prices may fall and where urban-biased governments may be tempted to use their access to these subsidized food imports as an excuse to postpone the adoption of growth-producing and income-generating farm development policies. If the politically vocal urban minority can be fed through subsidized imports, then it remains politically justifiable for these governments to continue ignoring the long-run farm development interests of the rural majority. Such a stance, however, is economically unjust and further postpones the broad-based income growth so important to long-term farm trade expansion.

Fortunately, the restraint of lavish farm export subsidy policies need not work any great hardship on U.S. agriculture because experience has shown that U.S. subsidies only tend to be nullified by the offsetting subsidies of other rich export competitors such as the EEC. These competitors usually can afford the budget cost of staying ahead in an export subsidy competition with a smaller total volume of foreign sales to defend.[9] Export credits and export subsidies therefore do little more than cheapen the cost of farm trade for importers and shift trade into less-efficient patterns. These interventions do give the farm state politicians who clamor for these subsidies an opportunity to claim that they are "doing something" in response to a farm trade crisis, but export credits and subsidies are neither a proven nor a cost-effective means of expanding U.S. exports. The unprecedented export gains of the mid-1970s, we should remember, were accomplished despite a momentary suspension of all U.S. farm export subsidies.

Food Aid Programs

As Clay notes in Chapter 7 on the subject, some U.S. food aid programs also have been poorly suited to building a partnership between U.S. agriculture and farm development in the Third World. Food aid is not always harmful to Third World farm development, as evidenced by the spectacular farm success of a number of former food aid recipients, such as South Korea and Taiwan. In theory, the public distribution of additional program food assistance even could provide the opportunity for developing country governments to offer higher farm prices to rural producers without raising prices for consumers while directing added budget and foreign exchange savings toward rural farm sector development. But program food aid (especially when sold directly into local market channels) also can provide leeway for recipient governments to do just the opposite—that is, to hold in place policies heavily biased against farm production, the very policies that probably made food aid necessary in the first place. Recipient country governments that have decided to launch politically difficult internal farm policy reforms can use program food aid to advantage, but so can governments that are looking for ways to avoid or postpone reforms.

At the donor end, program food aid usually is given because it is a means to dispose of surplus production. For this reason U.S. food aid tends to increase when it is least needed, when international markets are saturated, and tends to be cut back when international farm markets grow tight. The individual country distribution of U.S. program food aid also makes clear its frequently nondevelopmental motivation. Egypt—neither the poorest nor the hungriest of all African countries, but an important U.S. diplomatic client—has recently received more than one-third of all PL-480 Title I assistance. Farm development within Egypt is one stated purpose of this aid, but the Egyptian government prefers instead to use this free food to service the short-term needs of consumers while taking a "worry later" attitude toward its own lagging farm sector.

U.S. food aid is more likely to serve the needs of poor people in poor countries either when given through carefully targeted feeding projects or when made available as short-term emergency famine relief. In war-torn, drought-stricken Africa today (as in India in the mid-1960s, when large quantities of U.S. food aid helped the Indian government survive two bad monsoons and carry through with important domestic farm policy reforms), emergency food assistance programs that start and stop promptly can save lives without disrupting long-term farm development. This urgent function is by itself an adequate reason for the United States to maintain and improve its capacity to provide project food assistance and short-term famine relief.

U.S. Farm Import Policies

One U.S. farm trade practice that places an unambiguous burden on farm development in the Third World is the exclusion of efficiently produced developing country farm products from the U.S. market. Developing country sugar production, for example, is now admitted into the U.S. market under an ever tightening schedule of quotas. As a result of a new "no cost" provision (no cost to U.S. taxpayers) in the 1985 farm bill, this blatant device for protecting the relatively inefficient but politically powerful U.S. domestic sugar industry now will require that sugar imports from tropical countries be reduced, beginning in 1986/87, by perhaps an additional 600,000 short tons, or by roughly one-third.[10] Such quantitative farm import restrictions impose high costs on both U.S. consumers and on efficient farm producers and farm exporters in the developing world.[11]

Developing Country Domestic Policies

It would be an error, however, to explain lagging farm development in developing countries exclusively or even primarily by reference to U.S. farm trade policy constraints. On the one hand, U.S. farm trade policies usually have been much less protective and therefore much less damaging toward developing country farm development than those of other industrial countries, such as Japan or the EEC. On the other hand, the farm policy shortcomings of all the industrial countries put together probably are doing less damage to developing country farm development today than are some of the farm policies embraced by the developing countries themselves.

Particularly when dealing with developing country agriculture, there is a limit to what can be done, either good or bad, from the outside. The food and farm policies poor countries select for themselves often make the greatest difference, and until now most of those policies have not favored agriculture. If rapid farm development is ever to take place and to play its desired role in the stimulation of broad-based income growth, then political leaders and development planners within those developing countries will have to embrace agricultural pricing policies, land tenure policies, tax policies, public investment policies, credit policies, and exchange rate policies that are not so heavily biased against the interests of the majority of poor people living in the countryside.

Until developing countries abandon the practice of overtaxing their own weak farm sectors in search of revenues to sustain inefficient, inequitable urban consumption and inefficient industrial development patterns, there will be a limit to what these countries can gain from any farm trade policy changes initiated by the United States. These necessary internal policy adjustments will run against the grain of political convenience and ideological preference in most developing countries, so the embrace of such policies will be problematic from the start.

U.S. efforts to induce these changes from the outside will be more problematic. Such efforts at times have been successful in the past, most conspicuously in countries such as Taiwan and South Korea (after World War II and during the 1950s) when both countries embraced a sweeping land reform, invested in agriculture, eventually abandoned inward-looking, import-substitution development strategies, and devalued their currencies, all at least partly in response to advice and assistance from the United States. As a result, Taiwan and South Korea today are among the wealthiest developing countries as well as the most agriculturally successful. Both are also the best commercial customers in the developing world for U.S. farm exports.

But in other countries and under other conditions, U.S. officials may not be in a position to play such a decisive role. Inducement worked in South Korea and Taiwan because U.S. security interests were high enough to make unprecedented levels of per capita assistance seem affordable and because South Korea and Taiwanese security fears were also high enough to inspire unusual deference toward the United States. A variety of unique, unrelated internal political circumstances within South Korea and Taiwan added still more to the likelihood of success. In most developing countries today these preconditions for successful outside inducement are not to be found, and where they are absent, efforts at outside inducement can backfire.[12]

Efforts by the United States today to induce food policy changes within developing countries through the manipulation of today's much less generous development assistance programs are by no means certain of producing the intended result. The efforts of the Reagan administration to induce greater Third World reliance on the "private sector" are not only likely to be enfeebled by unprecedented aid budget cutbacks; these privatizing efforts, if they become singleminded, may not always be appropriate in any case. Well-designed *public* sector interventions, we should remember, played a key role in the original development success enjoyed by South Korea and Taiwan.[13] Once again, there is the sad tendency for all bilateral economic aid programs to be captured, sooner or later, by administrators who do not have developmental purposes uppermost in mind. In 1986, roughly one-half the entire U.S. foreign assistance budget went to just two not so poor countries, Israel and Egypt, and most of the rest went to a handful of other favored diplomatic clients and allies (Turkey, Pakistan, El Salvador, Greece, Spain, Philippines, Portugal, and Honduras). The hypothetical contribution that well-funded, well-constructed U.S. bilateral assistance policies might be able to make toward the inducement of farm development in the Third World probably is destined to remain largely hypothetical.

This politicization of development aid could be avoided if more assistance were channeled through neutral multilateral agencies, such as the International Development Association (IDA) of the World Bank. Unfortunately, congressional and administration support for multilateral development lending recently has been weakening. Largely because of cutbacks initiated by the Reagan administration, worldwide IDA contributions have fallen from $12 billion for IDA-6 (1981–1983) to only $9 billion for IDA-7 (1984–1986). Congressional misgivings about multilateral farm development lending in particular now have led to a legislative proposal that would oblige the U.S. government to withhold its support from all loans to poor countries that might bring increased competition for U.S. farm operators without thought to the income-generating potential of those loans.[14]

Beyond Farm Policy Change

Fortunately, narrowly defined farm policy changes are not the only means available to improve agricultural trade relations between the United States and the developing world. Agricultural trade does not only respond to the changing levels of farm production, the changing levels of income that might be driven by farm production, or the changing character of farm trade interventions by rich and poor country governments. Agricultural trade patterns also are responsive to powerful economic forces from beyond the farm sector. It is in this wider economic environment that a second category of policy remedies must be examined.

Observers often have failed to appreciate the decisive impact of non-farm policy forces on international farm trade. When developing countries suddenly began importing more food during the 1970s (the value of less-developed country, or LDC, farm imports nearly quadrupled between 1972 and 1980), most casual observers looked for a farm sector explanation. They assumed the developing countries were experiencing a decade-long setback in their own farm production. A small decline in developing country per capita farm production was registered briefly in 1972, but the sudden surge in imports was influenced more heavily by rapid income growth in the Third World (6.2 percent real GNP growth among the developing countries in 1972 that increased to 7.4 percent in 1973), plus a variety of changes in the global lending environment brought on by abundant petrodollars and a loose U.S. monetary policy (resulting at times in negative real interest rates). As a result of these nonfarm sector changes, many middle-income developing countries were able to borrow heavily during the 1970s to purchase a record volume of imported consumer goods, including food.

Setbacks in developing country farm production were not a primary driving force behind this change. The United Nations Food and Agriculture Organization (FAO) volume index of agricultural production for all developing market economies increased at a respectable 3.0 percent annual rate during the 1970s. In fact, although developing countries were importing more farm products during this remarkable decade of increasing trade expansion, they also were producing and exporting more. During the so-called "food crisis" decade of the 1970s, the traditionally positive balance of developing country farm trade actually strengthened (see Chapter 1).

When these developing countries suddenly stopped increasing their purchases of imported farm products after 1981, some observers again tried to draw the erroneous conclusion that a farm sector turnaround must have brought about the change. It became fashionable to talk about a sudden explosion in developing country farm output. But the comparison by White and his colleagues in this volume of developing country per capita farm production trends in the 1970s and in the 1980s indicates there was no such turnaround. Judging from the FAO volume index of agricultural production for all the developing market economies, developing country farm production gains actually slowed a bit during the first half of the 1980s—gains increased at only a 2.9 percent annual rate compared to the 3.0 percent rate of the 1970s.

The Global Macroeconomic Environment
The constraint on developing country farm imports in the 1980s was not the result of sudden farming success in the Third World or of anything to do with farm or farm trade policy. What changed was the condition of the larger global economy and the macroeconomic environment in which farm trade must function. When the cost of Organization of Petroleum Exporting Countries (OPEC) oil redoubled in 1979, thereby simultaneously dampening growth opportunities and driving up prices, the new leadership at the U.S. Federal Reserve Board suddenly resolved to curb inflation with a more disciplined U.S. monetary policy. In part because U.S. fiscal policy remained essentially undisciplined, this monetary approach was able to bring inflation under control only at the price of deep world recession.

It was high interest rates and the world recession of 1981/82 that put an end to U.S. farm export expansion in the developing world—not a surge in developing country farm production. In fact, these same depressing macroeconomic conditions also put an end to developing country farm export expansion. Developing country farm exports actually fell faster than imports in 1981 and 1982, thus producing a brief, unusual net farm trade deficit for the Third World. Africa's total export earnings include a large agricultural component, and during the 1970s, earnings increased more than sevenfold, but they suddenly fell by more than one-third during the first half of the 1980s.

Food import demand in the developing countries eventually fell even more than did their exports after the final collapse of GNP growth rates. Rossmiller and Tutwiler (Chapter 6) show that annual GNP growth among the developing countries, which had averaged a strong 6 percent during the 1970s, fell to 1.4 percent in 1981, to 0.9 percent in 1982, and to a dismal 0.4 percent in 1983. GNP growth per capita was negative.

Even if GNP growth in the developing world had somehow been restored during this world recession, the sudden inability of the developing countries to earn foreign exchange (in part because of newly protectionist industrial country trade policies) would have reduced sharply their ability to import farm products. Export earnings are even more decisive than income growth in determining the level of developing country farm imports.[15]

Given that the developing countries were unable to earn additional foreign exchange through exports, unable to borrow additional foreign exchange from abroad because of high interest rates, and obliged to use most foreign exchange on hand to service past debts, they understandably reduced their food and farm imports after 1980. Because this newly adverse global economic environment also brought with it high dollar exchange rates and hence relatively uncompetitive U.S. farm export prices, this developing country import reduction was felt most strongly by U.S. farm exporters.

Even with all of these difficulties, however, the developing countries have continued to be good customers for U.S. farm exports in the 1980s. Compared to others, in fact, they have actually become better customers. The developing countries did reduce their purchases of U.S. farm products early in the 1980s, but less so than other foreign customers in the developed world and among the centrally planned economies, as Table 8.2 indicates.

What these figures demonstrate is that the 1980s U.S. farm export crisis would have been even worse if it were not for the relatively dependable U.S. customers in the developing world. Furthermore, the future prospect is that the developing world will continue to provide the only dependable source of farm market expansion for U.S. exporters. Long-term trends indicate an increasing developing country reliance on farm imports. Developing countries imported about 15 percent of their total wheat and coarse grain consumption in the early 1960s, roughly 20 percent in the mid-1970s, and about 25 percent by the 1980s.[16] Among industrial nations, such as those of the EEC, long-term self-sufficiency trends have been in the opposite direction.

Table 8.2   Developing Country Farm Imports (as percentage of total U.S. farm exports)

Year	Food Grain	Coarse Grain	Oilseed	Cotton
1980	55	29	15	42
1983	67	42	19	44

Source: White et al., in this volume.

The argument I wish to make here is that U.S. producers and exporters ought not to give up on farm market expansion in the developing world. Developing country markets have fallen short of expectations lately, but not because of any inevitable or irreversible long-term transformation of the world's food or farm economy. The problem has been a sudden change in the global macroeconomic environment, traceable largely to nonfarm policy decisions, including some that have been taken in the United States. What recently has been lost through a sudden change in the nonfarm policy environment can at least partially be regained, if and when macroeconomic conditions rebound.

Reviving Mutually Profitable U.S. Farm Trade Relations with Developing Countries

Unfortunately, it is not possible for the U.S. government by itself to reverse all the macroeconomic circumstances and policy changes that originally helped throw world farm trade into its continuing recession. Oil prices at last have declined, which ought to give the Federal Reserve Board more flexibility to expand the money supply so as to bring down interest rates and dollar exchange rates without immediately reigniting inflation. Falling interest rates in particular are a tonic, both to the heavily indebted developing countries that purchase U.S. farm products and even more directly to the heavily indebted U.S. farm operators who sell those products. Falling dollar exchange rates in time will help U.S. producers recover part of their earlier competitive position against rival exporters and thereby ensure that when farm trade expands U.S. producers again will enjoy a respectable share of the profit.

However, the inflationary bias in U.S. fiscal policy is still with us in the form of federal budget deficits still projected into the $200 billion range. Until some fiscal policy discipline is restored, there will be a limit to how much U.S. monetary policy can prudently be relaxed.

Pending greater fiscal policy discipline in the United States, there are still a number of important nonfarm policy steps that might be taken to help revive mutually profitable farm trade relations with the developing world. The first of these is to encourage a more growth-oriented pattern of debt rescheduling in the developing world, and the second is to avoid a lapse into full-scale industrial trade protection at home.

Until late 1985, U.S. policies toward debt rescheduling in the developing world were focused too heavily upon the supposed need to balance static accounts. If developing countries balanced their budgets and their foreign trade accounts—even if this meant zero growth and a termination of imports—they were deemed more worthy of new lending. The damage done by this attitude to growth prospects within poor countries and also to growth prospects for U.S. exporters was needlessly severe. Finally in the fall of 1985, at the annual meeting of the World Bank and the International Monetary Fund (IMF), U.S. Treasury Secretary James Baker presented what he called a Program for Sustained Growth that placed greater emphasis upon dynamic growth initiatives in the developing world as a basis for asking the commercial banks and the multilateral banks to provide more funds for rescheduling. A more recent plan put forward by Senator Bill Bradley would stress lower interest and principal payments on existing loans but also would require added World Bank and development bank lending. Either plan will mean difficult requests to Congress for more funds to support lending and assistance to developing countries through multilateral channels.

A second needed initiative, which is just as far beyond the traditional realm of farm policy, is a reversal of the trend in Congress toward highly protectionist industrial trade policies. In May 1986, by a vote of 295 to 115, the House of Representatives passed trade legislation that would require, as its central provision, an across-the-board reduction of imports from trading partners that maintain "excessive" trade surpluses with the United States. The countries that would be most damaged by this trade provision happen to be among the best overseas customers for U.S. farm exports, including the EEC, Japan, and Taiwan. Despite the problems the EEC causes for U.S. farmers, it still takes more U.S. farm exports ($6.5 billion worth of purchases yearly) than anyone else. Japan is second ($5.4 billion) and Taiwan seventh ($1.2 billion). The punitive provisions of this bill easily could provoke these customers into a retaliation against U.S. farm exporters. This most recent manufacturer trade policy threat to U.S. agriculture was opposed before the House Ways and Means Committee by nearly a dozen organized agricultural interest groups.[17] Influential farm organizations and related agroindustries now will have to work hard to block similar action in the Senate.

Conclusion

The work that comprises this volume suggests that there need not be a contradiction between the goal of promoting Third World farm development and the goal of promoting U.S. farm trade expansion. With the proper policies in place, these two goals can be successfully pursued side by side.

These proper policies, which already have been discussed at greater length, are listed in summary fashion in Figure 8.1.

The four sequential steps that logically link together developing country farm production and U.S. farm exports are listed across the top of the figure. Greater developing country farm production makes easier the stimulation of broad-based income growth and dietary enrichment. This, in turn, facilitates the expansion of developing country farm imports and thus of U.S. farm exports. The function of public policy should be to support each of these four steps simultaneously.

Note that the policies listed in column 1 in support of more farm production in developing countries imply some measure of official policy responsibility. But the more difficult, more essential actions listed in column 1, such as farm market deregulation and much larger public investments in the farm sector, can only be taken by policy officials in the developing world itself. When we look to column 2, where the purpose is to promote broad-based income growth and dietary diversification in poor countries, the burden of necessary action shifts even more heavily onto the developing world. Without some of the social and institutional changes within developing countries that are listed here, there may be little in support of step 2 that even the most positive U.S. policy initiative can accomplish from the outside.

But as we move to columns 3 and 4, where international trade responses are more at issue, the policy burden begins to shift more clearly onto the United States, specifically onto those in the United States who make the macroeconomic and other nonfarm policies that do so much to condition the larger international farm trade environment. At these later steps in the sequence, if the essential U.S. nonfarm policy initiatives are missing, there may be little that even the wisest developing country policies can do to produce the final desired outcome.

Figure 8.1 has been designed to describe only the most desirable sequences of events, those that link more farm production in developing countries eventually to more U.S. farm exports. Several less-desirable sequences can occur, however. For example, steps 3 and 4 can sometimes be taken and U.S. farm exports to the developing world can sometimes grow, even without the successful completion of steps 1 and 2. In those poor countries where oil export revenues have led in the past to larger farm imports, for example, only the second half of the sequence has been in operation.

Also, note that if any of the intermediate steps in this sequence were missing, the final outcome could be reversed. Note that without step 2—that is, without the successful promotion of broad-based income growth and dietary enrichment—the impact of step 1 on steps 3 and 4 can be reversed. More farm production in such cases can have the effect of reducing farm imports from the United States instead of increasing these imports. Alternatively, in an unhealthy macroeconomic environment some developing coun-

Figure 8.1 Policy Matrix for Promoting Additional Farm Production and Income Growth in Developing Countries and Additional U.S. Farm Exports to Developing Countries

Categories of Political Action	STEP 1 Farm Production in Developing Countries	STEP 2 Broad-based Income Growth and Dietary Enrichment	STEP 3 Larger Developing Country Farm Imports	STEP 4 Larger U.S. Farm Exports to Developing Countries
Developing Country Actions				
Farm Policy	More public investment in agriculture	Social and institutional change to ensure more equitable access to land, grain, cattle, etc.		
	Fewer farm market restrictions biased against agriculture, thus giving producers access to market prices	Expansion of animal product production		
Nonfarm Policy	Tax policies, credit policies, wage policies, education policies, and exchange rate policies less biased against agriculture	Policies that diversify rural employment Policies that stimulate industrial growth	Development strategies built around openness to trade	
U.S. Actions				
Farm Policy	Increase bilateral and multilateral farm development assistance		Relaxation of quota import restrictions on tropical farm products, accompanied by structural adjustment to downsize domestic production of such products	Market-oriented commodity policies, including target prices as well as loan rates
	Less reliance on program food aid, especially for pursuit of purely farm export or foreign policy objectives			Trade liberalizing agreements with other developed countries
Nonfarm Policy	Increase bilateral and multilateral nonfarm development assistance	Foreign policies that tolerate rapid social and institutional reform in developing countries	Industrial trade policies, developing country debt policies, and domestic macroeconomic policies designed to produce world trade expansion, including expansion of developing country exports	International monetary policy coordination to stabilize and reduce dollar exchange rates

tries might fail to take step 3. They might feel obliged to cut farm imports and boost farm exports to help service foreign debts, and they might feel forced to pursue step 2 by using their own resources rather than by depending on expanded foreign trade. If so, step 4 may never be reached.

The sequence described in Figure 8.1 is therefore not the only one possible. But I have argued here that it is the most attractive sequence and one that will promote the desired partnership between the developing world and the United States. It is the sequence that U.S. policy prescriptions should be designed to encourage. The purpose of this chapter has been to outline these policy prescriptions and to list the various actions that public officials can take to promote a harmony of interests between U.S. and Third World agriculture. This, of course, is the easy part. Persuading responsible officials in the United States and in the developing world to act on this list of prescriptions will require much more effort.

Notes

1. Kenneth L. Bachman and Leonardo A. Paulino, *Rapid Food Production Growth in Selected Developing Countries: A Comparative Analysis of Underlying Trends, 1961–76,* Research Report no. 11 (Washington, D.C.: IFPRI, October 1979), 14.

2. John E. Lee, Jr. and Mathew Shane, *United States Agricultural Interests and Growth in the Developing Economies: The Critical Linkage* (Washington, D.C.: ERS, USDA, June 1985), 16.

3. Earl Kellogg, "University Involvement in International Agriculture Development Activities: Important Issues for Public Education" (Speech given at the 1985 Annual Meeting of the Association of U.S. University Directors of International Agricultural Programs. Athens, Georgia, May 31, 1985).

4. Richard Kodl (M.A. thesis, University of Illinois, Champaign/Urbana, 1985).

5. James P. Houck, *A Note on the Link Between Agricultural Development and Agricultural Imports,* Staff Paper 86-26 (Minneapolis: Department of Agricultural and Applied Economics, University of Minnesota, July 1986).

6. The argument that agricultural development followed industrial development, rather than the other way around, has been made in the important case of Korea. See Sung Hwan Ban, Pal Yong Moon, and Dwight H. Perkins, *Rural Development, Studies in the Modernization of the Republic of Korea: 1945–1975* (Cambridge, Mass.: Harvard University Press, 1980), 12.

7. Robert L. Paarlberg, *Food Trade and Foreign Policy* (Ithaca, N.Y.: Cornell University Press, 1985), 48.

8. Merilee S. Grindle, *State and Countryside: Development Policy and Agrarian Politics in Latin America* (Baltimore, Md.: Johns Hopkins University Press, 1985), 99–100.

9. For an extended review of this problem, see Robert L. Paarlberg, "Responding to the CAP," *Food Policy* (May 1986).

10. *Inside U.S. Trade* 3, no. 51 (December 20, 1985):1.

11. In a somewhat disingenuous fashion, some U.S. officials now have talked

about compensating the Caribbean Basin countries for this loss of sugar markets with additional free deliveries of surplus U.S. rice and corn. This sort of "compensation," obviously self-serving to U.S. agriculture, might only redouble the damage done to farm development in developing countries.

12. For some examples, see Sidney Weintraub, ed., *Economic Coercion and U.S. Foreign Policy* (Boulder, Colo.: Westview Press, 1982).

13. Jeffrey D. Sachs, "External Debt and Macroeconomic Performance in Latin America and East Asia," in William C. Brainard and George L. Perry, eds., *Brookings Papers on Economic Activity 2* (Washington, D.C.: The Brookings Institution, 1985), 545.

14. S.1810, the 1986 Foreign Agricultural Investment Reform (FAIR) Act.

15. Lee, *United States Agricultural Interests,* 11.

16. USDA, Foreign Agriculture Circular, FG-1-86 (January 1986):1.

17. Included among these were the American Soybean Association, Farm and Industrial Equipment Institute, Grain Sorghum Producers Association, Millers' National Federation, National Association of Wheat Growers, National Grange, National Soybean Processors Association, National Turkey Federation, Rice Millers Association, and the United Fresh Fruit and Vegetable Association.

Contributors

Chapter and Commentary Authors

Cheryl Christensen is chief of the Western Europe Division, and formerly headed the Africa and Middle East Division, of the Economic Research Service, U.S. Department of Agriculture, Washington, D.C.

Ramon L. Clarete is assistant professor of economics at the University of Western Ontario, Canada.

Edward J. Clay is director of the Relief and Development Institute, London, and a fellow of the Institute of Development Studies at the University of Sussex, Brighton.

Barbara Insel is a private consultant who was formerly with the Council on Foreign Relations and the World Bank.

D. Gale Johnson is Eliakim Hastings Moore Distinguished Service Professor of Economics at the University of Chicago.

Charles Y. Liu is president of International AgriBusiness Consultants, Inc. in Arlington, Virginia.

Michael Lofchie is director of the African Studies Center at the University of California, Los Angeles.

Gene A. Mathia is deputy director for regional analysis of the International Economics Division, Economic Research Service, U.S. Department of Agriculture, Washington, D.C.

C. Edward Overton is chief of the International Economic Indicators Branch of the International Economics Division, Economic Research Service, U.S. Department of Agriculture, Washington, D.C.

Robert L. Paarlberg is associate professor of political science, Wellesley College, and an associate at the Center for International Affairs, Harvard University.

George E. Rossmiller is senior fellow at the National Center for Food and Agricultural Policy, Resources for the Future, Washington, D.C.

James A. Roumasset is professor of economics at the University of Hawaii and research associate at the Resource Systems Institute, Honolulu, Hawaii.

Daniel E. Shaughnessy is president of TCR Services Inc. and president of the International Trade and Development Education Foundation, Arlington, Virginia.

M. Ann Tutwiler is a research assistant with the National Center for Food and Agricultural Policy, Resources for the Future, Washington, D.C.

Alberto Valdés is director of the International Food Trade and Food Security Program at the International Food Policy Research Institute, Washington, D.C.

T. Kelley White is director for regional analysis, International Economics Division, Economic Research Service, U.S. Department of Agriculture, Washington, D.C.

Larry Witucki is an agricultural economist with the Africa and Middle East Branch of the International Economics Division, Economic Research Service, U.S. Department of Agriculture, Washington, D.C.

Editors

Randall B. Purcell is director of the Curry Foundation, Washington, D.C.

Elizabeth Morrison is research coordinator for the Curry Foundation, Washington, D.C.

Acknowledgments

Special acknowledgments to the Farm Foundation, the Ford Foundation, Pauline C. Knox, Pioneer Hi-Bred International, the Rockefeller Foundation, the National Center for Food and Agricultural Policy at Resources for the Future, and the Agency for International Development at the U.S. Department of State for assisting this project through their contributions.

Index